THE ENIGMA *of* THOMAS WOLFE

THE ENIGMA of
THOMAS WOLFE

Biographical and Critical Selections

Edited by RICHARD WALSER

Harvard University Press, Cambridge, 1953

Grateful appreciation is hereby extended to Charles Scribner's Sons, to Harper & Brothers, and to Edward C. Aswell, Administrator of the Estate of Thomas Wolfe, for permission to reprint from the books of Thomas Wolfe those excerpts included in the essays throughout this volume.

All rights to the selections in this book are retained by the original authors and publishers.

Distributed in Great Britain by
GEOFFREY CUMBERLEGE
OXFORD UNIVERSITY PRESS
LONDON

LIBRARY OF CONGRESS CATALOG CARD NUMBER 52-13698
PRINTED IN THE UNITED STATES OF AMERICA

CONTENTS

PART III *THE COMMENTATORS*

PREFACE

Several years ago William Faulkner was quoted in the press as listing Thomas Wolfe at the head of contemporary American writers. During the time when I was gathering the selections for this book, I wrote Mr. Faulkner requesting that he expand the statement. His reply is of such significance that I wish to set down his letter here in full.

"I seem to have been misquoted," he wrote, "as apparently happens every time I open my mouth to newspaper people. I never said Wolfe was 'the greatest American writer of modern times.' I said, and this was several years ago, that among his and my contemporaries, I rated Wolfe first because we had all failed but Wolfe had made the best failure because he had tried hardest to say the most — a generalisation made rather in conversation than as a public statement, or so I thought at the time. I still support the statement, of course. Man has but one short life to write in, and there is so much to be said, and of course he wants to say it all before he dies. My admiration for Wolfe is that he tried his best to get it all said; he was willing to throw away style, coherence, all the rules of preciseness, to try to put all the experience of the human heart on the head of a pin, as it were. He may have had the best talent of us, he may have been 'the greatest American writer' if he had lived longer, though I have never held much with the 'mute inglorious Milton' theory; I believe it all gets said; that is, unless you are run down by a hit-and-run car, you say what you are capable of before you can persuade yourself to let go and die."

In many ways this statement epitomizes the various problems presented in this book. Though Thomas Wolfe's permanence in the history of American fiction is now generally assured, the exact nature of his literary status is hardly established — mainly because of the very matters of which Faulkner wrote. More than any other contemporary writer, Wolfe has been alternately glorified and damned. Such adjectives as "enormous," "discerning," "superb," "Gargantuan," and much of the time simply "great" have appeared in the same criticisms and reviews which employed such words as "bulky," "formless," "fatuous," "sprawling," and "undisciplined." The critical confusion, if it has entertained the academicians and cognoscenti, has had little influence upon those who read his books. Everybody knows by now — and librarians will be glad to tell him if he does not — that Wolfe's novels have kept in circulation, in fact have increased, far more than those of any other novelist of the thirties. As one critic noted, Wolfe seems destined to speak for and to each rising generation, regardless of the pro-and-con clamor.

An attempt to present evidence of this remarkable situation is the purpose of this collection of essays by those who knew Wolfe and wrote about him as well as by those whose criticisms of his books are straightforward and honest. It is no "memorial volume" by praising devotees, though that attitude has its place too. Nor is it a book of comments by smiling castigators, for that attitude has no place at all. Each of the contributors, it seems to the editor, has tried to fathom the complexities of Wolfe, to interpret him as sincerely as possible within the range of his own critical perspective. All writing, and criticism more so than any other kind, is a personal thing. Critics are the first to admit that complete objectivity is impossible, but most of them are continually striving toward that end. "We write it as we see it," they say; and the reader must agree or disagree as is his way.

The outline of this book is quite simple. The first part is a series of articles (with the exception of a few) by those who knew Wolfe. They tell about isolated instances in his life and, generally, only incidentally about the books he wrote. Wolfe is there himself, and his great friends, John Terry and Maxwell Perkins. This first series constitutes no biography. But we do see the man in all his sympathy and greatness, even his awkwardness and perplexity. The second section is composed of reviews of and comments on some of his books. The last part, which makes up just about half the collection, includes the essays of critical

writers generally viewing Wolfe's complete output by focusing
on some special phase of his talent.

It is inevitable that such a symposium will contain some dupli-
cation of comment; but it is hardly surprising that comment on a
single Wolfe problem by two writers is rarely ever repetitious in
idea. Wolfe's overflowing vocabulary, his autobiographical substance, his form or lack of form — all are favorite topics for discussion by the critical observers. His growth from the first novel
to the last — or his lack of growth — is referred to in most of the
essays. Few critics can deny themselves the opportunity of explaining Wolfe's symbols, or rather of interpretating them; for
though Wolfe left clues for identification, a translation from the
figurative into the actual can take a devious path and reach a
varied destination. Again the reader of this collection may choose
his favored guide or himself plot a course.

Inevitable, too, is the quoting of identical passages from
Wolfe to illustrate the critics' contentions. The prose-poem at
the beginning of *Look Homeward, Angel*, the note prefacing *The
Web and the Rock*, and the Credo which serves as the conclusion
of *You Can't Go Home Again* are notable examples of such passages; but he who knows his Wolfe will not bewail the reap-
pearances.

Some of those who know their Wolfe best will wonder at the
exclusion from this volume of certain material now well established in the Wolfe critical canon. Space, of course, is the answer.
An editor's most unpleasant decision is that which omits material
he would like to include. But a book can be only a limited number of pages, and thus a selection to fit those pages must be made.
Excerpts from the book-length studies of Wolfe by Herbert J.
Muller, Pamela Hansford Johnson, and Agatha Boyd Adams
would have lent attraction to this symposium; but those works are
still in print and are likely already known to those interested in
Wolfe. Discussions of Wolfe, particularly in books by Joseph
Warren Beach, Alfred Kazin, Harry Slochower, George Snell,
and Floyd Stovall, would deserve a place; but they, too, are easily
available to him who would pursue this interest further. Oscar
Cargill's "Gargantua Fills His Skin," Malcolm Cowley's "Wolfe

and the Lost People," Desmond Powell's "Wolfe's Farewells," and
John Donald Wade's "Prodigal" are articles — some of them now
in published volumes — which would expand anyone's under-
standing of Wolfe. Such biographical essays as Frederick H.
Koch's "Thomas Wolfe: Playmaker," and "Reminiscences of Tom
Wolfe" and "Further Memories of Thomas Wolfe" by L. Ruth
Middlebrook would have added considerably to the first section.
Interesting though not necessary should have been an appendix of
those short stories in which Wolfe serves as a character or in which
his spirit is implicit, such as Aline Bernstein's "Eugene," Ray
Bradbury's "Forever and the Earth" (which catapults Wolfe into
the field of science fiction), Fannie Cook's "Thomas Wolfe's
Wife," Clifton Fadiman's "Of Nothing and the Wolfe," and William Fifield's "Tom Wolfe Slept Here." Only a gleaning of even
the best Wolfe material is listed here; the number of titles could
of course be vastly enlarged. The piece, however, most noticeable in its absence is the much admired "Sorrows of Thomas
Wolfe" by John Peale Bishop. To those who have read it recently
the omission will not be surprising. Valid as it was in 1939, the
year of its composition, it seems somewhat out-of-date now in the
light of the subsequent *You Can't Go Home Again*. But, then,
there are perhaps other favorites. One can see that the field is
wide, the picking plenteous.

Some of Wolfe's great admirers will ponder the inclusion in this
volume of quite a few monographs unflattering to Wolfe on several accounts. As previously stated, the selections are not designed
to exculpate the novelist, but simply to present him. Generally an
attack on one page will be succeeded by a counterattack some
pages later. On that score, the book is rather a contest with the
reader acting as the entire committee of judges. It must be remembered, too, that the most perceptive critics reserve their most
stringent examination for the greatest artists. Nothing could be
less chivalrous than attacking a writer unworthy of any attack at
all. Sir Percivale might as well challenge a lackey. There is no
debasement here, the sides are drawn, the gavel has descended.
The enigma of the man and his work lies before the reader. And

it is well to recall that neither defender nor detractor is willing to call Wolfe less than a writer with the greatest endowments.

With the exception of obvious typographical errors, occasional emendations in punctuation or italicizing, and some few corrections in the quoting of Wolfe text, there has been little effort to edit the selections. Slight factual slips (such as that Wolfe died at the age of thirty-eight when actually he was a few weeks short of his thirty-eighth birthday) have been left uncorrected. They are of minor importance; the selections, after all, must stand on their own.

R. W.

by *THOMAS WOLFE*

1929 *Look Homeward, Angel*

1935 *Of Time and the River*

1935 *From Death to Morning*

1936 *The Story of a Novel*

1939 *A Note on Experts: Dexter Vespasian Joyner*

1939 *The Web and the Rock*

1939 *The Face of a Nation*

1940 *You Can't Go Home Again*

1941 *The Hills Beyond*

1942 *Gentlemen of the Press*

1943 *Thomas Wolfe's Letters to His Mother*

1946 *A Stone, a Leaf, a Door*

1946 *The Portable Thomas Wolfe* (edited by Maxwell Geismar)

1948 *Mannerhouse*

1949 *"The Years of Wandering in Many Lands and Cities"*

1951 *A Western Journal*

about *THOMAS WOLFE*

1943 *Thomas Wolfe, A Bibliography*, by George R. Preston, Jr.

1947 *The Marble Man's Wife, Thomas Wolfe's Mother*, by Hayden Norwood

1947 *Thomas Wolfe*, by Herbert J. Muller

1948 *Hungry Gulliver*, by Pamela Hansford Johnson

1949 *Thomas Wolfe*, by Pierre Brodin

1950 *Thomas Wolfe: Carolina Student*, by Agatha Boyd Adams

1950 *Thomas Wolfe, La France, et Les Romanciers Français*, by Daniel L. Delakas

1953 *Thomas Wolfe at Washington Square*, edited by T. C. Pollock and O. Cargill

PART I

THE WRITER

This sketch was written during the latter part of 1935 for "Portraits and Self-Portraits." When the book was published, about half of Wolfe's words had been deleted to make his article fit the allotted space. A dozen years passed before the full text was printed. The year 1935 was a difficult one for Wolfe, filled as he was with doubts and misgivings brought on by his too serious concern with those critics who had not showered praise upon the recently published "Of Time and the River." This circumstance doubtless accounts for the tone of apology so clearly evident in the sketch.

SOMETHING OF MY LIFE

by

Thomas Wolfe

I suppose the biographical facts about birth, home-town, colleges and so on, are available to the editors of this book, so I shall not bother to give them here. Since almost all the knowledge the world has of me, concerns me as a writer, perhaps it will be better if I try to tell something of the life.

I am thirty-five years old, and although I have written more millions of words than I should like to count — how many I don't know, but perhaps as many as anyone else my age now writing — I have published not more than a tenth of them. Nevertheless, the critics say I write too much — and I don't say that they are wrong. Although I suppose the desire to be a writer has been buried in

From the *Saturday Review of Literature,* 7 February 1948. By permission of the publisher and Edward C. Aswell, literary administrator of the Estate of Thomas Wolfe.

me for a long time — certainly the itch for it has been there, because I began to scribble when I was not more than fourteen
years old, I never dared admit to myself that I might seriously
proclaim my intentions until I was about twenty-six.

Before that, I had written a few plays and although I had hoped
they might find a producer, I don't think that even then, I had
sufficient confidence in my abilities to announce definitely to my
family that I actually intended to be a playwright and to hope to
earn my living that way. I didn't succeed, anyway. And it was not
until the twenty-sixth year that I began to write a book, which
occupied me for the next two or three years. During this time I
was employed at the Washington Square college of the New
York University as an instructor in English. I don't think that
even then did I concretely and reasonably assure myself that I had
found my life's direction in the work that I intended to do from
that time on. I certainly did dream of finding a publisher and a
public for the book, but it was really a kind of dream — a kind of
intoxicating illusion which sustained me during the period of
creation. I suppose I can say honestly that I wrote the book because I had to write it and after it was written and I saw the
tremendous bulk of it in the cold grey light of sober actuality, I
had the most serious misgivings and wondered what on earth had
ever possessed me to make me spend two or three years of my
life in creating such a huge leviathan or what moment of mad
unreason had deluded me into thinking that I could possibly find
a publisher and readers for it. My own dejected doubt was speedily
confirmed by the first publisher who read the manuscript, who
sent it back very speedily, with a very brief note to the effect that
it was too long, too autobiographical, too amateurish and too like
other books which he had published and lost money on, for him
to risk a chance. This seemed to summarize and confirm my own
most depressed feelings, now that the book was written and in
this frame of mind I went to Europe and almost forgot about
the book.

Within six months, however, another publisher had read the
manuscript and accepted it. I returned to America, taught at the
University and worked on the revision of the book which was

published in October, 1929, a few weeks after my twenty-ninth birthday.

So far as "early struggles" are concerned, my experience has been a fortunate one. The first book I ever wrote, and a very long one, too, was accepted and published by one of the first publishers who read it, and I understand that this is an extraordinary occurrence. I have had my struggles, however, and pretty desperate ones too, but most of them, so far as writing is concerned, have been of my own making. I have to struggle all the time against indolence — perhaps it would be more accurate to say against an insatiable and constantly growing interest in the life around me, my desire to get out and explore it with an encyclopedic thoroughness, my desire to travel and make voyages and see places, things, and people I have never known. I like companionship, food and drink, going to baseball games, and having a good time. I must also struggle constantly against self-doubt — lack of confidence in what I do and the many difficulties I encounter in doing it. My knowledge of the craft and technique of my profession is still very imperfect. I believe and hope that I learn something about it and about my own capacity as a writer all the time, but I learn very slowly and at the cost of almost infinite error, waste, and confusion. I do much too much of everything; I write millions of words in the course of shaping out and defining a volume of a few hundred thousand. It seems to be an element of my creative faculty that it has to realize itself through the process of torrential production, and although I hope to be able to control and guide this force as I go on, so that I will be able to achieve my work with more and more clearness and precision and economy, without such a waste of effort, time, and material, I think that the way I work will always remain in its essence pretty much as I have tried to describe it and that it will have to come out of me in this way.

I come from a class and section of American life which regarded writing — the profession of a writer — as something very mysterious and romantic and very remote from its own life and the world of its own knowledge and experience. For this reason, as I have said, it was twenty-six years or more before I even dared to admit concretely that I might become a writer and I was almost thirty before my own admission was concretely affirmed by publication. For this reason, perhaps, and for others — which I tried to mention — a kind of tremendous inertia in me and the tendency of human kind to put off and evade for as long as possible the thing it knows it has to do, the work it cannot avoid and without which its life is nothing — and a strong sense of direction and often a very confused sense of purpose. For all these reasons my development, I think, has been a slow one. And yet it has sometimes seemed to me that in all these apparent handicaps, there may have been certain advantages, too. The belief that I may be by nature somewhat indolent and the knowledge that I may allow a ravenous curiosity for life and new experience to come between the work I ought to be doing — and the fact that as hard and grim as work itself may be, not only the intensity of effort and concentration required, but the period of spiritual imprisonment that work necessitates — the very knowledge that once a piece of work has been begun, a man's whole life must be absorbed and obsessed by it day and night until he finishes it — all of these things, together with a certain goad of conscience, have driven me to face the fact of work, to try to meet it squarely and to do it as hard as I can once I am started on it. It has been said of much that I have written thus far that it was autobiographical. I cannot answer such a very debatable and complicated word in the short space that is allotted here and I shall not attempt to. I can only say that it seems to me that every creative act is in one way or another — autobiographical.

The kind of naked directness with which the young man writing his first book is likely to make use of his material, but as I have said, much of the trouble and misunderstanding may have come from the fact that I have not yet succeeded in being autobiographical enough, instead of the fact that I was, as many people say, too autobiographical. At any rate, as I go on, my tendency I believe is to make use of the materials of living experience with an ever increasing freedom of the inventiveness and the plastic powers of the imagination.

As far as the experience of work itself is concerned, I have found that so far from isolating one from contacts with reality and a living experience with the world around one, it enhances and enriches one's perceptions enormously. In fact, it seems to me that the core of an artist's life is his work, and his deepest knowledge, his greatest power, his profoundest social feelings come through the work he does as a great current of electricity pulses and surges through a dynamo. I suppose it is true that a man at twenty is likely to have an egocentric picture of the universe, is concerned with life very largely as it reflects and acts upon his own personality. And I suppose also that this concentration on his own immediate experience and interest is likely to show itself in his earlier work. But so far as my own experience is concerned, I believe that as one grows older, he becomes a great deal more interested in the life around him in terms of itself. His interests, and the adventures and experiences of his own personality, become valuable to him more in terms of their relation to the experience of all mankind. And his social feeling, his whole understanding and sympathy with the lives of people and with the whole human experience, becomes enormously enriched and deepened as a result of this. That, I hope, has begun to happen to me. At any rate, I am working.

When fifteen-year-old Tom Wolfe came down from the moun-
tains surrounding Asheville to the slightly rolling country of the
University of North Carolina at Chapel Hill, he began an under-
graduate career full of excitement, companionship, and finally
honors. His actual student days were vastly different from the
semi-autobiography recorded in the novels. Don Bishop, now
with the National Broadcasting Company, wrote this account as
a student at the University of North Carolina. He searched the
files of the campus publications which young Wolfe had helped
to edit and also talked widely with those who knew Wolfe as an
undergraduate.

TOM WOLFE AS A STUDENT

by

Don Bishop

There was nowhere a shred of evidence of collegiate mischief
in the room of Thomas Wolfe one night more than twenty-two
years ago when he loped into his fraternity house quarters in the
early morning hours. He prepared for bed unmindful of the dili-
gence of his fraternity brothers in arranging his iron bed for a
collapse the moment its six-foot-three occupant touched it. The
house and room were quiet as Wolfe knelt beside his bed and
began his prayer, but suddenly in mid-sentence, as the bed
crashed downward under his weight as though it were the
original one-horse shay, he volleyed a shower of oaths to finish
his words of reverence.

This outburst was the signal for the other members of Pi Kappa
Phi fraternity to rush in and have a good laugh at the expense of

---

From the *Carolina Magazine*, March 1942. By permission of the author.

their prize "Big Man on the Campus": Thomas Wolfe, editor of the *Tar Heel*, the student weekly newspaper; associate editor of the *Magazine*, the publication for literary men; and pioneer member of the Carolina Playmakers, since a world-reputed dramatics organization.

Half a decade later, when he was writing *Look Homeward, Angel*, had he chosen to use this incident in his semi-autobiographical novel, he would have pictured himself as a tormented and lonely fellow, mercilessly gibed by his closest "friends," and grossly misunderstood by all.

He would have used the practical joke of his fraternity brothers as an example of the misery of his life in the state university of Old Catawba, the University of North Carolina at Chapel Hill, North Carolina. In writing his novels he did just this, seizing upon some memory of discomfort or embarrassment and magnifying it to the gargantuan proportions of the character Eugene Gant. That was his method: to use an incident of his college days, but to twist it to fit his outlook five years later, after he had experienced bitter years at Harvard University in fruitless search for a career as a playwright; after he had found Paris too distracting for creative work; after he had suffered alone in New York City. Thomas Wolfe made himself Eugene Gant in *Look Homeward, Angel* and *Of Time and the River*, and George Webber in *The Web and the Rock* and *You Can't Go Home Again*. As he wrote each book he became the major character in each. The tortures of his heroes, the hunger for life of each, became a written account of the daily events of the life of the author. But he went further than this: he saw himself ten, fifteen or more years ago just as he pictured himself at the moment of writing. Wolfe the child and college student was the same as Wolfe the man of the world who was then discovering that he could not discover his place in society and in the world's ways. In his books he drew no line between his old and new personalities. He did not relate the true incidents of the four college years of conformity.

The truth is that Wolfe spent those four years at the University, from his sixteenth to his nineteenth year, observing and being a contented part of a small world. He sought the pleasures and

honors that college life could give a youngster with a lively
personality and a keen intelligence. He revelled in the joys of
being editor of the paper and handing down the Mount Sinaic
word to students and professors; he joined organizations and
reached for the titles that rewarded hard work and a jovial manner. Wolfe was a conformist; and he acquired all the fruits of
temporary pleasure that conformity could bring him. Then, disillusioned as he scrutinized this kind of life, he broke away from
the rut that would have carried him back to the small town for
small-town success. His restless soul, born hungry and not ap-
peased by the ointment of undergraduate attainment, turned to
the new, the different, and the faraway life of other lands and
localities.

Thomas Wolfe cursed volubly as he fell victim to the humor
of the fraternity funmakers, but there was no real rancor in his
expletives, for would not come shortly his turn to have a laugh?
He could always be relied on to father a practical joke at the expense of a college mate; so it followed naturally that he likewise
must feel the brunt of raw student humor.

On another occasion, when he had been tapped into the
Golden Fleece, the highest honor society, Wolfe was notified by
the initiators to be in his room every night at nine o'clock. This
regulation was extremely irksome to one accustomed to roaming
the campus until two or three in the morning, but he surrendered
to the rule and was in bed by the appointed hour, even though
there was no certainty that the initiation crew would arrive on
that particular night. Fraternity brothers took advantage of the
situation, cloaked themselves in sheets, and submitted him to
initiation ceremonies of their own creation. As usual, he fumed
at length over this maltreatment.

But Wolfe could not hold a grudge. He liked too well to be in
the center of life to think of breaking with the humor perpetrators.
He would sometimes become irritated while arguing with a
fraternity brother and would get up and stalk away. But his real
inclination was to remain in the circle, survive the thrusts of
humor, and retaliate. It had to be this way with a man of his
position. Known and liked by all, he must necessarily remain a

part of the body of students, and must master them with his own jokes, not run from theirs.

"In a broad sense, Wolfe was one of the most sociable persons I have ever seen," a fraternity brother declares. "He enjoyed meeting and being with people and talking with them. He liked to join organizations and be a part of them. If you read his editorials in the *Tar Heel* you will see Tom written into them."

Correctly, the fraternity brother probably should have said Wolfe enjoyed "talking *to*" people. He would drop into a friend's room, halt all activity, and launch a conversation that soon narrowed to a monologue from Wolfe. Driven away by the sleepy occupants of the room, he would wander on to an all-night café and there corner a jitney driver, an itinerant bum, or a café waiter who would listen to his interesting, but lengthy, discussion of any subject that seized him. In this fashion Thomas Wolfe was experiencing and enjoying the life that tumbled by him. His steel-trap memory was storing up the million scenes and faces that he later was to call part of his lost youth, but at this time he knew and appreciated them as links in the happy chain of collegiate camaraderie.

"My impression of him as a student after these years is that he was usually in a happy, jovial frame of mind, the center of every small group in which he happened to be for the moment," says LeGette Blythe, author and journalist, who was a schoolmate of Wolfe. He remembers the "long, gangling, awkward, stammering, grinning, lovable fellow with the mountains written all over him." Like so many others who knew Wolfe the collegian, Mr. Blythe loved him for himself, regardless of what crowns the future might lay upon his brow.

Wolfe's contemporaries loved him for the fellowship that he spread upon the campus. If they needed a humorous speech at a class smoker, a talk at a football pep rally, or a poem to be read at some special ceremony, the call went out to Tom Wolfe to fill the bill. His quick, ready wit was certain to respond. He "fitted in" and his fellow students looked up to him. Even in his freshman year, before he had blossomed as a writer, he was elected president of the Boo Loo Club, a group of freshmen whose wit and sharply defined personalities had singled them out for special "honor" by the sophomores.

In this and all organizations Wolfe followed the accepted pattern. He may have been conscious that he was forcing himself into the undergraduate straitjacket. If so, he was too engrossed in living with and as his fellows ever to desire a change. In after-college years he found the life of unorthodoxy most satisfying to his creative soul, but in the younger years, when he was a campus leader and sophomoric genius, he thrived on his daily experiences as a political wirepuller, happy-go-lucky friend of all, and practical joker extraordinary. He was harnessed to collegiate ways, but of his own volition.

His successor as editor of the *Tar Heel* says that, apart from the restraints imposed on him in his later years by his editors at Scribner's and by the fact that he was teaching classes in New York University, "Tom came as near being organized and harnessed to human organization during the time he edited the *Tar Heel* as during any other period of his life." He adds that the paper was far from systematic, but that at least Wolfe strove in that direction.

In certain respects Eugene Gant of *Look Homeward, Angel* was minutely like Thomas Wolfe, the campus thinker and activities man. Wolfe was none too careful of his appearance: trouser knees were baggy, tie was twisted, collar was dirty, and hair was uncombed. But these are not so much signs of incipient genius as they are evidence that his intensity often blinded him to such commonplace considerations as correct apparel and appearance. When the occasion demanded it, he would dress as well as anyone else. But occasions did not often present themselves nor did he often look for them.

If anything, Wolfe was overanxious that he be regarded as a regular fellow. He desired always to be the center of the circle, to keep his listeners laughing or seriously contemplative of his philosophizing. He sought companionship and held it with his effervescent manner. Seldom was he judged eccentric because of his antics, though his first book sounds this idea as the dominant theme of his collegiate life.

Indeed, he uttered wild "goat cries" as he strode across the lonely stretches of green campus, but what student did not in that isolated community? He was merely conforming when he gave vent to a cry, although his mountain-bred voice had more volume than most others. He disliked fraternities because of their snobbery? Hardly, for he joined one of the leading chapters of the college. He was disdainful of student politics? Not while he was part of it, for he was a powerful figure in parceling out offices, and he felt an awful jolt when his choice as his successor failed to win the editorship of the *Tar Heel*. In all these things — the components of the normal student life — he lived or acted his part well. He dramatized his deeds, he saw all life centered in the college community, with himself as a prime force. It was a comforting feeling to be one of the gears in the machine of life.

Wolfe was so intense in his desire to be a popular member of the mass that he often overacted the part. Thus were born some of the stories of his eccentricity.

As editor of the newspaper he wrote, "If a man sleeps till barely time to catch an eight o'clock class when there is work to do, he is a slacker." Yet he was notoriously delinquent in turning in class assignments or copy for the week's issue of the paper. He seemed to delight in putting off work until the last minute and then furiously driving himself until his task was completed. Classmates would marvel at their superman and this pleased him.

He would bolt into his dormitory five minutes before meeting time of the Dialectic Society, the student debating club of which he was an influential member and "behind-the-scenes" elections manipulator. Snatching at whatever writing material that presented itself, he would dash off a poem to read at the society meeting. He would arrive fifteen minutes late and be fined twenty-five cents; whereupon he would rise and explain that his tardiness was due to his prolonged effort on the poem; and he would read the poem as proof of the alibi. A henchman would then move that Wolfe be excused from paying the fine in view of the poem's excellence.

On one occasion he was designated by the editor of the *Tar Baby*, the humor magazine, to be guest editor of the publication for one issue. The regular editor hounded Wolfe for the copy week after week, but on the day before the material must be in the hands of the printer, he had still turned in nothing. The editor cornered Wolfe and demanded action. So he sat down after supper and wrote the issue from cover to cover, forty-five pages of satire modeled after one of the newspapers in the state.

One Saturday night he and other students were in the room of the secretary of the Young Men's Christian Association, arguing far into the night on nearly everything. Along about three o'clock Wolfe dramatically jumped to the center of the floor.

"My God, gentlemen, I've had nothing to eat since breakfast!" he shouted, and dashed off downtown to buy a hot dog.

No one was surprised, for this was Wolfe's way, and, whether natural or affected, his friends loved him for it.

He was especially popular with his professors. He did excellent work; in intellect he was up to many of them; and his humor won their hearts. With the late Professor Edwin Greenlaw, a noted scholar of English, he was a favorite. Invariably Wolfe would come to class late and Greenlaw would chastise him with a witty remark. But Wolfe always replied in kind.

One day he came to the classroom door and rolled in a long section of toilet tissue, letting it unfold his story as it proceeded toward Professor Greenlaw. As the class broke into an uproar, the professor calmly asked:

"Mr. Wolfe, are we to judge the quality of your story by the quality of the paper on which it is written?"

Wolfe's classmates recall particularly some of his antics in that class. When called on to read his theme, he would fumble in his pockets until he had found a sheet of paper. He would read this, run off the page in the middle of a sentence, fish into his pocket again, then locate perhaps a scrap of manila paper on which he had scrawled some sentences. Sometimes even a matchbook cover would yield a sentence.

In his newspaper, as well as in his personal actions, Wolfe demonstrated his strong urge to be "a regular fellow." Interspersed with the usual run of news and editorials would be bits of Wolfian humor that portray his boundless exuberance. An uncaptioned item on the front page read:

"Of the 15 patients in the infirmary at the present time nine have influenza, five are just sick and one was carried there just after he made a 'one' on Zoology II. He will recover, says the nurse."

The newspaper contained a long article on "The Experiences of Ethical Eddie," who is trying to decide whether to satisfy himself by eating onions, or society by leaving them out of his diet. After wrestling with the elements of the problem for several hundred words, Ethical Eddie comes to this rather logical conclusion:

"So there I have it, a moral situation which is intolerable and which must be solved. I can either eat onions and wrong society or pass them by and harm myself or do the diplomatic thing and act a lie. That is a problem which each one must work out for himself, solve it and you will be happy, fail and to hell you go."

There is no indication whether Ethical Eddie was Thomas Wolfe, but Wolfe did write about himself, seriously and in jest. Items such as this, by his own pen, refute the impression that he was unmercifully made the butt of jokes by others:

"Thomas Clayton Wolfe, editor of the *Tar Heel*, was on the Hill a few fleeting hours last Wednesday. Mr. Wolfe is taking a rest cure in Raleigh and Greensboro following a week of strenuous and nerve-racking examinations. It is thought that he is taking the Keeley cure."

A joke on the editorial page would cast doubt on whether Wolfe was really sensitive about his height:

"Fresh — It sure is a pity and loss to the varsity that Tom Wolfe doesn't play football.

"Campbell (the football coach) — Why?

"Fresh — He could fall down with the ball and make a touchdown every time."

Such tomfoolery he wrote often. Like any other normal college editor, he had frivolous as well as grandiose moments. It was all part of the process of being human and subject to the chameleon qualities of the undergraduate mind.

In his *Tar Heel* editorials, especially, he showed the sobriety and intensity characteristic of college editors. The Carolina Spirit, the disgrace of an unclean campus, and the unhealthiness of crowded dormitory rooms vied for attention from his pen. In his philosophy prize-winning essay, "The Crisis in Industry," he likewise spoke as one whose mission it is to save the world. He advocated for labor a practice of "self-determination" to decide on its "inner workings." It was unprecedented that such a commonplace subject as labor should win the Worth Prize, but Professor Horace Williams, one of Wolfe's most admired teachers, said in a foreword:

"If Philosophy shall be able to throw any light upon the problem of Industry, or aid in advancing gentler methods of progress, the effort justifies itself."

Thus to Thomas Wolfe in four years of college came all the superficial pleasure that he could aspire to. His full quota of honors was placed under his name in the 1920 yearbook, with this tribute:

"Editing the *Tar Heel*, winning Horace's philosophy prize when only a Junior, writing plays and then showing the world how they should be acted — they are all alike to this young Shakespeare. Last year he played the leading role in the 'Midnight Frolic' at 'Gooch's Winter Palace,' but this year it's the leading role on the 'Carolina Shipping Board.' But, seriously speaking, 'Buck' is a great, big fellow. He can do more between 8:25 and 8:30 than the rest of us can do all day, and it is no wonder that he is classed as a genius."

In this fashion ran the general opinion of Wolfe's classmates. They knew him as one who was extremely prolific, well informed, talented. He was genial and generous, a friend to all, and full of schoolboyish conviviality. By every standard he was a success as a college student.

Wolfe loved this life in which he was so triumphant. He basked in its spotlights and bowed gracefully to its plaudits; he was at a supreme moment as Mother Wolfe watched him dance around the ballroom floor at the final dances just before commencement. He had come silently from the mountains, a few weeks short of his sixteenth year, had found his way about the scholastic labyrinth, and had emerged with the fruits of the struggle. Book knowledge, special recognition, and thousands of opportunities to see and know people had come to him in the four years of development.

Yet he was on a plane above his fellows; he saw the shallowness of his attainment. The delight lay in the desire for recognition. In his possession the honors became tarnished and impermanent. Sooner than the usual college senior, he realized the ephemeral nature of undergraduate honors. He did not renounce them however; he bore them bravely and marked time until June, 1920, should bring graduation. The University and his undergraduate training had given him much and he would always love the place, but when he decided upon graduate study he selected Harvard University. From there, on November 26, 1920, he wrote to Professor Frederick H. Koch, who had directed him in his dramatic work with the Carolina Playmakers:

"I yearn for Chapel Hill at times — many times — but I know my bolt there is shot — I got away at the right time. Here, as there, I am a Carolina man, learning with sorrow today that Virginia beat us. It's the greatest place in the world, prof. That sums up all my findings."

After graduating from the University of North Carolina, Wolfe set out for Harvard University, where he spent three years. The fictional account of his sojourn in Cambridge is well known to readers of "Of Time and the River." The factual story of this germinal and stimulating period is here presented by Richard S. Kennedy, who as a Harvard graduate student wrote a dissertation on Wolfe under the direction of Professor Howard Mumford Jones. Kennedy is now on the faculty of the University of Rochester.

WOLFE'S HARVARD YEARS

by

Richard S. Kennedy

The earliest period of importance in Thomas Wolfe's productive career was that of the Harvard years, 1920–1923, during which he divided his time between graduate study for the A.M. degree and playwriting for Professor George Pierce Baker's 47 Workshop. Throughout this period, his mind absorbed the great literature of the world not only through his classwork, but also through his incessant reading and browsing in the Harvard College Library. It was at Harvard that he wrote "Welcome to Our City," his first creditable literary production, and it was at Harvard that he began to govern his life in preparation for a future writing career. Finally, it was in this period that he began to conceive plans of a

Based on Richard S. Kennedy's "Thomas Wolfe at Harvard, 1920–1923," in the *Harvard Library Bulletin*, Spring and Autumn, 1950, copyright by the President and Fellows of Harvard College. By permission. Excerpts from the manuscripts of Thomas Wolfe in the Thomas Wolfe Collection of William B. Wisdom in the Houghton Library at Harvard University are used by permission of Edward C. Aswell.

scope that made it necessary for him to repudiate the drama form and turn to prose narrative.

He worked under some of Harvard's most celebrated faculty members during the time he was enrolled in the Graduate School. If we examine a list of his courses, we may get some idea of the scope of his studies. First and most important, he was registered for three years in Professor Baker's playwriting course, English 47 and 47a. He also chose Baker's course "The Forms of the Drama," a survey of great works in the drama from the Greeks to the twentieth century, and Professor A. N. Murray's course, "The Drama in England from 1590 to 1642." Under Professor John Livingston Lowes, he studied "The Poets of the Romantic Period" and worked on "Studies in the Literature of the Renaissance" (the Renaissance literature of Italy, France, the Germanic countries, and England). He took Professor Chester Greenough's survey of American literature, and he audited Professor G. L. Kittredge's Shakespeare course. Nor did he stay entirely within the English Department. He took a course in aesthetic theory under Professor Langfield in the Philosophy Department and a summer course in British history under Professor McIlwain, and during his last term at Harvard he audited Irving Babbitt's famous "Literary Criticism of the Neo-Classic Period." He did almost all of his formal course work in the first year and a half, allowing more time for the Workshop and for extensive reading during the last half of his residence. However, even during his busiest terms, Wolfe had more time for reading than ever before. At Chapel Hill his many campus activities had taken all his spare time, but at Harvard, among students whom he found restrained and distant, he made few friends at first and he looked to the books of the Widener Library for companionship.

I have in the longer article on this subject given a brief profile of Wolfe's personality, his loneliness, and his quest for "fulness of life" through omnivorous reading and through variety of experience. Here I will only comment on one or two important points. Professor John Livingston Lowes was partly responsible for Wolfe's foraging in the library stacks. At the time Wolfe enrolled in the course in Romantic Poetry, Lowes was immersed in his study of the poetic process, using Coleridge's 1895–1898 Notebook as his principal document. As readers of Lowes's *The Road to Xanadu* know, he was able to demonstrate that Coleridge's vast reading contributed in an astonishing way to the creation of "The Ancient Mariner" and "Khubla Khan." The contents of myriad books lay for years in Coleridge's "deep well of unconscious cerebration" (Lowes takes this phrase from Henry James); and later, isolated words, phrases, images, and ideas rose from the chaos of twilight memory to be shaped into brilliant poetry. Wolfe, fascinated by Lowes's findings, wanted to put the secret formula into practice. He strove to stock his memory with a prodigious store of bookish turmoil from which great poetry might emerge when the imaginative faculty summoned. This is his explanation in a letter to Professor Edwin Greenlaw at Chapel Hill:

Professor Lowes book on Coleridge (not published yet I believe) which he read to the class last year, had a great effect on me. In that book, he shows conclusively how retentive of all it reads is the mind and how, at almost any moment that mass of material may be fused and resurrected in new and magic forms. That is wonderful, I think. So I'm reading, not so analytically but voraciously.

His aspiration to the fullest knowledge and experience is not inconsistent with another impulse, the desire to escape from the world about him (especially to escape such forces as family, custom, or social pressure that might retard his personal or artistic growth). In his Autobiographical Outline (one of the most valuable of the unpublished documents among the Wolfe papers in the Harvard College Library) he refers to this escape as a retreat behind a "wall." But this freedom, this "wall," is not an exclusive withdrawal from life, but is rather a withdrawal into a position where he would be free to select the experience in which he wished to participate. He wished to become an Everyman in order that his personal experience might be a touchstone guaranteeing the universal in his future writings. In the following jottings from the Outline, he shows that his idea of self-determination was suggested by Pater's *Marius the Epicurean* (chapter vi and elsewhere):

A growing belief and understanding of the selective principle (Marius the Epicurean) — a despair because those events and that knowledge which might mean most might not be ordered to come at the exact moment when it was needed, so that all experience became a perfectly governed stream expanding without wastage or confusion under a constant pressure — the extension of this to all life — to the persons one meets — to all that one sees or does — thus at twenty there was no wall except this enforced and growing solitude.

Although Wolfe thought of this withdrawal as a necessary preparation for the task of the artist, his loneliness resulted partly from his failure to fit into his new surroundings. Having been used to a small, closely knit college community at Chapel Hill, he did not adjust to the new life for almost two years. Moreover, his towering figure drew attention to the oddities of his appearance as he made his way about the Harvard Yard with long quick strides. Mrs. Baker remembers that she first saw Wolfe when he came to their house to ask Professor Baker for admission to English 47: he was a tall, thin, awkward youth with a coat too short for his arms and trousers too short for his legs. He did not concern himself with grooming: he frequently went to class unshaven, he seldom took time to bathe, he rarely had his hair cut. He dressed so shabbily that his Boston relatives worried about him.

He was extremely shy in class. Furthermore, the step from the chaotic give-and-take of the Chapel Hill playwriting class to the other extreme of mature criticism (and sometimes a vulgar oversophistication) made him feel at once hostile and inferior to the other older members of the class. Although English 47 was conducted informally, he seldom added to the class discussion, for he was overawed by the "concocted eloquence" of such members as his friend Kenneth Raisbeck. He was very shy with almost everyone. He spoke little, and when he did he stammered out his speech in halting phrases. At rehearsals of his plays he scarcely made himself known at all; anything that he had to contribute was spoken in a low tone to Professor Baker, who directed the plays. With friends whom he knew well, however, he talked at great length. He loved to corner a listener to whom he could unburden his feelings, opinions, and remembrances. As one friend expressed it, "He didn't talk to you, he delivered a speech at you." The rhetorical patterns of triple word, phrase, and clause found in Wolfe's writings were a part of his conversational habits. In his attempts to express himself, he would repeat himself many times, saying, "I know I'm saying this badly, but what I mean is . . ." The effect was that of a man passionately concerned with communication, but not at all sure of his penetration.

He lived in various rooming houses similar to those described in *Of Time and the River*. In his first year at 48 Buckingham Street, he had a third floor room under the sloping roof which became the model for Oswald Ten Eyck's garret in the novel. In his last year at 21 Trowbridge Street, he lived in the downstairs front room of Mrs. D. J. Casey, whose family became the "Murphys" in *Of Time and the River*. He made himself at home there, spending many hours in the kitchen telling the Caseys about Asheville and about his family or enlarging the vocabulary of Mr. Thong, a Chinese roomer, by teaching him the four-letter words he would not find in books.

His room was generally in a great disorder of books and papers. The floor around his desk was littered with pages (a penciled scrawl on yellow typewriter paper), hurriedly tossed aside during his nightly labors. Piles of manuscript, which Mrs. Casey was forbidden to touch, were scattered about the room. Around his favorite arm chair, books were stacked — some stuffed with paper markers, others turned face down, open to a chosen page.

His reading was extensive but not careful. However, with his remarkable memory, which he inherited from his mother, he was able to retain an enormous amount of his discursive reading. For his classes he tried to read the complete works of every poet or dramatist who was emphasized. His outside reading was not ordered in any way, nor did it reflect any particular tastes. He read what came to hand: books his friends were reading, books in the Farnsworth Room, books that were the chance result of browsing in the library stacks. Professor Lowes was much impressed by Wolfe's ability to cite from this great bulk of reading and he thought he would do well in the scholarly life.

I would distort the picture of Wolfe at Harvard if I left the impression that he was only the lonely, brooding, bookish young man during these years. The other side of his nature, warm, gay, gregarious, was here too. As time went on, he had more companionship — among fellow students in the Workshop and among the Southern boys at the University — and, of course, he often saw his Boston relatives on Sundays or at holiday dinners. In the homes of married Workshop members, Henry Carlton, Frederick Day, or Roscoe Brink, he would strain the endurance of his listeners, recounting his mother's parsimonies or describing his brother Ben's death. He found time for evenings with Wilbur Dunkel at the Copley Players or for late-hour carousing with Kenneth Raisbeck. He came to know Boston well and he loved its atmosphere, "the musty and delightful brownness over all." He knew the Fenway and the Esplanade, the Boston Museum and the Old Howard, Garden Street and Scollay Square, Beacon Hill and the Faneuil Hall Market, the Village Blacksmith Tearoom and Jake Wirth's. William Polk's description of Wolfe away from his books gives us a more full-blooded man than the self-conscious introvert we find in the Autobiographical Outline:

He was . . . full of mighty laughter and abounding energy which would cause him to split a door with his fist. . . He had a hunger for life, too, which would clothe him in a borrowed shirt — since he had forgot to send anything of his own to the laundry for a couple of months — send him out to the Parker House basement for a quart of surreptitious Scotch, to Durgin-Park's for a steak and to the Boston Common or to Wellesley for a girl or a young lady.

II

George Pierce Baker's 47 Workshop at Harvard had begun as a playwriting class in 1905, but no plays were actually produced until 1912. After this date, it operated as a theatre laboratory until Baker left Harvard in 1924. Selected plays were produced each year before private audiences who submitted criticism of the plays after they were performed. Thereby, the young authors were able not only to see their own work brought to life, but also to revise it in the light of audience criticism.

This was the time of the Provincetown Players, the Neighborhood Playhouse, and the beginnings of the Theatre Guild. These indications of new vitality in the American theatre, plus the fame of Professor Baker's Workshop, aroused Wolfe's eagerness to try his hand at playwriting at Harvard. Although he had told the administration of plans for a career in journalism, he went immediately to Professor Baker and was delighted to be admitted as one of "Baker's Dozen." Still it was not until he had absorbed the enthusiasm of the older students that he thought of becoming a professional playwright. After he had written his first play, "The Mountains," a one-act revision of a script begun in North Carolina, he remembers the discovery thus:

For the first time, it occurs to me that writing may be taken seriously — separated from home I realize that it is not a remote thing for me — that it is a very present thing — Life begins to live — in spite of the welter of events and reading.

Baker liked the play and promised to include it in the next year's program. It was presented first in a trial performance in January, and after revision it was included in the regular program of the Workshop performances, October 21 and 22, 1921. Since the dialogue was over-wordy and there was very little action, the play was a miserable failure. The written comment of the audience seemed even malicious to the self-centered young author. A notation in the Outline recalls his hopes and his disappointment: "The writing of my play — reading it to Ketchum — his generous enthusiasm — Alas the *generous* enthusiasm of Baker — But how they turn on you when it fails — the coldness, the neglect."

Wolfe was so discouraged he was ready to give up writing forever. Since Professor Lowes had suggested that he continue his graduate studies and plan for a teaching career, Wolfe began to consider this possibility. Years later he gave an account of this dilemma and of his appeal to an older friend for advice:

No one thought [the play] was any good, and most people took pains to tell me so. It was a very desperate occasion for me. It seemed to me that my whole life and future depended upon it, and in this state of mind I went to see a man on whose judgment, honesty and critical ability I relied to the utmost. I asked him what he thought of my abilities as a writer, and if he thought I would ever succeed in doing the thing I most wanted to do; and although he tried at first, out of the kindness of his heart, to evade the issue, he finally told me point blank that he did not think I would ever become a writer and that he thought my abilities were critical rather than creative and therefore advised me to devote my time to graduate study in the University, leading to a Ph.D. degree and a position in the teaching profession. . . I will never forget the almost inconceivable anguish and despair that his words caused me.

Wolfe went ahead with his studies, and by February of his second year he had completed his residence for the A.M. degree and needed only to fulfill the language requirements in French and German. In March he registered with the Harvard Appointment Bureau to teach English at a college or preparatory school the following September. Meanwhile, he was continuing to work on his playwriting. In spite of his failure with "The Mountains," he must have received some encouragement from Professor Baker with this play, for he had decided to enlarge it to three acts.

The most heartening incident of this second year was Professor Baker's request that Wolfe return for another year of study in the Workshop. However, Mrs. Wolfe had kept a tight grip on Tom's purse: her letters had been full of complaint about his expenses. Since Wolfe knew that his mother would never support him through a third year, he went ahead with his plans for teaching. In June he received an offer from Northwestern University for a position as instructor in English, but before the matter was settled Wolfe received news that his father was dying. He left immediately for Asheville. It was this new sequence of events that ultimately made possible his return to Harvard the following September.

III

Wolfe's last year at Harvard was his happiest. He now felt secure both in the Workshop and in the Cambridge community. He no longer thought the Boston families were cold and heartless, for he was now welcome in several homes. He was asked to Thanksgiving dinner at Professor Baker's and he often joined the evening gatherings in Professor Baker's library. But most of all he felt certainty and achievement in his writing.

In August 1922, Miss McReady of the Harvard Appointment Bureau received a letter from Thomas Wolfe about the teaching position for which he had applied the previous spring. He had decided not to take the job:

> Matters at home were in an extremely unsettled condition following the death of my father, and it was not until very recently that I knew absolutely whether I should stay at home with my mother, accept the offer from Northwestern, or return to Harvard for another year with Professor Baker. My finances are now in such condition as will permit me to return for another year at Harvard. Professor Baker has been so unfailingly kind and encouraging that I believe this extra year which is now made possible, will be of the utmost importance to me.

Since he had by this time earned his A.M. degree, Wolfe registered in September for only one course, the Workshop. He could now devote all his time to writing. Some of the fragments of plays still extant among the Wolfe papers no doubt belong to this period. The most important of these, entitled "The House of Bateson," foreshadows the Gant family in *Look Homeward, Angel*; here the characters who later emerged as Old Man Gant, Helen, and Ben may be seen in their early stage of development. Although Wolfe probably began work on "The House of Bateson" sometime after the death of his father in June 1922, he had been considering the story of his family as possible literary material ever since his first summer in Cambridge. In his history notebook, there appear preliminary plans for a play about the conflicts of a family surnamed variously Broody, Groody, or Benton, which begins: "The Broody's were a strange family. They never saw each other's good points till one of their number died."

At the beginning of the term, he brought to class the first act of six different plays within a two-week period. His head was full of ideas, and he was experimenting with assorted techniques. Professor Baker withheld praise for his efforts, merely requesting that Wolfe concentrate on one project and bring in a second act to any one of the plays. This little discipline was evidently the bridle Wolfe needed, and during the term, the play "Niggertown" began to emerge, presumably from one of the first-act experiments.

Wolfe had come upon the idea for his new play about a year previous to its final production. In June 1922, when he had gone home for the first time in two years, he found that Asheville had changed. The boom years had come. That fall in a letter to Mrs. J. M. Roberts, his beloved prep-school teacher, he thundered out his complaint:

Coming home this last time I have gathered enough additional material to write a new play, — the second fusillade of the battle. This thing I had thought naive and simple is as old and as evil as hell; there is a spirit of world-old evil that broods about us, with all the subtle sophistication of Satan. Greed, greed, greed, — deliberate, crafty, motivated — masking under the guise of civic associations for municipal betterment. The disgusting spectacle of thousands of industrious and accomplished liars, engaged in the mutual and systematic pursuit of their profession, salting their editorials and sermons and advertisements with the religious and philosophic platitudes of Dr. Frank Crane, Edgar A. Guest, and the American Magazine.

This was the situation that set him writing "Niggertown," the play in ten scenes which was produced by the Workshop May 11 and 12, 1923, under the title "Welcome to Our City." The play, covering the life of a Southern town, tells the story of a real-estate group who, together with civic authorities, contrive to buy up all the property in the centrally located Negro district of the town. They plan, after evicting all the tenants, to tear down the old property in order to build a new white residential section. When the Negro group resists eviction, a minor race riot breaks out, and the militia comes to restore order. Since Wolfe tries to picture a cross-section of the town life, much of the dialogue does not pertain to the central action, but with the exception of the last scene the play reads very well. Wolfe employs a variety of techniques (even including stylized pantomime) as the play ranges in mood from broad comedy to tragedy at the death of the Negro leader. His characters include all classes and ages, both colored and white. Here too he brings in for the first time some of the "humorous" characters, in the Jonson-Smollett-Dickens tradition, which he drew with such success in his novels. His satire is broad in scope, attacking Southern politics, backward universities, evangelical preachers, small-town boosters, provincial little-theatre groups, and even short-sighted humanitarians. Yet for production, such scope and variety presented problems. Professor Baker had always urged students to make use of materials which they could handle, using characters and situations of a class or a region well known to them. But he also taught that dramatic presentation was based upon highly selective parts of this particular action. When Wolfe wrote a synopsis for "Welcome to Our City," he included the youth and background of certain characters, problems that had arisen in the city in recent years, his own ideas on the race question, and so forth. But when he began to turn it into acts and scenes, even a selection still included a great many characters, a number of side issues, and a couple of scenes not pertinent to the action. However, all this was part of his plan to present a complexity of life surrounding his main problem.

Although Baker agreed that his idea of presenting the background to his conflict was a good one, he pointed out that Wolfe must give his audience a more compressed story, for an over-supply of undeveloped action would crush their interest in his central problem. Wolfe, on the other hand, maintained that if the materials were true to life an audience would continue to give their attention, no matter how long the play or how full the list of characters.

The basis of this disagreement was the question of the distinction between the two forms, the novel and the drama. The problem had often arisen for Wolfe's consideration since he had been working under Professor Baker. The lectures in the course, "Forms of the Drama," had stressed the differences; a question in a mid-term examination had forced Wolfe to write about it; and Baker had called it directly to his attention at least once, in a penciled note beside an elaborate stage direction and character description in Act I of "The Mountains": "Aren't you anticipating your text and writing as a novelist?" In "Welcome to Our City" Wolfe needed to restrict his approach to actuality to meet stage limitations if he was to write a successful play. However, Baker recognized his potentialities in narrative, his zest for detail, and his interest in the full development of minor characters; and he pointed out to him that his aims suggested the novel form rather than the drama. But at this point Wolfe conceived of himself in the role of the artist as playwright, not the artist as novelist, and he was sure his play would be a success. Though he was already pushing the limits of the drama form, in a note to Baker (when he submitted his script for production) he indicated future plans of even larger scope:

I have written this play with 30 odd *named* characters because it required it, not because I don't know how to save paint.

Some day I'm going to write a play with 50, 80, 100 people — a whole town, a whole race, a whole epoch — for my *souls* ease and comfort.

He wished to write something on the scale of *The Dynasts*, but he also counted on stage production.

"Welcome to Our City" was marked for production in the spring, and Wolfe worked hard to put his scenes into shape for performance. He tried to cut down his material, make his scenes more compact, and economize as much as he thought possible; he attempted to follow Baker's advice and at the same time to retain as much of his own conception of the play as he could. He stated his position in the note to Baker:

I would be sorry to think that a close eye on the relevancy, the direct bearing of each scene and incident on the main problem, that of the negro, would conceal from you the fact that I knew what I wanted to do from the beginning to the end. With what success I did it I cannot venture a guess.

But will you please remember this: a play about the negro, a play in which each scene bore directly upon the negro, a play in which the negro was kept ever before you, might be a better play; it would not be the play I started to write.

But the play was still too long and still contained some portions that were far below the quality of the whole. It was Professor Baker's policy to refrain from editing scripts that were to be produced for his private audience. Let professional producers deal with scripts as they must, this was the one opportunity for a young playwright to see his play produced exactly as he had written it. Of course, Baker offered criticisms to the young writers, and in most cases his suggestions were adopted. But now he was dealing with a young man who felt that the truth of his realism would carry over any dramatic shortcomings. Wolfe would not cut the play, and after successive conferences, Baker had to do some cutting himself in order to reduce the excessive running time. Although Wolfe even lost his temper a couple of times during the shaping of the final script and was ready to withdraw the play, in the end he submitted to Baker's cutting, because he wished to get his play produced. Not much was dropped out, but the concluding scene was considerably shortened.

"Welcome to Our City," as produced in Agassiz Theatre in May 1923, was one of the most spectacular productions ever undertaken by the Workshop. It made use of seven different arrangements of a unit set and had a cast of forty-four people, with thirty-one speaking parts (Wolfe himself put on blackface to take part in the crowd scenes). The performances were very exciting; yet the play was not a complete success. It was original in its presentation of several strata of town life and in its forthright treatment of the race problem; but some of the scenes extraneous to the main action were far too lengthy for their purpose. The chief fault, however, was that the moral positions of the antagonists — Rutledge, the white leader, and Johnson, the Negro leader — were not clear, probably because Wolfe's views on the race question were not clear in his own mind. Since the play was still far too long, and the set changes were not made with the necessary speed, the performances, which began at eight, did not end until midnight. Most of the written criticisms from the audience remarked on the unnecessary length, and some were critical of Wolfe's boldness in putting the realities and brutalities of race conflict on the stage, but on the whole the audience comment was favorable. As a piece of writing, it was the best work that Wolfe had done: the characters were the first lifelike creatures he had ever drawn. But he had also used real-life models for the first time. One of the guests in the audience, Miss Laura Plonk from Asheville, was astounded as the plot

unfolded. After the show, she rushed backstage to Dorothy Sands
to exclaim with horror, "I know every person in the play!"

Wolfe would not state his opinion of the production even to his
mother: "I won't say whether my play was good or bad!" but he
was angry that part of the audience failed to give his work its
deserved acclaim. However, the productions were supposed to
be laboratory experiments, and the young playwrights could
profit by the criticism. Bearing in mind the staging of their
scripts, they might be better able to revise their plays into condition worthy of sale to Broadway producers. Baker saw that
Wolfe's play had excellent possibilities if it were judiciously
tightened. He told him that he thought the play had a better
chance for commercial success than Elmer Rice's *The Adding
Machine*, which was just closing a three months' run in New
York, and he asked the Theatre Guild to give the young man's
play a reading.

Quite naturally, Wolfe was excited. Now he really began to
conceive of himself as an artist and as a successful one. Already
he was planning a trip to Europe with the money he would make
on his play. He wrote to his mother in a frenzy of self-dedication,
"I know this now: I am inevitable. I sincerely believe that the
only thing that can stop me now is insanity, disease, or death,"
and further, "I will go everywhere and see everything. I will
meet all the people I can. I will think all the thoughts, feel all the
emotions I am able, and will write, write, write." But this faith
in himself, which provided the necessary power and energy to
carry out his later literary projects, brought about his downfall,
at this point, as a playwright. He was convinced that his play
with the scope of a novel would prove acceptable to a New York
audience. Instead of applying the blue pencil, he restored all the
cuts that had been made in rehearsal and, late in the summer, set
off for New York with great hopes. The final outcome of his
contacts with theatrical producers was that "Welcome to Our
City" was never sold.

Wolfe's troubles with the drama form did not end at Harvard.
Three years were to pass before he wrote Mrs. Roberts that he
had begun a new project — "a novel to which I may give the title

The Building of a Wall." At last, he was able to make use of his long preparation: he was able to convert that knowledge and experience which he had so furiously sought into his portrait of the artist. No longer bound by the limitations of the theatre audience, he was able to represent all the levels of society moving about his central character. Since the narrative was based on his personal life, one of its principal elements was its theme of escape.

It was to Harvard that Wolfe had made this escape and there began his attempt at the self-determined life preparatory to a writing career. At Harvard he first put into practice his own conception of Edwin Greenlaw's theory of "literature as a transcript of life." As a result he met problems that ultimately forced him to write prose fiction, although it was in the drama workshop, spurred by the encouragement and discipline of Baker, that he did his first mature writing. Wolfe never acknowledged what the University meant to him except as an atmosphere of learning and of books. He felt bitter about his failure to be a playwright. But during these three years he fed his mind with books, and this is the happy remembrance of Harvard that he kept. Even in the arrogant tone of his Autobiographical Outline, this is his summary:

What can I say of Harvard? A deficient enough place but for three years I wallowed in books there, performing as prodigious a feat of reading as has ever been performed by a living mortal before or since — having no elections to win, no popular favor to court, no particular student tabu to obey — I found it as free a place for thinking as I have ever found in America — God knows, I went around slovenly enough, — unbarbered, untailored . . . I lived in a kind of dream — at first a species of nightmare — at last — (particularly during the last year) — in a radiance — drunken with joy and with power — To me it was only vaguely a "University" — to me it was a place heavy with the noble enchantment of books — all the beauty, all the power, all the wonder was there for me — the centre of the place now, the first picture that comes to me, is of the Farnsworth room — the luxurious couch — and the books . . . Was not a university for me a wall. . .

Wolfe left Harvard in 1923 with a degree in English and set out for New York to sell the plays he had written at Cambridge. His failure to find producers led him to accept a teaching position at New York University. One of his young colleagues there was Henry T. Volkening, a graduate of both Princeton and Harvard. The friendship which developed at the time extended beyond their professional association. Volkening, a member of the New York Bar, is now a literary agent of the firm of Russell and Volkening.

PENANCE NO MORE

by

Henry T. Volkening

It was at the end of a dreary winter's day some twelve years ago. I had not long been teaching at New York University on Washington Square, though long enough already to have lost some early unreasonable enthusiasm.

One of the instructors, a poet of sorts, seriously asked, "How do *you* teach appreciation?" And a huge, black-haired man at a desk nearby squirmed and looked incredulous. He had just returned from Europe, they told me, to teach in the spring term, though he'd been here before.

Then the minister's son from the open spaces, one of the most self-assured and emancipated of our staff, started to bellow at us for the hundredth time that Samuel Butler's *The Way of All Flesh* was the best novel in English, nearest to the essential bitter truth, and so forth. I rose for rescue toward the water-cooler, just as

From the *Virginia Quarterly Review*, Spring 1939. By special permission of the author.

the huge man with the wild black hair tilted his head to bellow back, "And since then, by God, nothing whatsoever has been written!" He jumped up, and with what seemed like but three giant strides, stood over me at the water-cooler, looking fierce, his whole face compressed, swaying with hands on his hips. "Look," he said, pointing his finger into my eye, "I don't know you but you're new here, aren't you? I'm Thomas Wolfe and it's time to eat something, isn't it? Let's get out of here. I know a good place." And his face relaxed as we turned to go. "Tired?" he asked, smiling suddenly.

By three of the next morning he had stopped talking, and after that we often escaped together, having found the way. Sometimes others joined us, and always Tom talked, endlessly, joyously, bitterly, humorously, lyrically, with never any compromise with what he saw as the truth, never at a loss for words or subject, and never, of course, with the slightest regard for the lesser vitality and strength of his auditors, whom he would always leave in a state of happy and dazed collapse.

But there were times when he became quiet and confidential. Then he would tell of his hopes and longings, of little amenities and pleasures, of his tastes and friends and affections. Then he would no longer be tortured by the demon of the writer in him, and he would be kind, compassionate, and just. It was this side of him that is unknown, that appears rarely in his books, and that was as much a part of him as the ruthless and driven artist in him, who never knew peace or rest.

Those were the days when he was quite poor, or at least felt himself to be, when I used often to go to see him, sometimes alone, and sometimes with Natalie, my wife, at his "hole," as he called it, on West Eleventh Street, where he had a perfectly tremendous and very attractive three-room apartment, a part of which Aline Bernstein occasionally used as a workshop for her stage-designing. The place was in incredible disorder, as Tom's homes usually were, with a minimum of furniture, and with manuscripts and books and hundreds of "Freshman themes" thrown everywhere.

There he would entertain his visitors, often in a bathrobe, or in blue shirtsleeves, with talk, apologies, and tea — always tea, on a big cluttered table, served in enough unmatched cups to go almost around, with lump sugar from the original package, or from the table. And he'd pace about, distressed at having been interrupted in his work, and yet very happy.

At first he was principally concerned with his teaching and with what he conceived to be the false values of many of his colleagues, their preciosity, their limited experience, their knowing small-talk, spoken in a kind of code, and their concern with tea-cup tempests — these things, and most particularly their prejudices and bad literary judgments, he found hateful in them. "Look," he would say, pointing to a shelf of books above his working table, "there in one small row is much of the best that has even been written, and half of those they've never really read." And there were Burton's *Anatomy of Melancholy*, Melville's *Moby Dick*, Dostoevski's *Brothers Karamazov*, Heine, Shakespeare, Donne, Goethe, Homer, Plato, Euripides, Walt Whitman, Joyce's *Ulysses* (freely marked-up), the Bible, Swift, Boswell's *Johnson*, Voltaire's *Candide*, Milton, Coleridge (including the essays), Herrick, De Quincey, Anderson's *Winesburg, Ohio*, DeFoe's *Moll Flanders*, Bennett's *Old Wives' Tale*, Fielding's *Tom Jones*, and a few others which I have forgotten.

The actual classroom work he enjoyed hugely, but he was none the less always talking of the day when he would be freed from the economic necessity of teaching. Most of his students discouraged him profoundly, though I never heard him say an unkind word about any one of them. I believe that they thoroughly disgusted him, but he was always patient with them, gave them of his very "heart and guts," and was conscientious in his study of their efforts at composition, to a degree which was surely appreciated by very few. Chiefly he was sorry for them, especially for the "tortured intellectuals," which, he said, "so many Jewish students are."

Tom was then in such difficult financial circumstances that he could not afford to do more than dream of complete freedom from his duties at the college. (He always thought of himself as being poor, for that matter, and as coming of poor parents, though his father is said to have left a very substantial fortune, which was subsequently all lost.) He had only just graduated from a room on Eighth Street, which he described as being a mere attic in a deserted house, from the ground floor of which he had nightly to chase the derelicts, of whom there were often a dozen, for fear of their leaving cigarettes that would burn him to death. Then he would barricade the house, and get to work again on themes, and on *Look Homeward, Angel,* a large part of which he wrote on those nights, with a can of beans, coffee, cigarettes, and long shadows for company.

He worked like a man literally possessed, impatient with every petty interruption, so forgetful of time and friends that he would rarely remember an engagement for more than an hour or two, and would resent anyone's efforts to "tie him down" to a social obligation, much though he wanted companionship. I remember his phoning me at eleven o'clock one evening, to ask if I could have some dinner with him, embarrassed and confused to discover the hour.

Work, and more work, that was his only god, and his only faith was in his work, and in himself. That was why he was so bitter against not only every critic who doubted his power, but even against people who ignored his efforts, or who held views which, if sound, would by necessary inference impugn his own convictions. His attacks were often based upon a chance remark of the victim, or upon an attitude or a look, so that his conversation and writing were packed with a most unjust destruction of character, when it was only some characteristic or mannerism that had unpredictably annoyed him. Whenever he detected affectation, dullness, sterility, duplicity, or formalism, his annihilating rhetoric slaughtered wholesale, in the names of integrity and justice.

The æsthetes who needed what they called inspiration before they could work, and who would of course never work, he despised as much as he did those who would have literature serve an irrelevant cause, such as Communism or Fascism. The "business boosters," invariably caught in their self-made periodic crashes; lawyers, with their frustrating technicalities and machinations and delays; the gossip columnists and their readers; "the café-society swine, with a sense of values so distorted that, like the giraffe, you couldn't believe it if you hadn't seen it"; dentists and doctors; actors, for their sole interest in boring you with being either somebody else or nobody at all; "the whole damned theater crowd"; most modern painters, "painting theories because they are too incompetent to paint man or nature"; self-styled music lovers; pedagogues, opera singers, and "men who wear pearl-gray hats"; psychoanalysts and their pathetic patients, "suffering from nothing but too much money and too little to do, without the sense to know that it is all in Plato, in understandable language not especially manufactured for the trade"; those mystics "to whom their own otherwiseness is sufficient evidence of the existence of a God, maybe even with a beard"; women, for "their inherent incapability of detached and impersonal thought," and for "their feeling a right to possess you forever when you've done them a favor, especially a sexual favor"; telephone chatterers, other than himself; the women's-club favorites; most Southerners, as distinguished from the South; all the sophisticates among the writers, except Aldous Huxley; book reviewers, on principle; creative critics, who, "having no talent themselves, annihilate beautifully those who do"; and those people of Asheville who were bitterly disappointed that they could not threaten to horse-whip him for their not being in *Of Time and the River* — all these he castigated with a wonderful nobility of passionate invective.

Still, despite his talent in the character of a vengeful god, Tom's lighter satire always seemed to me more truly like him. There was the picture postcard from Atlantic City, for instance, exhibiting the broad rear-ends of four monstrous bathing beauties, on which he had written, "Here for the weak-end." He used to compare Atlantic City with Washington, D. C., to the disadvantage of the latter, as "last resorts for the amusement of ciphers." One Fourth of July he wrote, from New York, "The free Americans have been shooting off firecrackers all day; it's about all they can do." From England: "I am looking forward to a real old fashioned London Christmas — that is to say fog, rain, and a sodden wet woolly stuff they call air." Little academic notes: "Did you know they are dividing N. Y. U. up into colleges according to the Oxford plan? I've been appointed Master of Hoggenheimer Hall."

— The year at N. Y. U. is over and gone (with my prayers) to oblivion. When I saw the boys last many had turned slightly green, yellow, and purple from stored-up poison and malice." A suggestion to the traveler: "Why don't you go to Italy and follow the spring north? It would be so pleasant getting cheated in Sorrento in April." And another: "I am glad to be out of France — the people are cats: I don't mean anything against them, they are cats. . . ."

At times like these, I think, he was his lovable self. But when a black mood was on him, induced always by some trouble or irritation that kept him from his work, and on occasion exaggerated by too much alcohol, he would descend upon even his best friends with an unforgivable ferocity absolutely unwarranted by anything they had said or done. And these tirades would be the more embarrassing because they were invariably followed by stuttering and painful contrition, and by great lengths of effort to make amends.

He did have a genuine interest in his friends, and in all they thought or did. I remember with what fascination he entered into plans for an extended European trip which my wife and I were outlining late in 1928, how he would pore over maps with us late into the night with as much enthusiasm as if this were going to be his own trip, telling of places and pictures and sights that we especially should not miss: Naples, Pompeii, Sorrento, Rome, Florence, Vienna, Munich, Nuremberg, Montreux, Bath, York, the English Lakes, the Trossachs, Fountains Abbey; the paintings of Michelangelo, Rembrandt, Dürer, Grünewald, Hals, and particularly Breughel. In February, 1929, he even wrote a spontaneous little note from the Harvard Club, on what must have been one of his few leisure evenings: "I'm working on a huge book for Henry and Nat — a Glutton's Guide, a Sensualist's Handbook of seven countries with all about where to eat, drink, sleep — and how to avoid Rhodes Scholars, bedbugs, Ph.D.s — and other itinerant vermin. You can call the book 'Profiting,' by Tom's Mistakes."

A month later Tom came to see us sail at midnight on the *Vulcania*. It was a happy time for him, for Scribner's had accepted

Look Homeward, Angel, after several other publishers had turned it down. His good will, toward us and toward the world, was boundless, and he had a great affection for the ship too, for when he had last been abroad he had come home on her, on her maiden voyage. We toasted one another and explored the boat from bow to stern. Tom showed me what had been his quarters, "with three miserable wops, only slightly deloused, and always seasick." And he introduced me to his steward, to the bartender, and to a host of sailors, who seemed to remember him, and acknowledged his effusive greetings with the puzzled and frightened look of people about to be engulfed. We visited our little inside cabin, which, I thought, disappointed Tom in being not quite regal. He had somehow vaguely believed that we would be traveling in one of those private-veranda apartments reserved for "the fabulous women of the fabulously rich." It was on these apartments and their women that he glued devouring eyes. (I always thought he looked at women as if they were juicy steaks.) As we slowly drew from the pier, we could see his huge and lonely figure towering above the others, his arm waving awkwardly until the night swallowed him.

We heard from Tom, not frequently but usually at length, for writing letters bothered him so much that when he once managed to get around to the task he filled page after page in a kind of frenzy to make quick and worthy amends for weeks of silence. From New York, July 4:

Your letters and postals have given me the greatest pleasure. I cried out for joy at your rapturous letter from Vienna: I had a great personal pride in it, as if I had discovered the place. . . . Long, long ago I wrote you . . . wrote page after page, but never finished it. . . .

My other letter was filled with news — which I've forgotten. I feel splendid, and am fresh and fat. My proofs are coming in, my story appears in the magazine next month (get it in England if you can — Scribner's for August), book's out in the fall, and Scribner thinks it a grand thing and that it will go. I hope it makes a splash — not a flop! — but that it splashes me with a few dollars. Also, writing some short stories that they have asked me to write. . . . Loaded to the decks with my new book. — Thank God I'm thirty pounds overweight, it's going to kill me writing it.

Again from New York, August 9:

Please forgive me for not having written you more and oftener. I've been in Maine and Canada for several weeks. . . . Maine was lovely and cool. — I was at a wild little place on the coast. I fished, corrected proofs, and read John Donne and Proust all day long. . . . I am going to buy an island there surrounded by woods and the Atlantic Ocean. — I have already saved $1.25, and need only $2,998.75 more.

I envy you everything on your trip except the hordes of tourists who are, you say, beginning to swarm around you. I note you are going to Paris. . . . Whenever I think of the French . . . I control myself and mutter "Voltaire! Voltaire!" — And, after all, that is how a civilization should be judged — by its best, not by its worst, but its worst is pretty damned terrible, and unfortunately it requires superhuman fortitude and vision to see through to Ronsard when one is struggling to escape the snares of ten thousand petty rascals. Nevertheless, I have thought of France recently more than of any other country. — It is physically the most comfortable and civilized of nations, and its highest and best spiritually is magnificent. The greatest evil in the national temper, I think, is "glory" — what they call "la gloire." — It accounts for the flag waving, "France has been betrayed," speech making, singing the Marseillaise, going to war, et cetera. — It represents what is cheap and melodramatic in them. I could go on like this indefinitely, but you can hear the other side from any of the fourteen thousand American epic poets, novelists, dramatists, composers, and painters now in Paris. They all "understand" France, and will point out my treason. . . .

My story came out in the August Scribner's — also a picture of the author in the back and a brief write-up of his romantic life — how he has a "trunkful of MSS.," "forgets all about time when working," and "goes out at three A.M. for his first meal of the day." I was more madly in love with myself than ever when I read it.

I had expected convulsions of the earth, falling meteors, suspension of traffic, and a general strike when the story appeared — but nothing happened. . . . Nevertheless I am still excited about it. Proofs of the book will be finished in a day or two. The Book-of-the-Month Club heard of the book. . . . There's not much hope of its being their selection. They have pure and high-minded judges like William Allen White and Christopher Morley — and they may find some of the stuff too strong. Besides I am an unknown writer and they have hundreds of MSS. — but if! but if! but if! *Then*, of course, I should immediately accept the Abe Shalemovitch Chair in Anglo-Saxon Philology at N. Y. U. . . .

Scribner's have been magnificent, their best people have worked like dogs on the thing — they believe in me and the book. To have found a firm and association with men like this is a miracle of good luck. . . . I tremble, now that the thing's done. — I loathe the idea of giving pain, it never occurred to me as I wrote, it is a complete piece of fiction but made, as all fiction must be, from the stuff of human experience. Perhaps I may have to wear false whiskers and smoked glasses. Again perhaps no one will notice it. This too is a complicated thing about which I shall talk to you.

I am aching with a new one — it's got to come out of me, I loathe the idea of not writing it, and I loathe the idea of writing it — I am lazy, and doing a book is agony — sixty cigarettes a day, twenty cups of coffee, miles of walking and flying about, nightmares, nerves, madness — there are better ways, but this, God help me, is mine.

Forgive me — I have talked only about myself. . . .

In September we returned home and we soon saw him again. He talked about our trip, about himself, and about the book which was to be off the press in a few days. There were many dinners and visits, and he seemed, on the whole, quite happy.

I remember his infectious and childlike excitement on the day when Scribner's window first displayed *Look Homeward, Angel*, when he told of pacing back and forth in front of the piles of gay covers, admiring the colors, the arrangement, and the prominence accorded "this baby of mine." He frightened other passersby, and attracted the attention of the cop on the beat by his "strange weavings and ogling." He stopped in at book stores to ask whether people were buying it, and he avidly read all the reviews he could lay his hands upon, cursing every one that did not shower it with unqualified praise. He told of riding on a bus next to a girl who held a copy of the book, which was the first time he believed that people were really reading it, and of his not quite daring to speak to her, though he never so much in his life wanted to speak to anyone. And finally he began to see, despite initial misgivings, despite neglect in some quarters, and despite some stupid vilifications, that his first child had not been stillborn, and that his faith in himself and in his work had substance in the eyes of the world.

I saw Tom often that fall, usually in his tremendous one-room "hole" on Fifteenth Street, just west of Fifth Avenue, with its long row of casement windows facing north on comparatively quiet backyards. His book was "selling"; it brought him some money and a bank account, and the chance to lay his long deferred plans to relieve himself of the burdens of teaching. Those critics and writers whose opinions he valued were showering encomiums upon him with a liberality that should have gladdened the heart and soul of any man. But, paradoxically enough, it seemed to be this very success which distressed him most, which drove him to work ever harder upon his next book, while misgivings about its reception were already crowding themselves into his spirit. The suggestions by some of the reviewers that in *Look Homeward, Angel,* so patently autobiographical, he had possibly written himself out, maddened him with a determination to prove to others the faith he had in himself that as long as he might live he could never write himself out. He would "show them too that he could compress, maybe like Dostoevsky," that he could write short stories to conform to "any damned acceptable pattern they wanted." He said he would write a Gargantuan fable for them, without a recognizable person in it, with New York as setting, portraying the struggles of an artist against the attempts of literary people to cheapen and kill him: a modern *Gulliver's Travels* that would make Swift seem all sweetness and light. And he would even scores too with those noble Southerners of the old school who were driving him insane with their scores of threatening letters, and this he would do by becoming so famous that these same people would be "building monuments to me, comparing me with O. Henry (hah!), naming their children after me, and nigger children too (hah!), and stuffing me with food, just so they can get a good look at me, and tell me of my great contribution to the great literature of the South (hah!). But I do wish," he would say with a sudden sadness, "that they would try to understand, and that they would let me alone."

One day he phoned me to come over to help him resist "a boy from back home" who was about to stop in to sell him some life insurance. There was a comical desperation in his plea, for the simple fact was that he could not have paid premiums, and yet he could not deny people on merely logical grounds. And another time he spoke of "the strange songs and melodies in my head,

which I intend some day to set down"; strange they must have
been, for he seldom spoke of or listened to music, or even hummed
or whistled. He often talked about women, of those who came to
see him and to stay with him, of the many he had slept with and
the none he had known, of the two worlds in which men and
women live, speaking different languages, never to understand
each other.

But he was far from being a Don Juan. I have always felt that
his wild habits were nothing more than one expression of an
insatiable and overwhelming vitality. At heart he was pathetically
and naïvely domestic. He wanted, or thought he wanted, a wife,
a home, and children. "It is only through his work and children
that man can achieve immortality, and even the work, no matter
how good, will die, in time. You see what I mean, don't you?"
He wrote me once, "I have begun fondly to meditate a loving
wife, my own — this time! — and a few little ones, but where to
start searching for these simple joys is beyond me." He profoundly
envied the supposedly quiet and simple lives of the happily
married. "I notice," he said in a letter, "that people who have
never been alone for five minutes in their lives cheerfully banish
you to solitude, assure you there's no life like it, how they envy
you, and it is all for the best, after all, et cetera. But I've had
thirty years of it!"

The tension and speed of his life continued unabated. He went
everywhere where life was: along Fourteenth Street, "one of the
most horrible and hopeless streets in the world, where the faces
have lost every last trace of human dignity and striving"; and
into the wild wastes of "endless Brooklyn, a city so desolate as
to be unbelievable"; into, through, and out of every subway in
New York; to neighboring towns and cities; into Pennsylvania,
where some of his ancestors had lived, unaccountably fearful of
finding a Jewish name among them, and relieved at finding none;
to baseball games when Babe Ruth was playing, to enjoy his "tremendous rhythmic swats"; to park benches to "stare at my naval,
and feel vaguely uneasy, like all Americans, that I was not doing
something"; to "lit'ry teas" when he could not help himself, to
confound anemic dilettantes, and probably also to scare them

nearly to death, by shouting parts of the *Iliad* at them, in Greek, to prove that he knew what he was talking about and that they didn't; through the chasms of Wall Street during the stock market crash of 1929, expecting the bodies of suicides to fall upon him; to restaurants and speakeasies without number; and then back to his "hole" again, to reflect upon and to tell and to write about it all, and to lament the sad fact that "the artist can never freely enjoy any experience, for he is forever studying life in terms of translating it into something finer. And yet," he would say, "the artist must have first-hand experience. That is one thing I never could quite understand about Irving Babbitt, though he was in many ways a great man. I would rather listen to Coleridge, who comes to me sometimes in dreams, shadowy in a darkened room, sitting at a piano, looking at me — and like me."

The spring of 1930 brought the end of Tom's last year of teaching, and he escaped to Europe from troubles at home, for what he hoped, as he always hoped, would be a rest and vacation, but which turned out to be a time of hectic adventures and heartache more terrible than any he had known before.

I first heard from him in July, from Montreux:

There is nothing to do here. I read a great deal, an English feller named Shakespeare, the poems of Heine and Gooty, Donne . . . also Racine and Pascal — both sublime and dull.

My book is minutely outlined, and I have learned so much about brevity and condensation that it will not be over 600,000 words long. I am quite serious. It will be a very good book if I live to finish it. There are four parts and each is longer than an average novel.

I am reading "War and Peace" at the repeated suggestion of Maxwell Perkins. He is quite right about it; it is a magnificent book. . . .

In September came a letter from Strasbourg:

I've written you three enormous letters, none of which I have been able to finish. In the first two I couldn't say anything I wanted to say, and in the last one I said everything. . . . I have had some of the worst and also, I think, some of the best moments of my life these last four or five months. On the whole it's been a pretty bad time for me, but I am now out of the woods. For eight weeks now I have not spoken with one person that I knew — yes, I did see for one night a man I knew. . . . It would be better if I had never seen him at all:

he has played me one series of shabby tricks this summer, and also
made some very pretty speeches about character, courage, honor, et
cetera. . . . He . . . saw romance where it did not exist — or if it
did exist, it existed in bloody and sorrowful depths that he will never
fathom.

Now I am going to a place where I shall have a place of my own
and there are two or three real friends (I believe) that I can trust and
talk with. I need both. I have been alone long enough now, it has been
bitter medicine, but it has done me good, and I am back on my feet
again. . . .

In January, 1931, arrived a young book from London:

I am rapidly becoming a great authority on the subject of *Work*,
because I . . . have done some — "and penance more will do." By
the way, that would be a good title for almost any book — "Penance
More" — for that, I think, is what it takes to write one. . . . I have
not only worked but I have worked with spiritual bellyache, tooth-
ache, headache — as well as with something like a virulent abscess
just over my left lung, and I think now that I shall probably work
under almost any kind of conditions. . . . Buy a book written by one
Anthony Trollope, Esq., who wrote about ninety-seven other books in
addition. It is called "An Autobiography." . . . Brother Trollope
with great good humor and some cynicism describes his methods of
work, and tells how he managed to write fifty or sixty novels while
riding all over Ireland and England in the Civil Service, going hunting
twice a week, entertaining many friends, and in general leading a hell
of an active life. . . .

I shall never write fifty books or learn to write in railways or on
boats, nor do I think it is desirable, but it is certainly a damned good
idea to get ideas of steady work, and I think this is a good book to
read. I am able to do thirty or thirty-five hours a week — thirty-five
hours is about the limit and if I do that I am pretty tired. If a man will
work — really work — for four or five hours every day, he is doing his
full stint. Moreover, I find very little time for anything else. — I practically spend twenty-four hours getting five hours work done: I go out
very little. But it soon gets to be a habit. — I wish sometimes I were less
homesick, less lonely, and sometimes less heartsick; I could certainly imagine better conditions for work, and I am firmly decided (between us!)
that the "going-abroad-to-write business" is the bunk. — I went to
Paris Christmas; it is one of the saddest messes in the world to see all
these pathetic ********* who are beginning to get ready to commence
to start. Why a man should leave his own country to write — why he
should write better in Spain, France, England, or Czechoslovakia than

at home is quite beyond me. . . . It seems to me that one of the most important things a writer can have is tenacity — without that I don't see how he'll get anything done. Someone told me a year or two ago that the pity about modern writers is that the people who have the greatest talent for writing never write, and an embittered and jealous Irishman told me that one of the people Joyce wrote about in Ulysses was a much better writer than Joyce if he wanted to write — only he didn't want to. All this, in the phrase of my innocent childhood, "makes . . . ."

There can be no talent for any writing whatever unless a man has power to write: tenacity is one of the chief elements of talent — without it there is damned little talent, no matter what they say. Which I suppose is only another way of saying Arnold's dogma: Genius is energy. I think I would agree that the best writers are not always the people with the greatest natural ability to write. For example, I have never felt that Joyce was a man with a great natural ability. — I don't believe he begins to have the natural ease, fluency, and interest of, say, H. G. Wells. But he had an integrity of spirit, a will, and a power to work that far surpasses Wells. — I don't mean mere manual and quantity work; Wells had plenty of that, he has written one hundred books. — But I mean the thing that makes a man do more than his best, to exhaust his ultimate resources. That is the power to work and that cannot be learned — it is a talent and belongs to the spirit. At any rate, the only way out . . . is work — work under all circumstances and conditions. I am sure of that!

But . . . I am not nearly so easy and certain as I sound — but I am sure what I said about working is right. I do not know whether what I am doing now is good or bad — the impulse and idea are very good — but, as *always* between us, I think I have been on the verge of the deep dark pit for two years, and I am just beginning to get away from it. I am tired of madness and agony. I am willing to let the young generation have a fling of it — after all, I'm an old fellow of thirty and I deserve some peace and quiet. If work will do it I'll come through: I'll work until my brain and the last remnant of energy go. I suppose some people would say I have never spared others, but I should say that I never spared myself, and on the whole I think other people have done pretty well by me. I have given away what I would never sell if I had it again for diamond mines — years out of the best and most vital period of my life — and I find myself today where I was ten years ago, a wanderer on the face of the earth, an exile, and a stranger, and by God, I wonder why! I can't help it if it sounds melodramatic — it is the simple truth. . . . I am tired of . . . Europe . . . . I know it is all wrong — but where to live on that little strip of 4000 miles of earth is the question. . . . I confess now to a low craving for companionship, the love and affection of a few simple ******** and evenings spent by the ingle nook. . . .

Most of the people I like and a great many I dislike are in New York, but I can't go back there: it would be like walking around with perpetual neuralgia at present — the place is one vast ache to me — and I've offered quite enough free entertainment to the millions of people who having no capacity for feeling themselves spend their lives on the rich banquet some poor hick from the sticks (like myself) has to offer: I've learned a few things and the next time the ******** want to see a good show they're going to pay up!

I am going to see the Four Marx Brothers tomorrow with my English publisher — they are here in the flesh and the swells have suddenly discovered they were funny — so I suppose I shall have to listen to the usual horrible gaff from the Moderns: "You know there's something very grand about them — there really is, you know. I mean there's something sort of epic about it, if you know what I mean. I mean that man who never says anything is really like Michelangelo's Adam in the Sistine Chapel, he's a Very Grand Person, he really is, you know, they are really *Very* Great Clowns, they really are, you know," et cetera, et cetera, et cetera. . . . The dear Moderns, you will find, are cut from the same cloth and pattern all over the world. — Unplatitudinously they utter platitudes, with complete unoriginality they are original. Whenever they say something new you wonder where you heard it before, you believe you have not heard it before, you are sure you have heard it forever, you are tired of it before it is uttered, the stink of a horrible weariness is on it, it is like the smell of the subway after rush hours. . . . I am tired of these weary ********: they hate life, but they won't die.

The literary business in America has become so horrible that it is sometimes possible to write only between fits of vomiting. If you think that is extreme I mention a few names. . . . Keep away from them: don't talk about . . . writing to anyone, don't tell anyone what you're writing, and go with doctors, architects, bootleggers — but not with writers. This is not bitter advice: it is simply good advice — no one has ever written any books about America — I mean the real America — I think they bring out ten or twenty thousand books a year, but no one has ever written about America, and I do not think the "writers" will. . . .

I did not hear again from Tom, until one morning in spring he phoned from the end of Brooklyn to tell me that he had just docked. We met in Tom's room at the Prince George Hotel, and set out to spend the day, drinking and eating. It was impossible to leave him for mere office appointments, when it was so obviously refreshing his soul to tell of his happiness to be home, with all of the bitter experiences of Europe behind him, feeling freed again, for a little while at least, from entanglements and madness and despair. His chief anxiety was to get out of Manhattan as soon as possible, where old wounds might reopen, and to find an apartment on Brooklyn Heights, where "people would let me alone, for the mere name Brooklyn frightens them with visions of great distances."

He soon found spacious quarters, in no less than two floors of a house with a pleasant backyard, not on the Heights, but no farther than a long walk from there. Later he moved to Columbia Heights, to a place only a few minutes from Brooklyn Bridge, across which he often walked at sundown. And from the Heights he finally came back to the city and rented an apartment on one of the upper floors of a modern First Avenue building. In 1935 he took a short trip to Europe, principally to spend some small German royalties which could not be exchanged, and to enjoy his fame in Germany, where, he wrote, "People overwhelmed and exhausted me with friendship, et cetera. The only place I was ever famous. . . ." There he enjoyed "all the social gaiety I have missed for the last thirty-four years." The newspapers even took pictures of him getting on and off trolleys, he as big as the trolleys, and everyone roaring delight.

When *Of Time and the River* finally appeared, it was an instant success, so that Tom was for a time financially happier, and better able to live and dine well, even extravagantly. But troubles seemed to pursue Tom Wolfe more than they did most men. There was a suit against him brought by a former agent, about which I thought he was both needlessly generous and relentlessly bitter, and a libel action which brought him more into conflict with his flabbergasted attorneys than with the plaintiff, and a suit which he had to institute for the recovery of some manuscripts which he had very unwisely given into the possession of a young boy. His disrespect for the law became almost epic, for these troubles kept him from having a free mind for his work, they cost him more money than he could afford, and they brought about several lamentable clashes which had only remotely to do with their causes. There were few occasions when I met or talked to him when he was not in a murderous rage about some recent interview with a lawyer.

But of those few occasions, one especially stands out in my mind. It was in the early summer of 1937, late in the afternoon, immediately following a brief but terrific rain and thunderstorm. As I walked down First Avenue I saw him standing at the window of his apartment, high over the city, leaning upon the open upper sash, smoking vigorously as his searching eyes took in the beauty of the sudden clearing at sunset. He spoke, when I arrived, of the "clean glory" of the scene, and I felt that it must have refreshed his very soul, for that evening he too saw and felt "cleanly," and forgot his struggles for a few hours. At dinner he talked of his plan to go south to live for a while on a farm outside Asheville, with a good Negro servant all to himself, and with a sign at the front entrance: "Visitors welcome, without firearms." He was apprehensive about his reception, but he hoped that time would have softened much bitterness, and that there would be few "envious and defeated people." He spoke of his disgust at some hardhearted intellectuals for their sentimental sympathy for far-off Loyalist Spaniards about whom they knew nothing. "The miseries of home, I suppose, are not romantic enough, not noble enough, and, above all, oh dear yes, not ideological enough." He talked of death, and asked if I had ever seen a man die: when I told him yes, he asked me to tell him everything I saw. "Did he give any sign of — of — anything? I suppose not. I suppose no one ever really has."

Late that night we walked to Scribner's, where he gathered some mail and brought down a copy of *The Story of a Novel*, which he autographed under a street lamp on Fifth Avenue. I never saw him again.

He phoned me once after that, to say that he had just changed publishers. He seemed pained and confused and elated about it, and he sought to justify his action by telling of advice he'd had

from some writers' organization, of the folly of mixing business
and friendship, and of his hope that he had lost no friends who
mattered. He felt unwell, he said, and very tired.

Some months later he went west to Washington, where he'd
always wanted to go, and there he contracted the pneumonia
which ultimately led to his death after a brain operation in Baltimore, in the same hospital in which his father had died.

His last conscious words were characteristic of the faith and
hope that he always had. When Tom was almost gone, in the
hospital, and his brother Fred sought to encourage him with
assurances that he'd come through all right, Tom answered, from
the subconscious depths of approaching death, "I hope so, I hope
so."

His faith might have faltered at times, when things seemed
against him, and his spirits were sometimes low — but never for
long. And hope he always had, no matter how many and terrible
the doubts. This is what he wrote in my presentation copy of
From Death to Morning:

Dear Henry:

I'm a little sad as I write you this. I've just read the first review of
this book — in next Saturday's Herald-Tribune — which pans it and
sees little in it except a man six foot six creating monstrous figures in a
world of five feet eight. — I do not think this is true, but now I have a
hunch the well known "reaction" has set in against me, and that I will
take a pounding in this book. — Well, I am writing you this because I
believe that as good writing as I have ever done is in this book — and
because my faith has always been that a good thing is indestructible
and that if there is good here — as I hope and believe there is — it
will somehow survive. — That is a faith I want to have, and that I
think we need in life — and that is why I am writing you this —not in
defense against attacks I may receive — but just to put this on record
in advance with you, who are a friend of mine. — So won't you put this
away — what I have written — and keep it — and if someday it turns
out I am right — won't you take it out and read it to me?

Yours —
Tom

When Wolfe failed to return from a trip to Europe in February 1925 to meet his classes at New York University, John Skally Terry was selected to replace him. Terry had been a fellow student of Wolfe's at Chapel Hill; and when Wolfe finally came back to the university, the acquaintance was renewed and cemented. Terry was a friend of both Wolfe and Maxwell Perkins when the controversy began over how much Perkins' editing was responsible for the success of Wolfe's novels. Terry, still at the Washington Square College of New York University, is now designated Wolfe's official biographer.

WOLFE AND PERKINS

by

John Skally Terry

When Fate, in the person of Madeleine Boyd, the literary agent, brought Thomas Wolfe's manuscript of *Look Homeward, Angel* to Maxwell E. Perkins, editor of Charles Scribner's Sons, there began an association which will perhaps become as famous as that of Dr. Samuel Johnson and James Boswell. Perkins was immediately enchanted by the book. He and his office staff read it avidly; all agreed as to its importance.

Perkins wrote to Wolfe in Europe, Wolfe hurried to New York, and the shaping of the manuscript for the press began. In a memorandum on Wolfe submitted by Perkins to the Harvard College Library, to accompany the William B. Wisdom collection of Wolfe's letters, bills, documents, notebooks, and manuscripts, Perkins explained, without ado, that he and Wolfe began "to

---

Published under "En Route to a Legend" in the *Saturday Review of Literature*, 27 November 1948. By permission of publisher and author.

work upon the book." He then told how, at the very beginning, in order to give the book unity, they agreed to cut out the opening scene first used — that which showed W. O. Gant and his brother, both then little boys in Pennsylvania, as they watched passing soldiers who were soon to take part in the Battle of Gettysburg. This cutting was done so that the book might begin with the memories of the character about whom the book was to revolve, Eugene Gant, rather than with the memories of the father. Perkins explained how this wonderful first scene was later woven most effectively in *Of Time and the River* into the memories of W. O. Gant as he lay dying in the hospital in Baltimore.

This work of shaping Wolfe's writing for publication at conferences between Wolfe and Perkins has led to false beliefs, some of them ridiculous. Therefore, some clarification is necessary.

According to Perkins the work they shared brought him some of the happiest hours he ever spent. The coöperation between author and editor continued from 1928 until 1935, when *Of Time and the River* was published. Wolfe then, in gratitude to Perkins, acknowledged his debt in one of the strangest and most moving tributes in literary history, *The Story of a Novel*, issued in 1936. This book brought further confusion as to the part played by Perkins in preparing Wolfe's material, and led to the outcropping of innuendo and falsehood which had something to do with Wolfe's leaving Scribner's in 1938 and, before his last Western journey, turning over his eight-foot-high pile of manuscript of unpublished material to Edward C. Aswell, then editor of Harper and Brothers.

The extent to which the Wolfe-Perkins efforts were, and still are, misunderstood, was illustrated in *The Saturday Review of Literature* for February 7, 1948. This issue carried an autobiographical bit written by Wolfe for Georges Schreiber. An accompanying illustration showed parts of two pages of the manuscript with interlinear corrections and deletions. A legend explained that the two pages were "a working example of the Maxwell Perkins — Thomas Wolfe editor-author relationship," and there were further explanations that this was the first published demonstration of how the two worked. One of the pages photographed was signed and dated by Wolfe in his own handwriting.

Perkins had let me use, in my work as the official biographer of Wolfe, a post to which he and the Wolfe family appointed me, the whole mass of personal material left by Wolfe and now in the Harvard College Library. Since I went over all of this material most carefully and recorded what I would need, I came to know Wolfe's handwriting and methods intimately. I had, of course, before Wolfe's death, read much of his handwriting. Therefore, when I read the legend below the manuscript illustration in *The Saturday Review*, I knew that a mistake had been made. All the editorial changes and deletions in the two pages had been made by Wolfe himself. Perkins certainly had made no editorial changes in these particular pages of manuscript.

I also knew that Maxwell Perkins, according to his own declaration to me, never made any changes in words or style; and that he never changed a sentence of Wolfe's. I had been aroused by a somewhat similar error made in the *New York Herald Tribune Book Review* of January 13, 1946. In a review by Horace Gregory of *A Stone, a Leaf, a Door*, which was a rearrangement of some of Wolfe's prose into poetic form, Gregory stated that Perkins wisely had often edited out some of Wolfe's rhetorical flights. I immediately asked Perkins if he had ever done any such thing. He assured me that he had not; that he never rewrote a single sentence of Wolfe's; that he never changed a word. What he did, he said, was give advice about material which was out of perspective, or which gave too much importance to side issues. Then he recalled to me how, once, when he asked Wolfe to work over some material on the sickness and death of the father, W. O. Gant, Wolfe brought in a magnificent piece on the doctor who treated the father; none of the material, however, really belonged in the piece, for it did not fill the gaps that required filling.

I knew as almost any careful reader of Wolfe must know, that no one could hope to change Wolfe's sentences without having the changes stand out like proverbial sore thumbs. Wolfe's lines were as personal and individual as those of a poet.

The two men, Wolfe and Perkins, working together for years, and both being very human, did not always agree; sometimes they argued violently. But stick together they did until the first two great novels published in Wolfe's lifetime, were issued. Their method of working was routine. Perkins would take home the sections of manuscript which Wolfe gave him, and read them carefully. Then, after office hours, that is, after four or five P.M., Perkins and Wolfe would meet in Perkins's little office, or they would go to the lounge of the Chatham Hotel, known as Chatham Walk, and Perkins would give his advice. The nearest he ever came to writing on a Wolfe manuscript was in drawing a line in a margin by some passage; sometimes he would merely bend down the corner of a page. Then Wolfe and Perkins would discuss the ideas held by the editor, and Wolfe, if he found the suggestions good, would take the manuscript home for rewriting or revision.

Perkins kept after the work and also after Wolfe until the final unity achieved was pleasing to both. However, Wolfe was never ready for his books to go to press and Perkins had to use heroic measures to convince the author that he must finally consign his words to the printer.

Wolfe, as before stated, was not always happy about the changes suggested. He explained in *The Story of a Novel* the way in which *Of Time and the River* took form. He first brought Perkins two enormous manuscripts, one over 1,000,000 words; they faced the task of bringing order out of chaos, for Wolfe had the job of revising, weaving together, and shaping and cutting. He told how during 1934 he and Perkins took the first of the two manuscripts, how he wrote a thoroughly detailed synopsis and slowly, by adding needed material and cutting out superfluous matter, they got the book ready for the press by 1935. Cutting, he admitted, was always most difficult to him and his tendency was always to write rather than to cut.

Wolfe's very soul revolted at some of the cutting he knew was necessary. I remember that, one spring morning in 1934, my phone rang at two A.M. I recognized Wolfe's agonized voice.

John [he said] I've written all that one could write, or need ever write, about a train; and it's one of the best things I've ever written.

But, by God, they tell me I've got to cut it. I just don't see how I can do it. This ought to stand as a final piece of writing about a train.

He talked to me for over two hours about the passage and how he felt. As I listened, I visualized him sitting alone, in his fourth floor walk-up apartment at 5 Montague Terrace, Brooklyn, five blocks from where I lived. He just had to pour out his misery to someone.

In Wolfe's *The Story of a Novel* he explained that the section about the train was 100,000 words long, and that, while it was important in itself, its function was subordinate and it had to be fitted for its place in the manuscript being planned for publication. In further explaining his task of revising the whole manuscript, he said that he wrote over a half a million words, of which only a small part was used.

A short while after Wolfe called me about having to cut the passage dealing with the train, I asked Perkins why he did not take the section and publish it as a unit in itself. He replied that to do so would not be practical and that in the long run Wolfe would use the material somewhere. . . .

The work on which these two collaborated was at an end when *Of Time and the River* was issued in March 1935. They never got together on another project, and some resentment arose in Wolfe toward Perkins and Scribner's. Wolfe had begun to write about both in a new section of a novel; in a letter to Perkins he accused Perkins of criticizing him for planning to use such material. Perkins denied having made any such criticism; Wolfe wrote that someone had told him that Perkins threatened to disappear if Wolfe used him in his fiction.

Wolfe's frankness in his *The Story of a Novel* has led people with little understanding to accuse Wolfe of being entirely dependent on Perkins, and incapable of writing alone. Perkins regretted such accusations deeply. Wolfe became convinced that he must show his independence. This conviction and other unfortunate circumstances led to rationalizations in Wolfe's mind which gave him courage to break with his first publisher and editor. The move was most painful to both author and editor; however, it was to bring Wolfe the friendship of another great editor, Edward C. Aswell, who was, as already stated, at that time with Harper's; Aswell, after Wolfe's death, performed a herculean task as editor and devoted friend, in bringing order to thousands of pages of manuscript, which were published as three posthumous books, *The Web and the Rock, You Can't Go Home Again,* and *The Hills Beyond.*

Aswell dismisses as absurd the charge that Perkins ever made any detailed changes in any Wolfe manuscript. Moreover, Irma Wyckoff, who was Maxwell Perkins's secretary during the time of the Wolfe-Perkins association, declares unequivocally that Perkins never edited in detail or rewrote a particle of Wolfe's copy.

The whispered accusations of his dependence on Perkins, as well as that ideological difference expounded in a letter to Foxhall Edwards in "You Can't Go Home Again," determined Wolfe to break with Scribner's. In the fall of 1936, when the severance seemed inevitable, Perkins wrote Wolfe: "I can't express certain kinds of feelings very comfortably, but you must realize what my feelings are toward you. Ever since 'Look Homeward, Angel' your work has been the foremost interest in my life." That Wolfe's deep love for Perkins remained after the complete break is evinced in the letter to Perkins written during Wolfe's final illness. Perkins died in 1947, regarded as the greatest creative editor of his time.

SCRIBNER'S AND TOM WOLFE

by

Maxwell Perkins

When I knew that Tom Wolfe had died, as I knew he must after the day of his operation at Johns Hopkins — and before that it had seemed inconceivable that one so vibrant with life could die young — a line kept recurring in my mind as a kind of consolation: "He hates him that would upon the rack of this tough world stretch him out longer." For he was on the rack almost always, and almost always would have been — and for one reason. He was wrestling as no artist in Europe would have to do, with the material of literature — a great country not yet revealed to its own people. It was not as with English artists who revealed

From the *Carolina Magazine*, October 1938. By special permission of the Estate of Maxwell E. Perkins.

England to Englishmen through generations, each one accepting what was true from his predecessors, in a gradual accretion, through centuries. Tom knew to the uttermost meaning the literatures of other lands and that they were not the literature of America. He knew that the light and color of America were different; that the smells and sounds, its peoples, and all the structure and dimensions of our continent were unlike anything before. It was with this that he was struggling, and it was that struggle alone that, in a large sense, governed all he did. How long his books may last as such, no one can say, but the trail he has blazed is now open forever. American artists will follow, and widen it to express the things Americans only unconsciously know, to reveal America and Americans to Americans. That was at the heart of Tom's fierce life.

It was a gigantic task, and Tom was a giant in energy and in power of feeling as well as in physique. His too great dimensions seemed to represent the difficulties that almost drove him mad: he could not fit a book to the conventional length, nor produce one in the usual space of time. He was not proportioned to these requirements, but neither was his subject, the vast, sprawling, lonely, unruly land.

It is said his books are formless, but I do not think he lacked a sense of form. Is it wanting, for instance, in "The Web of Earth"? In a large way he knew where he was going, and given twenty years and many volumes, I often thought, he might have fully achieved a proper form. But as he had to fit his body to the doorways, vehicles, and furniture of smaller men, so he had to fit his expression to the conventional requirements of a space and time that were as surely too small for his nature as they were for his subject.

Four years after the publication of *Look Homeward, Angel* about Christmas time in 1933, he brought me the huge manuscript, two feet high, of *Of Time and the River*. And he was desperate. Time, his old enemy, the vastness and toughness of his material, the frequent and not always sympathetic inquiries of people about his progress toward another book, and financial pressure too — all were closing in on him. I thought, "this book has to be done," and we set to work. I, who thought Tom a man of genius, and loved him too, and could not bear to see him fail, was almost as desperate as he, so much there was to do. But the truth is that if I did him a real service — and in this I did — it was in keeping him from losing his belief in himself by believing in him. What he most needed was comradeship and understanding in a long crisis, and those things I could give him then.

After I had read the manuscript and marked it up, we began a year of nights of work. The book was far from finished. It was in great fragments, and they were not in order. Large parts were missing. It was all disproportioned. Tom, who knew all this, would come in at eight or so, and I would point these things out, part by part. But I could tell Tom nothing, if it were right, that he did not easily see, and perhaps had already seen. But his whole natural impulse was outward, not inward — to express, not compress, or organize — and even though he realized that something had to be cut, as extrinsic, or otherwise superfluous, he could not easily bear to have it done. So every night we worked and argued in my boxstall of an office over Fifth Avenue, often accomplishing nothing, and strewed the floor with cigarettes and papers. The night-watchman and the scrubwoman forgave us, because there was that in Tom that established a fellowship with all good sound people. And there was his humor too, always, except in the mortal struggle with his material.

Once I argued for a big deletion, late on a hot night, and then sat in silence. I knew he must agree to it for the reasons were strong. Tom tossed his head about, and swayed in his chair, and his eyes roved over the office. I went on reading in the manuscript for not less than fifteen minutes, but I was aware of Tom's movements — aware at last that he was looking fixedly at one corner of the office. In that corner hung a winter hat and overcoat, and down from under the hat, along the coat hung a sinister rattlesnake skin with seven rattles — a present from Marjorie Rawlings. I looked at Tom. He was eyeing that group of objects, and the rattlesnake stood out. He waved his hand at them: "Aha," said Tom, "the portrait of an editor." We worked no more that night. After the laughter we went to the Chatham Garden which

Tom loved — and where the waiters all knew him as a brother —
and talked and argued for an hour under the summer stars.

Such cutting was one thing, but there were the gaps, and Tom
filled some of them in there and then, writing in his huge, heavy
scrawl, on the corner of my desk. When we came to the point
where Eugene's father died, I said that it must be written about,
but that since Eugene was away at Harvard, Tom need only tell
of the shock of the news, and of Eugene's return for the funeral —
a matter of perhaps five thousand words. And Tom agreed.

The next night he came in with some thousands of words about
the life of the doctor who attended Gant. I said, "This is good,
Tom, but what has it to do with the book? You are telling the story
of Eugene, of what *he* saw and experienced. We can't waste time
with all this that is outside it." Tom fully accepted this, but
still, the next night, he brought in a long passage about Eugene's
sister Helen, and her thoughts while shopping in Altamont, and
then at night in bed when she heard the whistle of the train. I
said, "How in God's name will you get this book done this way,
Tom? You have wasted two days already, and instead of reducing
the length and doing what is essential, you are increasing it and
adding what doesn't belong here."

Tom was penitent. He did not argue back as he almost always
had done. He promised he would write only what was needed —
and yet the next night he brought in thousands of words about
Gant's illness, all outside of what I thought was wanted. But it
was too good to let go. I said so. It was wrong, but it was right,
and Tom went on, and the death of Gant is one of the finest things
he ever wrote. Thank God I had sense enough to see it that early,
even though it seemed to me to violate the principle of form.
But I do not think I could have stopped Tom anyhow. He had
agreed that I was right, but underneath he knew what he was
doing and had to do it.

All this perhaps sounds grim and desperate — and it should,
for that it often was — but it gives no picture of Tom. It presents
him as he was in the heat of struggle. After *Look Homeward,
Angel* was published he was happy, and after the great success of

Of Time and the River, when he came home from Europe, and
before he began the next long battle that ended last May when
he set out on the tour of the Northwest that ended in his fatal
illness, he was happy too. In that last interval he lived on First
Avenue off Forty-ninth Street, and we had a house two blocks
away, on Forty-ninth. Then we had many happy times before the
struggle with his new book grew too fierce. The block between us
and First Avenue was almost slum like. Boys played some exciting
adaptation of baseball, and then of football, in the street, and the
sidewalks were crowded with children. They all knew Tom.
When he went by in his long, slow, country stride, looking at
everything, they would call out, "Hello Mr. Wolfe." And the
police all knew him too. Once my wife said, "A flower-pot has
disappeared from one of our window boxes. I can't understand
how it happened." The window box was too high for anyone to
reach, you would think, and who would want a geranium? Long
afterward, one night Tom said: "I meant to tell you, I took one of
your geraniums. I was coming in but the house was dark so I
just took a flower pot, and a cop saw me and said, 'What are you
doing?' I said, 'I'm taking it home to water it.' He just laughed."
This was New York. Was the cop afraid of Tom and his great size?
No, he knew him, and understood him: that human quality in
Tom had made him friends with everyone around, and they knew
he was one of them.

Tom was always one of them, the regular people, and he liked
them most. His talk was beyond any I ever heard when he was
not in the torment of his work. He would tell you of the river Cam
in Cambridge, England, and the mist over it so that you knew the
magic Tennyson felt; or of the tulip fields in Holland; or the
paintings he liked in the galleries of Europe so that if you knew
them you saw them again and afresh; or of that ruined monastery,
Fountains Abbey near York, in its old forest — and you knew it as
it was when it was all alive. He could have talked to anyone
about anything he had touched at all, but what he wanted, or
thought he did, was to be one of the regular people. He was lonely.
He inspired fellow feeling, but it could not embrace him enough.
He wanted the simple, hearty life of Gant in his best times, the

wife and children, and coming home for lunch, and the fire roaring up the chimney. (No door!)

He could not be like other people. He was not built on their
scale. Everyone important to him in his life seemed to know that.
His was not the conventional story of neglected, unrecognized
genius at all. His school teachers, the Robertses in Asheville,
knew, apparently, when he was a child, that he was different from
the others, and so did all his family, there in the mountains, and
they enabled him to go to college — I think Americans can be
proud of that. Only the inescapable slings and arrows of life betrayed him, the petty obligations and duties, and the lawsuits.
They maddened him because they kept him from his work. All
that infuriated him in its injustice. The one important thing in the
universe to him was his work, and this was so simply because it
was so. It was not due to ambition in the cheap sense, and it was
not what is generally meant by egotism. He was under the compulsion of genius, and all the accidents of life that got in the way
of its expression seemed to Tom to be outrages and insults. He
knew in his mind that man was born to trouble — that everyone
was beset with anxieties and thwarted by obstacles — but that
this work which he was bound to do should be interfered with by
trivialities, was maddening. And so was the struggle with the
work itself.

From this came the dualism in Tom that made him the one
man I ever knew of whom extreme opposites were true. He was
proud as Lucifer and yet utterly humble. He was full of kindness
and the most gentle consideration, and yet ruthless. He was
totally without a sense of humor, many said, but there never was
a more humorous man. And how could this be? Because there was
the man Tom and this dreadful *and* beautiful obligation in him.
He was not proud of anything he had ever done — not of much he
had written — but the consciousness of this great thing in him that
he had to do made him so. He was ruthless, as in writing about
real people, not because he did not realize as Tom, the pain he
might give but because this obligation in him made him feel that
the pain was relatively trifling and brief, and was caused by
conventional standards, and that what he was about was beyond

all that. He was without humor often in his writing about Eugene — though a magnificent humor pervades his writings otherwise — because Eugene, being Tom, was engaged in the same deadly serious business, was obsessed with the mortal struggle to master material.

And Tom was always harassed by time. He had always "thoughts that he must cease to be before his pen had gleaned his teeming brain." It was this that made him strive to read all the books in the Harvard library in a year or so, and sent him on his wild odysseys of Europe and the South and the Pacific Coast, and New England, and then the Northwest. And this largely it was that gave him his love of quantity, for its own sake as it seemed. He didn't have time enough, and somehow seemed to know it. One early morning when 49th Street was silent and empty, Nancy Hale who lived there heard a deep and distant chant. It grew louder, and she went to the window. A great, loose figure of a man in a black slouch hat and a swaying raincoat was swinging along in Tom's slow stride and he was chanting over and over: "I wrote ten thousand words today. I wrote ten thousand words today." Old Time was riding him, but that day Tom had won.

When I first saw Tom with his wild black hair and bright countenance as he stood in my doorway hesitating to enter — in those days Tom had more respect for editors — I thought of Shelley (who was so different in most ways) because of that brightness of his face and the relative smallness of his head and the unruly hair. Just before his illness took its fatal turn he scribbled me a letter in pencil, though he should not have done it. The last of it suggests how things sometimes seemed and looked to Tom. He recalls a good happy time we had on the day he returned from Europe several years ago, a hot Fourth of July when just before sunset we "went on top of the tall building, and all the strangeness and the glory and the power of life, and the city was below."

During the early months of 1938 Wolfe worked desperately to complete the huge manuscript later to be divided into "The Web and the Rock" and "You Can't Go Home Again." Though the pages were by no means ready for the printer, Wolfe put them in order and deposited them with his publisher for safe-keeping. Then he set out in high spirits for an extended trip to the West Coast, which he had visited only briefly in 1935. His first stops at Purdue University and Chicago are related here by William Braswell, now professor of American literature at Purdue.

THOMAS WOLFE LECTURES AND TAKES A HOLIDAY

by

William Braswell

The first time I saw Thomas Wolfe I immediately accepted as fact all that I had thought of before as "the Wolfe legend." I had known that he was tall, but I had not expected to see a man six feet six inches tall who weighed over two hundred and fifty pounds. Nor had the pictures of him that I had seen shown the baldness at the back of his head or his tendency toward a large belly. But perhaps I was more surprised by his halting speech than by his appearance. He stammered a good deal, especially at the beginning of his address, with an impediment that reminded me more of Luke Gant than of Eugene. And his voice was so deep and throaty that the loudspeaker relayed it but poorly to the more distant of the three hundred people who had come to hear him. When he began to talk, I noticed some frowning and shaking of

From *College English*, October 1939. By permission of the author and publisher.

heads in the corner where I was, and one man sitting near-by got up and moved closer to the speakers' table. I missed a word here and there, but never enough to lose the thread of thought. As Wolfe himself said by way of preface, he was not a good speaker. Yet he had a rugged force because of the naturalness, the sincerity, and the energy with which he spoke. As a matter of fact, his manner made perhaps as much impression as what he said.

The occasion at which he spoke was the Annual Literary Banquet at Purdue University on the evening of May 19, 1938. Just a handful in the audience knew that this was the second such address that Wolfe had made. And of course no one suspected that this was to be the last public appearance of this huge, robust man who stood there straining at articulation and occasionally sawing the air with a heavy arm.

In response to the toastmaster's query about the place of writers in the world, Wolfe had begun by saying that the writer has just as definite a place to fill as the engineer, the lawyer, or the businessman. Writing, he affirmed, requires a man to work as hard as any other occupation. Humorously, he said that when he told his mother of having sold a story for fifteen hundred dollars, she replied: "Boy, you're the only one in the family who can make that much money without working." Just as his father's hands had developed calluses from working with mallet and chisel on stone, so his own fingers had become toughened by writing. Some people did not realize that a writer had to write and had to keep writing. Here Wolfe touched upon a matter that he later discussed at length in conversation: various groups had asked him to parade in front of this legation, to picket that concern, and the like, and he had refused, not because he was without sympathy and convictions in regard to the points at issue, but simply because he felt that, as a writer, he could spend his time better by writing. (In conversation he grew eloquent in ridiculing "old ladies" who continually invited him to costly tea parties where they voiced their pity in "ah's" and "oh's" and fished up a few dimes for Spanish orphans or for "the poor, poor Chinese.") He had never heeded the golden trumpets of Hollywood because he considered what he was doing more important than writing scenarios.

He emphasized the necessity of the writer's working with material that he knows thoroughly, and told how he himself had tried to write from his own experience. He admitted that he had made mistakes, one of which was that he had taken no pains to conceal the identity of certain people whom he had used as characters in his earlier works. When he had recently visited Asheville to see his mother, an old friend had taken him to task by saying: "It's all right to use a man as a character in a novel, but there's no need of giving the man's name, address, and telephone number!" His mistakes, he said, had taught him a great deal. As anyone familiar with the book may already have surmised, the essence of much that Wolfe said may be found in his *The Story of a Novel.*

One point that he made with some humor was that he could not tell anyone else how to write stories and articles that would make money because he did not know how to write them himself. He said that when he sold a story to the *Saturday Evening Post,* he thought his financial troubles were over: now that he knew what the *Post* wanted, all he would have to do to sell a story for a high price would be to sit down and turn one out according to his formula. But the next story he sent to the *Post* was rejected. This surprised him: he had thought this story would be "surefire," because it had the Civil War and everything else in it. He submitted it to several other magazines that paid unusually well; yet it was always returned. Finally it was accepted and published by the *Yale Review,* and he was very happy that it was, for he had great respect for that journal. Nevertheless, he added, he was not unaware that if the *Saturday Evening Post* had bought the story, he would have received about fourteen hundred dollars more for it.

Another anecdote that he told was about a hopeful Belgian woman who eagerly inquired when German soldiers invaded her town: "When do the atrocities begin?" The tight-lipped silence of a few elderly women was a futile rebuke amid the loud laughter that the story touched off. In fact, the audience was as responsive throughout the address as the speaker could have wished it to be.

At a brief reception held just after the banquet, Wolfe was

pleased when complimented on his talk. Modestly repeating that he was no speaker, he went on to tell how a friend in New York had laughed at the idea of his being paid to give an address. His friend had exclaimed: "You know you can't deliver a speech!" Wolfe had replied: "No, but I can d-d-do a hell of a lot of stammering for th-th-three hundred dollars."

When he had been engaged to come to Purdue, he had made no pretenses about what he expected to do. Something of his plan is indicated in his correspondence with a member of the department of English at Purdue whose house guest he was to be.* On April 11 he wrote, from New York City, about a telegram that he had sent the official who had engaged him:

. . . I explained to him that I was hard at work on a new book and that I would not, therefore, be able to take time off for the preparation of a formal speech. But I also tried to explain that I thought what I had to say might be more interesting if I talked informally, and out of my own working and writing experience. That is really what I have in mind; since my present life is largely writing — for even when I am not actually engaged in it, I am thinking about it — it seems to me that anything I had to say might be more interesting if I drew it out of my own experience, and from the work I do.

He also humbly asked for information as to what was expected of him. His next letter, written April 15, contains an interesting note on a previous address he had made:

Thanks very much for writing me so promptly and giving me an idea of what is ahead of me. I feel much easier about the whole thing now, and believe I can swing it well enough. Of course, I am no sort of public speaker, but I did speak to a gathering similar to this at the University of Colorado two or three years ago and, after the first few minutes of fumbling and stumbling around, I got hold of what I wanted to say and did very well. The only trouble was that after I did get wound up it was hard to stop: I offered to at the end of three-quarters of an hour, but they very generously told me to go on. But I know what a bore a long-winded speaker can be on an occasion like this, at a banquet; so I will try to hold myself down within reasonable limits.

* Herbert J. Muller, who has kindly permitted me to quote from this correspondence. My friends the Mullers, the Kendall B. Tafts (of Chicago), Robert Liddell Lowe, William S. Hastings, and Albert R. Fulton gave me valuable aid in recalling many details used in this article. — W. B.

His humility in the face of what was coming became somewhat amusing when he asked whether "one pretty good blue suit and a tuxedo" would be enough to "meet the sartorial requirements of the occasion acceptably."

On May 16 he wrote of his happiness over the task he was leaving behind him. His frequent use of the word "tremendous" in this letter suggests his state of mind about the book he was shaping:

. . . I have driven myself without limit steadily for seven months now, and with only a brief interval for a long time before that. For the past week, my secretary and I have been engaged on the labor of assembling, putting in sequence, typing and binding the manuscript of my new book. It has been an enormous task, for it involved sorting and going over piece by piece a large portion of the manuscript I have written in the past four years — I should judge several million words.

I was up until five o'clock this morning working on it, and although there is still a tremendous quantity of manuscript left, I begin to see light, and feel a tremendous amount of comfort and satisfaction as the thing begins to shape up. Of course, the book is not finished yet — a tremendous labor of writing and revision is before me — but for the first time since I began it, I begin to feel a sense of wholeness: I have at least articulated a tremendous structure. All of this will be bound and minutely titled section by section and given to the editors at Harper's tomorrow to read and to hold for me until I come back and go at it again, and the remainder will be boxed up and kept in storage.

I have been thus tedious in telling you about all of this because I wanted to explain to you that I am not only very tired, but very happy, also. This trip is really a kind of momentous celebration for me, and that is why I am looking forward to it with so much pleasure.

The "pleasure" did not start until Wolfe had finished playing the role of lecturer; then, at his host's, he really began "relaxing" from his seven months' labor. One suspected that he wanted to take off his stiff collar and the bow tie that someone else had to tie for him, but he contented himself with taking off his coat. Then he leaned back in an easy chair, and, with a tall Scotch and soda in his hand, conversed leisurely. His speech was in harmony with his now informal appearance; he used a good many colloquialisms and occasionally he spiced a remark with a bit of profanity. He talked perhaps a little more than anyone else, but only because others led him to; he was quite as good at listening as at talking, even asking, when he missed a commonplace remark, "What?" or "What did you say?" His ears were tuned to catch outside noises as well as those in the room, for more than once he paused to listen to the whistle of a train: "I've always liked to hear them," he said. And as he conversed, his alert eyes, glancing here and there, seemed to be taking in the whole room. For several hours that night, and then the next afternoon, when the circumstances were similar, he conversed on many topics, most of them the trivial ones that academic groups usually talk about.

One subject that he discussed with keen feeling was the Spanish situation, which at the moment was causing much international concern. He expressed strong sympathy for the Loyalists and was perturbed by recent advances that the Insurgents had made. His interest in politics in the broad sense had increased greatly, he said, in the last year or two. Affairs in Spain had moved him only a few days before to write his first letter for publication to a periodical. This letter, which appeared in the *Nation* for May 21, referred to the report of General Franco's provisions to care for the tourist trade in Spain during the coming summer and noted his ordering of "forty new and brightly painted char-à-bancs" to convey the tourists:

. . . In addition, it is understood that he has not only taken considerable pains in the work of restoring and preserving the most notable of the ancient ruins, but has also shown extraordinary ingenuity in the creation of new ones. For my part, although I by no means share the too general lack of veneration for the monuments of antiquity, I must confess that on the whole the evidences of the modern spirit are more exciting to me. If I had to choose between the two sets of ruins, I should be inclined to visit the new ones rather than the old.

To mention but a few that have already suggested themselves to my awakened curiosity — I should like to visit the various craters and ruined masonries throughout the town of Barcelona, paying particular attention to the subway entrance where a bomb exploded and killed 126 men, women, and children. I should like to visit the ruins of Madrid, the ruined villages around Teruel; and being of a religious turn of mind, I should like to pay a visit of devotion to the chapel, a photograph of which was recently reproduced in the press, where

General Franco's wife and daughter go to offer prayers for the success of the Defender of the Faith.

I have quoted this letter at length because it reveals so clearly the spirit that characterized Wolfe's many oral comments on the Insurgents.

He talked a good deal about contemporary authors. Not that he pretended to have read their recent publications, for he admitted that he had not read many books in the past few years. "I used to read everything," he said, "but now I don't read books; I'm too busy working on my own." His critical comments bore out this statement. He praised MacLeish's early work but did not know his later work. He called *A Farewell to Arms* a first-rate novel, but he was not familiar with *To Have and Have Not*. He regretted that he had never had the opportunity to meet Ring Lardner, whom he praised for his canny insight into human nature and his fine satire on American types; he especially liked "The Golden Honeymoon." Having admitted the flaws usually pointed out in Dreiser, he expressed his admiration for the massive sincerity with which Dreiser had written about life. Of Masters' prose works he singled out the biography of Lindsay as an excellent book. He said that Lewis was one man who knew a great deal about American life and that Dos Passos was another. While he admitted Priestley's cleverness and skill, something in Priestley made him inveigh against British authors who, after a brief stay in America, say: "You know, old chap, what's wrong with you Americans is . . . ." Of *The Ring and the Book*, which he had lately reread, he exclaimed with an emphatic swing of his arm, "God, what a book!" He told anecdotes about Masters, with whom he had had friendly talks in their hotel in New York, and related with especial relish Masters' curt, acid comments on certain celebrated but pompous authors. He chuckled as he gave an account of the curious fight between Hemingway and Eastman that took place in Scribner's editorial offices. It was in connection with this story that he spoke with much fondness of "Max" Perkins, who had aided him so in his craftsmanship and whom he was to make his literary executor.

One of the most amusing anecdotes that he told was about himself. When he was visiting James Thurber one evening shortly after the two had become acquainted, some member of the household was suddenly stricken with appendicitis and had to be rushed to the hospital for an emergency operation. During the operation and even afterward Wolfe stayed at the apartment, thinking, he said, that he was being "a great help," whereas he really was making Thurber more and more nervous. Finally, at a very late hour, when Wolfe was stretched out on a couch rosily enjoying still another drink, the mild-mannered Thurber left the living-room, only to return in a moment without coat and tie. With a look of melancholy and almost complete despair, he said to Wolfe: "I'm sorry, but I'll have to ask you to leave; I *must* get some sleep." Wolfe rose up and replied: "This is a h-h-hell of a way to treat a man. Is this what you call h-h-hospitality?" Someone more diplomatic than Thurber stepped in and gently persuaded Wolfe to leave. A week or two later a friend of Wolfe's told him of a cartoon that Thurber had drawn on the wall of a restaurant frequented by writers but as yet undiscovered by the public. Wolfe went to see the drawing. There on the wall was a large, hulking figure with Wolfe's features confronted by a little man standing on books piled in a chair, saying: "Mr. Wolfe, if you don't leave at once, I'm going to throw you out!"

If any of us had thought that Wolfe might prove difficult to associate with, as Eugene Gant sometimes was, his friendliness soon removed the fear. At the end of the second day he was calling all the group by their first names and insisting that they call him "Tom." There was no Rotarian hollowness in his doing this; his warm, natural manner would have made continued formality seem ridiculous. He appeared interested not only in those about him but also in people they mentioned. "Who is he?" "What does he do?" he would ask. Only once did I see him when he appeared oblivious of others, and that was when he stood for almost a minute looking into a mirror. He rubbed his hand over his face as a man does when he does not want to shave but thinks perhaps he ought to, he thrust forward his bottom lip in a characteristic way, and then he leaned over and looked deep into his eyes. What he was thinking, God knows.

Toward evening of the second day Wolfe began urging the whole group to go with him to Chicago, where he was to meet friends from the East. Everyone had been so kind to him, he said, that he wanted to give a big party: "I've just made three hundred dollars and y-y-you've got to help me spend it." He kept talking about that party.

Finally several of us set out in an automobile for Chicago, one hundred and twenty-five miles away. Speeding through the night with Wolfe, who was now in the gayest of moods, recalled the train ride so memorably described in *Of Time and the River*. "Look at this man drive!" he said; "look at this man drive!" He took part in all the group singing, whether he knew the words or not; and once he sang as a solo one of his father's favorites: "I Wonder Who's Kissing Her Now." But the song that delighted him most was the dwarfs' "Heigh-ho" song from *Snow White and the Seven Dwarfs*. This was to be his "theme song" for the weekend. He sang it even walking across a quiet street in Chicago, and, for his mediocre voice, with a ludicrously serious look on his face. And he kept singing it after some of its original charm had worn off.

Upon arriving in Chicago, we had a midnight supper, and then at Wolfe's request we drove to the Auditorium Hotel. "Ever since I traveled as a child with my mother," he said, "I've w-wanted to stay in this hotel, and now I'm going to do it." When we met him the next day to take him to lunch, he was exuberant about his large room overlooking Michigan Boulevard and the lake — "big enough for me to give my party in," he said. He was exuberant, too, because he had just seen his letter on Spain in the current issue of the *Nation*. When we were greeted at our friend's apartment, which we had visited the preceding night, Wolfe rumbled: "You can't keep the Wolfe from the door."

After lunch we listened intermittently to the broadcast of a baseball game between the New York Yankees and the Chicago White Sox. Wolfe had earlier grown so ecstatic about baseball — about its being the great American sport, the symbol of life itself

— that someone who thought Wolfe must lately have written something about baseball had said teasingly: "That would sound good in a book, wouldn't it?" Wolfe had momentarily looked odd and smiled. Now he showed himself to be an ardent supporter of the Yankees. When someone mockingly reproached him for backing the strongest team in the big leagues, he defended himself by saying: "But the Yankees have always been my team — even b-b-back in the twenties when they had bad years." He admired their power, their sudden, spectacular feats. He was delighted by their one-to-nothing victory that afternoon and pretended to gloat over winning a twenty-five-cent bet on it.

During the course of the afternoon Wolfe wandered into the kitchen with his host and there shook hands with the colored servant, whom he talked with for several minutes about herself and her family. The effect of his friendliness upon her was not fully revealed until her mistress told her in the fall of Wolfe's death. Then she compared him with the world's heavyweight boxing champion, whom she knew personally: "What a pity!" she said with real emotion. "He was jus' like Joe Lewis — so big, and yet so nice and kind."

When asked whether he wished to meet any of the local "celebrities," Wolfe replied: "This party's big enough for me." And two or three times when asked what he would like to do for entertainment, he answered: "G-g-gosh, I want to do whatever the rest want to do."

At his hotel room and later at a restaurant, Wolfe that evening got a great deal of pleasure from playing the attentive host. But at a dull cabaret which the party visited briefly he was particularly bored. It was here that he had one of those unpleasant experiences such as he recorded in "Gulliver," a sketch which tells how his height made him the butt of crude curiosity and jeers. When he went out to the bar to avoid having to watch the convulsive writhing of a woman dancer, a partially drunk man came up and tried to engage him in conversation. Although Wolfe at first looked very much annoyed, he covered up his irritation and patiently talked with the man for two or three minutes. But as Wolfe walked away, the man pointed after him with outstretched arm and, with a brazen, drunken grin, looked around at his neighbors, as if he wished all other normal, good fellows like himself to join him in laughing at this freak, this monstrosity. Fortunately, Wolfe was spared seeing this. And the only remark he made about the man's conversation was: "Oh, he didn't mean any harm. He was just drunk." It was also in this cabaret that Wolfe said in a hurt way to someone who paid the check: "You can't do this to me! Th-this is *my* party!"

Back at his room, just as the last of us were taking our leave, Wolfe did something so incongruous that it struck us as very amusing. After telling an inquiring maid at the door that he needed no more towels, he dashed to his bed, stepped up on it, took a couple of huge strides across it, and exclaimed: "My God! That was the ugliest face I've ever seen." Anyone who ever saw Wolfe can easily imagine what an astonishing sight he made as he walked upright across the bed.

The next afternoon Wolfe went with a small group to the Brookfield Zoo. As we drove through the West Side of Chicago, his eyes seemed to be recording all that lies behind the façade of Michigan Boulevard, which he called "the greatest shirt-front in the world." He craned his neck to see grotesque buildings, and he virtually counted the innumerable railway tracks. For all its ugliness, this sprawling, powerful city fascinated him as the metropolitan center of an abundant farming region. "The Middle West," he said, "reminds me of the back of a fat, sleek hog."

At the zoo he went from one exhibit to another with as much apparent delight as anyone else in the shuffling Sunday crowd. He was a bit disappointed because he could not find a baboon with so colorful a rump as one he had seen when he was a boy: "It was like a rainbow." And the baby giant panda was distressingly dull that day: all she did was to sit on a log and chew a stick. But the polar bears made up for any disappointment. Like almost everyone else who stopped before the open-air inclosure of these bears, Wolfe was fascinated by one that begged for favors from the crowd by climbing to a boulder above the pool, sitting back on his haunches, leaning slouchily with his "elbow" on an adjoining ledge, and then waving his right paw as he looked about at the people. Since the other bears were very adept at stealing the gifts, Wolfe laboriously threw several boxes of Cracker Jack before he felt that he had sufficiently rewarded this genial performer.

Watching and listening to the people also pleased Wolfe. He smiled at some of their actions and their remarks, such as one man's saying to another about the giraffes: "Oh, but you know they're highly exaggerated." The remark of a colored woman to her companions, "Heah some mo' bea's ovah heah," caused him to smile and say: "Isn't this a great country!" On being told that it was up to him to express that greatness, he said: "I'm going to do all I can, but the rest of you will have to help." Thus colloquially he affirmed what he had said in closing *The Story of a Novel*:

. . . Out of the billion forms of America, out of the savage violence and the dense complexity of all its swarming life; from the unique and single substance of this land and life of ours, must we draw the power and energy of our own life, the articulation of our speech, the substance of our art.

At dinner that evening, at the famous old German restaurant, the Red Star Inn, Wolfe told how during his long visits in Germany he had come to love that country — not the government, which he denounced, but the people, for their cleanness and their solid ways of living, and the land, for its beautiful forests and valleys. And at the end of the meal he insisted: "Now everybody *m-must* have German pancake for dessert."

When we finally said goodbye to Wolfe, he spoke again of his intention to go to the Northwest after visiting in Colorado, and then to stop in Chicago for another party on his way back East. Standing there in front of his hotel, he was the only one in the group who did not seem a little tired; his energy and exuberance gave one no thought of anything but life. We later heard that just before leaving Chicago on the "Zephyr" he was full of boyish anticipation in regard to his first ride on a streamlined train; he even reserved a berth, knowing how little comfort it would give him. "By God, I m-m-might as well go the whole hog," he said.

From Denver he wrote on May 31 to his host in Lafayette:

I'm late in writing you to say hello and thanks again; and to let you all know that I think about you and the good time we had together, and the hope that we will do it again. I've been here almost a week — I came for just a *day*! — the whole town has been swell to me — so swell that for the first few days we just eliminated sleep as a despicable luxury. But I'm beginning to feel ironed out again, and if I can only keep my fingers off the cursed quill for another week or two — which I doubt! — I should be in fairly good shape for the struggle when I go back East. Am still resolute in my intention to push on to the North-west, although my friends here now lift their eyebrows and smile skeptically when I speak of it! And I'm still hoping to stop over in Chicago long enough to see you all again. Meanwhile, I send love and best wishes to you all.

Sincerely,
Tom Wolfe

P.S. Take care of the polar bears!

The next news was that Wolfe was critically ill with pneumonia in Seattle. After this came a report of his journey across the conti-nent to Johns Hopkins in the care of his mother and sister. And then his death.

Wolfe died at Johns Hopkins Hospital in Baltimore, 15 September 1938. They brought him home to bury him — home to Asheville, where he was reviled after the publication of "Look Homeward, Angel," but home nevertheless to one who had said "you can't go home again." Jonathan Daniels and Wolfe had been fellow students at Chapel Hill, and Daniels went up to the mountains from Raleigh to serve as a pallbearer at the funeral. Here is the story of the funeral and here is the story of Wolfe's Asheville. Daniels, editor of the Raleigh "News and Observer," is the author of "A Southerner Discovers the South," "The Man of Independence," and many other books.

POET OF THE BOOM

by

Jonathan Daniels

Neither of us was thirty then. The Pullmans from New York and Raleigh had been put together on the train to Asheville somewhere while we slept, and Tom Wolfe and I had met on the platform between the cars, unexpectedly. That was in the late summer of 1929, when he went home for the last time before his first big book came out which was to make him, so Sinclair Lewis said in Stockholm the next summer, one of the greatest American writers. It was also, Tom himself said later, to make him seem in Asheville a Judas Iscariot, Benedict Arnold and Caesar's Brutus, the bird that fouls its own nest, a viper that an innocent populace had nurtured in its bosom, a carrion crow preying upon the blood and bones of his relatives and friends, an unnatural ghoul to whom nothing is sacred, not even the tombs of the honored dead,

From *Tar Heels*, published by Dodd, Mead & Company. Copyright, 1941, by Jonathan Daniels.

a vulture, a skunk, a hog deliberately and lustfully wallowing in the mire, a defiler of pure womanhood, a rattlesnake, a jackass, an alley-cat and a baboon.

That was his own catalogue put together afterward. That summer morning we had breakfast together as the train twisted up the long sinuous curves of his mountains. Three times, on different levels, we went by that familiar fountain which seems set there by the railroad not so much to improve the view as to prove the writhing engineering. I remember we ate heartily. I think Tom was in the choicest part of all his fame then. He was not famous at all in the world's eyes. His first book had not yet been published, but it was in the presses, and Max Perkins, of Scribner's, who became his great friend and editor, and others had read it and pronounced it, Tom told me, a richer and more powerful story of an American town than *Main Street* had been. He had become a writer. He had met other writers as one of them. I remember, particularly, that among them he mentioned James Boyd, author then of *Drums* and *Marching On*, who had come with other authors to live in Southern Pines (there were others in Tryon in the mountains) and give North Carolina a literature before it had native writers of its own. Tom had been tremendously impressed by Boyd.

"He has a lot of ideas," he told me. We were a couple of kids over breakfast there on the train talking about ideas worshipfully, as we had done at Chapel Hill in the "bull sessions" which Tom had liked so much.

One thing Boyd said impressed him especially: that flat lands make a flat and colorless people. That may have been something Boyd said casually, a detail in a conversation. But to Tom, it seemed, that morning, a tremendous and satisfying idea. As a huge, dark-haired mountaineer himself, he looked beyond his scrambled eggs at his mountains. They were good. Eagerly then, he was coming home. But I thought afterward, when he had composed his catalogue of the things Asheville said he was, that perhaps even then he realized some little of the storm he was going to make over his Asheville — his Altamont — his Libya Hill — and had come home to say good-by.

I thought about that again, when I came up the same way and had breakfast alone nine years later, on the way to his funeral. I came by the same fountain as the train twisted up the huge green hills. They are as magnificent as Tom knew them and wrote them. In them, also, were those people along the way Tom had seen in his homeland: the slattern people gaping at the stations (the boy and girl in the convertible coupé, too), the lean farmers, the dawdling Negroes, the gap-toothed yokels (also the preachers and the choir singing women at the religious assemblies), and, yes, a hard, sallow woman with a grimy baby. These were his hills and his people. It seemed strange to be coming to bury him who had been of all of us the most alive. I remember on the train, going too, a sad man from New York and a woman with him talking on the way to Tom's funeral about North Carolina's virtues, if any, for hay fever sufferers.

Places, as Tom knew, better perhaps than the rest of us, are never merely items in geography, but memory as well, and change, too. So when I came back, when Tom was two years dead, to write this book, inevitably he was in my head. When I came into Asheville, which is circled with such magnificent mountains and is so steeply tawdry within, I thought that Wolfe himself was a part — almost the essence — of driving, hungry, resort-town frenzy which stripped all the prettiness, all the dignity, off the town. His own book, written with the same eager fury which his mother gave to real estate, hit the town almost like the collapse of the real estate boom and left people almost as naked. And it left nobody so hurt and naked as himself — in loneliness under anger — even if the book also clothed him, at last, with the appreciation he so much wanted and which his work so deserved.

He was a part of it and he never escaped, a part of a town properly famed for the loveliness around it, and, also, a town fated to violence and pettiness, greed and frustration. Tom himself saw a coincidence, which he pointed, in the appearance of his book little more than a week after the great American stock market crash, and a connection between his own disclosure of his people and their disclosure of themselves in the cheap madness of real estate speculation, taken second-hand from Florida. His

Asheville, in the empty ludicrousness in which it was left, seemed almost the exaggeration of the deflated comedy of the dropsical country.

There the mountains pushed beauty up higher. There was the resort where emotions are loosed more freely than in unchanging towns. In Asheville the hard-headed mountaineers counted at first on the mythical millionaires, who were going to have villas in Florida in the winter and around Asheville in the summer, to hold the bag if there was ever to be any end of filling the bag with hope. Two millionaires, who came before Tom Wolfe was born, may have been responsible for making Asheville the very tragic and comic picture of America which Tom put into his books. Only one of them lived long enough to hold any of the bag, but both helped blow it up.

The millionaires were George W. Vanderbilt, who had inherited his money from the old Commodore, and E. W. Grove, who made the money he spent in the mountains out of a tasteless chill tonic which he sold to the poor in the lower malarial regions of the South. A patriot, wanting to exculpate the natives and the neighbors, as Tom Wolfe properly did not, could make out a case to show Vanderbilt and Grove were the men who corrupted Asheville and created all the brilliant festering which Tom remembered and came back to find again at home. Mr. Grove and Mr. Vanderbilt were both honorable men, but Mr. Vanderbilt was the old millionaire play-acting as feudal lord and Mr. Grove was the new millionaire eager still in speculation. Both found native mountaineers ready to follow the patterns they set.

The palaces of Newport in the nineties were not sufficient to satisfy George Vanderbilt. He came to Asheville in 1889 and began the building of the greatest private palace in America. He bought 100,000 acres of land in the mountains and, in 1892, put a twenty-seven-year-old young fellow named Gifford Pinchot (later Governor of Pennsylvania) in charge of the first large-scale reforestation project in the United States. That was excellent. Also, under the direction of Architect Richard Morris Hunt, with imported artisans, he erected a residence still unequaled anywhere in the United States, modeled after the Châteaux at

Blois and Chambord. The house, which took five years to build, covers four acres with a frontage of 780 feet. It contains a grandeur of furnishings which must be catalogued to be indicated.

Important to Asheville, however, it became what he built, a lord's house; and even I am old enough to remember, long after Vanderbilt had died, in 1914, how the society of Asheville graded itself almost on the degree of acceptable subserviency to the great widow in the great house. It is empty now. The great lady married a Senator from Rhode Island after a North Carolina Governor tried unsuccessfully to marry her. I regard as pure legend the story that she turned him down after he tried to spit his tobacco juice out of her limousine window, not knowing it was closed.

The daughter of the house departed after she left her aristocratic British husband who was permitted to remain. Nobody is there now but a gate-keeper and fee-taker. It is so big that even a millionaire had difficulty heating it in winter. But you and I or anybody else can go there and go in for a two-dollar sightseer's fee. Left behind are only the aristocratic notions put down in a simple mountain town by a millionaire who built the greatest stage-set for snobbery this country has ever seen. (The Vanderbilts were never as guilty of it as some of the people who got inside their door and afterward came into rude contact with people who had not.)

Mr. Grove did not only come to spend his chill tonic profits. Like everybody else in Asheville, he was willing, also, to make a profit out of the mountain real estate. He helped the rising town in 1912 when, on the west slope of Sunset Mountain which runs down to the city, he built the huge Grove Park Inn. It resembles a Swiss mountain hostelry built by giants out of the big boulders on the mountain side. In its big lobby are fireplaces in which are burned logs like tree trunks. It was — and is — a great resort hotel. All around it Mr. Grove spread his real estate development of Grove Park. His activities did not stop at its borders. Just about the time when the Florida real estate boom of the twenties began to spread across the Carolina mountains, in terms of the very logical idea that if there were enough millionaires to buy all the lots in Florida for winter homes, there were enough of them, also, to fill with their villas the Carolina mountains in the summer, Mr. Grove stirred in speculation greatly and again.

In all Tom Wolfe's memory and mine, too, one of the pleasantest places in old Asheville was the Battery Park Hotel, a rambling wooden structure which sat on the top of its own small mountain almost in the heart of Asheville. At a time when men were making islands in Florida, it did not seem strange to raze a mountain in North Carolina. Mr. Grove did that. With the aid of an army of men mechanized with steam shovels, he pulled the mountain down, flattened it off for business property and made more property by dumping the erstwhile mountain into a neighboring ravine. Mr. Grove had wrought. But what Asheville called his "glorious building schemes" Tom Wolfe saw as an ugly flat of clay paved with a desolate horror of white concrete. But nobody was paying much attention to the Wolfe boy then. His book had not appeared. It was not to appear until the same thing had happened to the building boom that Mr. Grove did to the mountain.

There is something strange about the mountains, I thought, when I went up this last time and passed one of the State's best-known beauty spots and found that I would have to pay a dollar to drive to it. That is not peculiar to North Carolina. The Natural Bridge, in Virginia, has a fence around it and cheap souvenir and drinks stands around it, too. And it is probably not merely the mountains. In this commercial age there seems sometimes almost something in beauty which breeds prostitution. It may be with scenery as with women; an ugly girl may not be more virtuous than a pretty one, but she will not make a very good living as a whore. It is also true of places. Nobody fences in a dump.

But in North Carolina, they have put a fence around Blowing Rock, in South Carolina around Caesar's Head. And too often around the fences and the views are the cheap souvenir stands, the hamburger house, the trained bear that will drink the soda pop the pop stand owner will be glad to sell as essential to the spectacle. Beauty is not always prostituted. But wherever there is beauty in scenery on this earth, there are generally people prepared to sell it. Some of them are very nice people. They do not dirty up their roads any more in the mountains than most of us do below them, but it is hard for the visitors to realize that people live in scenery and treat it no better than the visitors treat the lands they call home.

If a traveler looks carefully in the lush growth by the road sides — sometimes rhododendron, sometimes blackberry — even now, on the roads around Asheville, he can sometimes see the crumbling archeology of the boom, the stone pillars put together with cheap mortar, the brick gates to real estate developments. Even on dirt roads, miles from the nearest firewagons, fire hydrants rose in the woods where dwellings, they said, if not hotels, were soon to follow.

For nearly ten years, on the top of Jumpoff Mountain, above Hendersonville, twenty miles from Asheville, the stark steel skeleton of the Fleetwood Hotel stood above rusting radiators, corroding bathtubs and empty building lots. It was the monument to a restless hope until junk dealers took it down. Now Florida, from which the contagion spread, has recovered, but the Carolina mountains, lovely still and lovelier now with the auction signs worn down, are still speculatively cast down. But they can look back. And sometimes, when they think about the great Blue Ridge Parkway, already on its way to completion to the Great Smoky Mountains National Park, old restlessness stirs again, or still.

It was grand while it lasted. Tom Wolfe was a $2,000 instructor teaching city boys to write at New York University then.

"I was sports editor," an Asheville newspaperman told me, "and you know sports editors don't get rich on their salaries. I quit, and the first six months I was in the real estate business I made $35,000 in cash. In the next six months I spent and lost $50,000."

He grinned, glad to be back on the pay roll. Everybody was in it. Tom Wolfe's mother, who as a native mountain woman had the speculative land fever in her blood when Tom was a wondering child, was in it. Everybody was going to get rich. The end did not come quickly like that stock market crash, which Tom regarded the week before his book was published as making an end and a beginning for both himself and America. As North Carolina said, the boom petered out. Actually, there was a crash there waiting in a gutted boom which did not fall in because

city and county bond-borrowed millions were kept in the house
of bad paper which still called itself the Central Bank and Trust
Company, the biggest in the western part of the State. Its overdue
failure was the first big bank crash in the series which began in
1930 in the State. (Tom sailed for Europe on a Guggenheim
Fellowship that year.)

The mayor was run out of office by clamoring citizens, a good
many of whom had participated in the mess which made the
mayor's perhaps corrupt use of city funds to save the bank seem
necessary. The bank president, who was the town's first citizen in
politics and finance, went down to Raleigh to become a convict.
Six months after the bank failed, the ex-mayor went to the men's
room on the floor above his law office and with a 45-caliber
revolver — and approximately as Tom has described it in *You
Can't Go Home Again* — blew half his head and brains all over
the room. Also, as Tom wrote, a blind man found the body when
he went in the room and stumbled against something on his way
to the urinal.

It is over. But it is easier for a people to get over a boom than
to escape the hunger and the hope and the desires which were
there for it to stir up. Maybe boom was in the blood. Tom drew it
there in his portrait of Eliza Gant long before any alien fever
came up from Florida. It is over, but the monuments remain.
There is the new hotel where the old mountain was. The big
public building skyscrapers, properly gaudy, which were part of
the big debt the speculators and politicians together helped to
erect, still stick up into the sky close to the labyrinthine web of
nigger town where Tom's young Eugene Gant had his paper
route. It is over; the community has made adjustment with
creditors. It left the town changed, and there was other change
as the shift in emphasis in the treatment of tuberculars from
climate to rest helped close some of the sanatoria to which men
used to come who had a frightened lust for life and not for land.

There is a new emphasis on industry. The Dutch gentlemen
who run the huge rayon plants at Enka on the road west came
during the boom, but were not of it. They walked between the
land speculators, appraised the land they wanted and reported

to the representatives of the rising, roaring mountain metropolis. "It is worth so much," the Dutchman said. "We will pay that." Asheville felt that the Dutchman had a very unromantic notion of land values, but Asheville had a very realistic idea of the value of the Dutchman. They got the land for what their appraisers, who were not looking for home-site speculations, said it was worth. The difference in the price was made up at home. Also, about that time, the Beacon Blanket Company, which makes cheap articles for the cheap trade and employs 1,500 to 2,000 people, moved from old New Bedford, in Massachusetts. They remain. They are cherished. But they are something strange and new in the town from which Tom Wolfe, at manhood, went away. And yet, maybe Tom did not go away. Eugene Gant was Eliza Pentland Gant's son. There was in him not only the rhetorical thunder of old Oliver, his father. He had the mountains in his blood which was Pentland. And sometimes I think there was the same magnificent, mountain and human, lustful and lost quality about the town and about Tom Wolfe, also.

It was the evil old blind man (honestly evil beside the booster crooks, philosophically evil by their hard calculation) who told George Webber (who was almost as much a figure for Tom himself in his last two big novels as Eugene Gant was in his first two) that he could not come home again. He came home to change undoubtedly then, but to home, still. And Tom Wolfe again came home undoubtedly, at last. Even when he was gone, I think his voice was his own, his home, his very human mountain roaring. When people live where so much land is steep and hard — too hard to use or hold — people seem to live it more. And love being always the strange thing that it is, a man or a woman can use it for speculation or a story. The same mountain blood may run to both ends.

The fact is, for all the blind man's talk, that he did come home, if, in truth, he ever left it. The road ran back always, and the big trains that he loved. No catalogue of epithets from those and their friends who recognized characters as people in his book could drive him away. I think he was as hurt as they were. He wrote eloquently in explanation, largely to himself I think, about what he had done. He seemed to become almost suddenly aware of the fact that he had put live people in a book, without the shadow of disguise, along with their weaknesses and indignities, follies and desires. He drew elaborate distinction between himself as Man-Creating and Man-Alive. The trouble was that the characters, as he realized, were only Men-Alive and squirming and angry.

His distinction was good literary criticism; it will be valid in the history of literature. It was scarcely satisfying to those who were not concerned about literature but did understand when they were pilloried in their own town. And even the charitable at home felt that Tom had worked off a few young grudges in his mature literature. He was sorry. That he undertook at such extent to explain, indicates that. And because he was sorry — because what people said at home was important — he never escaped from it. What they brought him back to was home, at last. They brought him home, after the futile operation at Johns Hopkins, to what was, in every aspect, a Tom Wolfe chapter in a Tom Wolfe book. It will not be written.

"Only Tom's hand, reaching from the grave, could adequately chronicle that day," an Asheville woman, who knew him and understood his work, said of the funeral. "And wouldn't he have enjoyed it?"

His body lay in the old boarding-house where he had spent his boyhood. "Dixieland," he named it. The Wolfes were not poor, but his mother was, to say the very least, thrifty. It is now, as Tom said it was then, a rambling, unplanned appearing, old wooden house on a pleasant, sloping, middle-class street, close to the business section. Its back hangs over one of the mountain town's ravines. It is the same house where, Tom wrote, before his mother bought it from an evangelist who had turned to drink, one boarder had hanged himself, a tubercular had stained the floor in hemorrhage, an old man had cut his throat. The boy was ashamed of it. In it he discovered that the poverty in which he lived "belonged to the insensate mythology of hoarding." It was the house where he had seemed to lack the dignity of any place because of the steady invasion of all the rentable rooms by diverse company of the boarding women and men, girls of "nigger-drawling desire from South Carolina," coughing secretly tubercular Jews, Negresses quartered in dank, windowless rooms in the basement.

As pallbearer, I looked at him lying against the crinkly undertaker's satin in that Dixieland tourist home. If they had not told me, I would not have known that after he died a wigmaker had to make a wig for him to be dead in. They did tell me. They told me, also, that there had not been in Baltimore a coffin big enough for the six-foot-six length of him. The oversized one, that had to be assembled in New York, filled half the front room, which was hall also, of the old boarding-house. Above it there were long cracks in the yellow plaster ceiling. He was home.

"Those melancholy cracks in the yellow plaster looking down at him!" the woman who was his friend said. "I know he fled from those cracks, and there he lay helpless while they triumphed over him."

I am not sure. I am not even sure I know what triumph is. But in little cities in North Carolina you can see a tribe. The matriarch stood beside the coffin of the man. She was both the mother Tom put in the book and the living woman who seemed to have walked out of it. Tearless and strong, she stayed through the morning and talked, as one to whom the realities of living and dying are alike unterrifying, about the operation on Tom's brain. (It was tuberculosis, they found, which had developed in a killing rush inside his skull after what they thought on the West Coast was pneumonia.) The brothers were there, in the house where the brother Ben had died. The sister Tom loved most of all, who had nursed him across the continent on those roaring trains he loved too, was there — vigorous and talkative and overwhelmed together. She did not go to the funeral.

"I went out with a bang," she told me.

All of them were not only Wolfes, tremendously alive, native North Carolina mountain people; they were also Gants out of the book, utterly true. Tom had come home to them. Man-Dead and Man-Creating did not seem very far apart. The distinction between art and life was scarcely perceptible.

A great many flowers came from far away, but not many people. Professor Frederick H. Koch was there. Tom was one of his boys. Tom had taken his playwriting course at Chapel Hill the first two years Koch was there. Paul Green had been in his classes then, too. There was a suggestion in Koch's whole manner that he was beginning in North Carolina — after a brief start in North Dakota — a folk drama movement which would rival — maybe exceed — the Irish dramatic renaissance. There was a good start in Green and Wolfe. Wolfe only turned to the novel after the theater turned him down. But there have been no Greens and Wolfes since those first two years.

I remember I was one of the three members of the cast of Tom Wolfe's second play, "The Third Night." We put it on in the Chapel Hill High School. Tom was his own hero, a degenerate and bad, bad Southern gentleman. I was his henchman. Fred Cohn, who was, when Tom died and after, head of information in the North Carolina WPA, played a tough half-breed. I have forgotten what happened to us. But it was a stormy night in a lonesome place. One of us, I think, got killed, but for the life of me I cannot be sure whether it was Tom or Fred or I.

Professor Koch's mind centered on the first play. "Proff," as he liked to be called, was a delightful person. One of his more devoted students said that he had been a great success teaching drama because he knew nothing about the drama. That is slander. But his great virtue, undoubtedly, was an unquenchable, child-like enthusiasm for even the worst possible one-act plays produced by his boys and girls. A part of that enthusiasm was a beautiful, generous egotism. He liked everybody and he liked to hear everybody liking him. Tom liked him, and at Tom's funeral he was almost desperately determined in dramatics that he must find violets to send to the funeral from the Carolina Playmakers, because Tom had mentioned violets in his first Playmakers play. Elizabeth and Paul Green tried, in vain, to help him find them.

Not many others of Tom's literary friends were there. Clifford Odets had been, I think, in Tennessee and came over the mountains. Hamilton Basso, little, able, dark Louisiana creole who lives at Brevard, was there as another pallbearer. Olive Tilford

Dargan, North Carolina novelist and poet, was at home in her Asheville. Phillips Russell, biographer and Tom's friend, too, had come up from Chapel Hill. Maxwell Perkins, who had been Tom's first and great editor, stood on the edge of the funeral party like a man hurt and as lonely as the saddest spirit in Tom's books.

The rest of us were a part of Tom's native land. Three of us were pallbearers who had been with Tom on a party at my house not many months before. In my closet there's still a quarter-bottle of an American absinthe Tom had picked up in New Orleans. There were Asheville people — a few bewildered and uncertain ones, some boarders in the house, people of the big Gant-Wolfe tribe; and there were thousands who stayed away and hardly knew he was dead. But there were enough to fill the Presbyterian Church and to make it look like the funeral of a prominent local insurance man. I remember there was a smooth young preacher. We sang lusty hymns. And then there was the old preacher who knew Tom was saved because he had always come to call on him when he was in Asheville.

The coffin was heavy. There was a steep terrace up to the lot in the cemetery, and we cut the turf on it with our shoes. I remembered while we moved toward the long hole in the yellow clay that O. Henry was buried somewhere in the same cemetery and that he had looked at the mountains around us without getting an idea into his head. But Tom had been a mountain man who could see city streets as well and people in cities and in the mountains also. Perhaps he was home in both. It was a magnificent day. In the late afternoon sun there was mist on the mountains, or perhaps it was smoke from the noisy trains which run down the valley of the French Broad. Their whistles had been forever in Tom's head.

Some of us went back to the hotel afterward and had drinks. It was the hotel which old man Grove had built after he hacked the mountain down. Not long before a little Northern girl had been brutally murdered in her room by a bellboy thief. All around us, in a circle about the city, were the mountains. The sun came down on them. In the room, I tell the truth, we were strangely gay. All of us wished that Tom could have been there to tell us about the people who were at his funeral and who helped make it the funeral of a small city's son, son accepted, son forgiven, son somehow saved for the Presbyterian Church. For years, while he lived, they would not let his books lie on the shelves of the public library. But Asheville lies in those books, beautiful, maybe damned, but home, too.

Afterward Paul and Elizabeth Green and Olive Tilford Dargan and I went to a restaurant and sought the biggest steak we could find.

"The size Tom would have liked," I said.

Mrs. Dargan does not eat meat, but that night she did. The steak was not big enough. We told Mrs. Dargan good-by afterward. Paul had his car and we drove all night long down the mountains, across the Piedmont to Chapel Hill. It did not seem long since Tom was there, a big popular campus philosopher and campus politician, too. He was on his way from home then. But I don't think he ever got away. Sometimes hill people cuss each other as Man-Creating or Man-Alive, but in their hearts they never hate the hills. They are home.

The fragment here published for the first time can be found in the original in the Thomas Wolfe Collection of William B. Wisdom at the Houghton Library of Harvard University. To students of Thomas Wolfe it is interesting for several reasons.

JUSTICE IS BLIND

by

Thomas Wolfe

NOTE: After he became famous, Tom was forced to waste much time as well as a great deal of his seemingly limitless energies fighting lawsuits and threats of suits brought against him on flimsy or trumped-up grounds. Such things angered him to an almost unbearable degree. To defend himself he consulted various lawyers at one time or another, and he came away from these encounters with a deep and abiding distrust of the legal profession. Lawyers advised him, for practical reasons, to settle suits for nominal sums, saying that it would cost him much more to fight them through the courts. Tom would have none of it. For the principle of the thing, he was for fighting every time.

Tom was both fascinated and outraged by the legal mind whenever he encountered it, and one result of these encounters was that he formed the idea of some day writing a book about lawyers. He told me of this intention seven or eight months before he died. After his death, therefore, I searched through his manuscripts to see whether he had done anything about carrying out his plan. The present fragment was the only existing evidence that he had done more than think about it.

In this manuscript a character is introduced by the name of Spangler. We are told very little about him. Who was he? Shortly after *Of Time and the River* was published, in 1935, Tom decided to abandon the central figure of his previous books, Eugene Gant. He

Printed by special arrangement with Edward C. Aswell. All rights retained. Wolfe's typescript, under a different title and with corrections in his own hand, is deposited in the Thomas Wolfe Collection of William B. Wisdom in the Houghton Library at Harvard University.

thought of at least half a dozen new names for Eugene before he finally settled on George Webber as we find him in the later books. Spangler was one of the interim candidates for this honor, so Spangler as he appears here was simply Thomas Wolfe himself. — Edward C. Aswell, Administrator of the Estate of Thomas Wolfe.

There used to be — perhaps he still exists — a purveyor of *belles lettres* in the older, gentler vein who wrote a weekly essay in one of the nation's genteeler literary publications, under the whimsical *nom de plume* of Old Sir Kenelm. Old Sir Kenelm, who had quite a devoted literary following that esteemed him as a perfect master of delightful letters, was a leisurely essayist of the Lambsian school. He was always prowling around in out-of-the-way corners and turning up with something quaint and unexpected that made his readers gasp and say, "Why, I've passed that place a thousand times and I never *dreamed* of anything like that!"

In the rush, the glare, the fury of modern life many curious things, alas, get overlooked by most of us; but leave it to Old Sir Kenelm, he would always smell them out. He had a nose for it. He was a kind of enthusiastic rubber-up of tarnished brasses, an assiduous ferreter-out of grimy cornerstones. The elevated might roar above him, and the subway under him, and a hurricane of machinery all about him, while ten thousand strident tones passed and swarmed and dinned into his ears — above all this raucous tumult Old Sir Kenelm rose serene: if there was a battered inscription anywhere about, caked over with some fifty years of city dirt, he would be sure to find it, and no amount of paint or scaly rust could deceive his falcon eye for Revolutionary brick.

The result of it was, Old Sir Kenelm wandered all around through the highways and byways of Manhattan, Brooklyn, and the Bronx discovering Dickens everywhere; moreover, as he assured his readers constantly, anyone with half an eye could do the same. Whimsical characters in the vein of Pickwick simply abounded in the most unexpected places — in filling stations, automats, and the corner stores of the United Cigar Company. More than this, seen properly, the automat was just as delightful and quaint a place as an old inn, and a corner cigar store as delightfully musty and redolent of good cheer as a tavern in Cheapside. Old Sir Kenelm was at his best when describing the customs and the whimsical waterfront life of Hoboken, which he immortalized in a delightful little essay as "Old Hobie"; but he really reached the heights when he applied his talents to the noontime rush hour at the soda counter of the corner pharmacy. His description of the quaint shopgirls who forgathered at the counter, the swift repartee and the Elizabethan jesting of the soda jerkers, together with his mouth-watering descriptions of such Lucullan delicacies as steamed spaghetti and sandwiches of pimento cheese, were enough to make the ghosts of the late William Hazlitt and Charles Lamb roll over in their shrouds and weep for joy.

It is therefore a great pity that Old Sir Kenelm never got a chance to apply his elfin talents to a description of the celebrated partnership that bore the name of Paget and Page. Here, assuredly if ever, was grist for his mill, or, in somewhat more modern phrase, here was a subject right down his alley. Since this yearning subject has somehow escaped the Master's hand, we are left to supply the lack as best we can by the exercise of our own modest talents.

The offices of the celebrated firm of Paget and Page were on the thirty-seventh floor of one of the loftier skyscrapers, a building that differed in no considerable respect from a hundred others: unpromising enough, it would seem, for purposes of Dickensian exploration and discovery. But one who has been brought up in the hardy disciplines of Old Sir Kenelm's school is not easily dismayed. If one can find Charles Lamb at soda fountains, why should one not also find Charles Dickens on the thirty-seventh floor?

One's introduction to this celebrated firm was swift, and from an eighteenth-century point of view perhaps a bit unpromising. One entered the great marble corridor of the building from Manhattan's swarming streets, advanced through marble halls and passed the newspaper and tobacco stand, and halted before a double row of shining elevators. As one entered and to the charioteer spoke the magic syllables, "Paget and Page," the doors slid to and one was imprisoned in a cage of shining splendor; a lever was pulled back, there was a rushing sound, punctuated now and then by small clicking noises — the whole thing was done quite hermetically, and with no sense of movement save for a slight numbness in the ears, very much, no doubt, as a trip to the moon in a projectile would be — until at length, with the same magic instancy, the cage halted, the doors slid open, and one stepped out upon the polished marble of the thirty-seventh floor feeling dazed, bewildered, and very much alone, and wondering how one got there. One turned right along the corridor, and then left, past rows of glazed-glass offices, formidable names, and the clattering cachinnation of a regiment of typewriters, and almost before one knew it, there squarely to the front, at the very dead end of the hall, one stood before another glazed-glass door in all respects identical with the others except for these words:

PAGET AND PAGE
Counsellors at Law

This was all — these simple functions of the alphabet in orderly arrangement — but to anyone who has ever broached that portal, what memories they convey!

Within, the immediate signs of things to come were also unremarkable. There was an outer office, some filing cases, a safe, a desk, a small telephone switchboard, and two reasonably young ladies seated busily at typewriters. Opening from this general vestibule were the other offices of the suite. First one passed a rather small office with a flat desk, behind which sat a quiet and timid-looking little gentleman of some sixty years, with a white mustache, a habit of peering shyly and quickly at each new visitor over the edges of the papers with which he was usually involved, and a general facial resemblance to the little man who has become well known in the drawings of a newspaper cartoonist as Caspar Milquetoast. This was the senior clerk, a sort of goodman Friday to this celebrated firm. Beyond his cubicle a corridor led to the private offices of the senior members of the firm.

As one went down this corridor in the direction of Mr. Page — for it is with him that we shall be principally concerned — one passed the office of Mr. Paget. Lucius Page Paget, as he had been christened, could generally be seen sitting at his desk as one went by. He, too, was an elderly gentleman with silvery hair, a fine white mustache, and gentle patrician features. Beyond was the office of Mr. Page.

Leonidas Paget Page was a few years younger than his partner, and in appearance considerably more robust. As he was sometimes fond of saying, for Mr. Page enjoyed his little joke as well as any man, he was "the kid member of the firm." He was a man of average height and of a somewhat stocky build. He was bald, save for a surrounding fringe of iron-gray hair, he wore a short-cropped mustache, and his features, which were round and solid and fresh-colored, still had something of the chunky plumpness of a boy. At any rate, one got a very clear impression of what Mr. Page must have looked like as a child. His solid, healthy-looking face, and a kind of animal drive and quickness in his stocky figure, suggested that he was a man who liked sports and out-of-doors.

This was true. Upon the walls were several remarkable photographs portraying Mr. Page in the pursuit of his favorite hobby, which was ballooning. One saw him, for example, in a splendid exhibit marked "Milwaukee, 1908," helmeted and begoggled, peering somewhat roguishly over the edges of the wicker basket of an enormous balloon which was apparently just about to take off. There were other pictures showing Mr. Page in similar attitudes, marked "St. Louis," or "Chicago," or "New Orleans." There was even one showing him in the proud possession of an enormous silver cup: this was marked "Snodgrass Trophy, 1916."

Elsewhere on the walls, framed and hung, were various other evidences of Mr. Page's profession and his tastes. There was his diploma from the Harvard Law School, his license to practice, and most interesting of all, in a small frame, a rather faded and ancient-looking photograph of a lawyer's shingle upon which, in almost indecipherable letters, was the inscription: "Paget and Page." Below, Mr. Page's own small, fine handwriting informed one that this was evidence of the original partnership, which had been formed in 1838.

Since then, fortunately, there had always been a Paget to carry on partnership with Page, and always a Page so to combine in legal union with Paget. The great tradition had continued in a line of unbroken succession from the time of the original Paget and the original Page, who had been great-grandfathers of the present ones. Now, for the first time in almost one hundred years, that hereditary succession was in danger of extinction; for the present Mr. Page was a bachelor, and there were no others of his name and kin who could carry on. But come! — that prospect is a gloomy one and not to be thought of any longer here.

There exist in modern life, as Spangler was to find out, certain types or identities of people who, except for contemporary manifestations of dress, of domicile, or of furniture, seem to have stepped into the present straight out of the life of a vanished period. This archaism is particularly noticeable among the considerable group of people who follow that curious profession known as the practice of the law. Indeed, as Spangler was now to discover, the archaism is true of that curious profession itself. Justice, he had heard, is blind. Of this he was unable to judge, because in all his varied doings with legal gentlemen he never once had the opportunity of meeting the Lady. If she was related at all to the law, as he observed it in majestic operation, the relationship was so distant that no one, certainly no lawyer, ever spoke of it.

In his first professional encounter with a member of this learned craft, Spangler was naive enough to mention the Lady right away. He had just finished explaining to Mr. Leonidas Paget Page the reason for his visit, and in the heat of outraged innocence and embattled indignation he concluded:

"But good Lord! They can't do a thing like this! There's no Justice in it!"

"Ah now," replied Mr. Page. "Now you're talking about Justice!"

Spangler, after a somewhat startled pause, admitted that he was.

"Ah now! Justice — " said Mr. Page, nodding his head reflectively as if somewhere he had heard the word before — "Justice. Hm, now, yes. But my dear boy, *that's* quite another matter. This problem of yours," said Mr. Page, "is not a matter that involves Justice. It is a matter of the Law." And, having delivered himself of these portentous words, his voice sinking perceptibly to a note of unctuous piety as he pronounced the holy name of Law, Mr. Page settled back in his chair with a relaxed movement, as if to say: 'There you have it in a nutshell. I hope this makes it clear to you.'

Unhappily it didn't. Spangler, still persisting in his error, struck his hand sharply against the great mass of letters and documents he had brought with him and deposited on Mr. Page's desk — the whole accumulation of the damning evidence that left no doubt whatever about the character and conduct of his antagonist — and burst out excitedly:

"But good God, Mr. Page, the whole thing's here! Just read these letters! She can't deny it! As soon as I found out what was going on, I simply had to write her as I did, the letter I told you about, the one that brought all this to a head."

"And quite properly," said Mr. Page with an approving nod. "Quite properly. It was the only thing to do. I hope you kept a copy of the letter," he added thriftily.

"Yes," said Spangler. "But see here. Do you understand this thing? The woman's *suing* me! Suing *me!*" the victim went on in an outraged and exasperated tone of voice, as of one who could find no words to express the full enormity of the situation.

"But of course she's suing you," said Mr. Page. "That's just the point. That's why you're here. That's why you've come to see me, isn't it?"

"Yes, sir. But good God, she can't do this!" the client cried in a baffled and exasperated tone. "She's in the wrong and she knows it! The whole thing's here, don't you see that, Mr. Page?" Again Spangler struck the mass of papers with an impatient hand. "It's here, I tell you, and she can't deny it. She can't sue me!"

"But she is," said Mr. Page quite tranquilly.

"Yes — but dammit! — " in an outraged yell of indignation —
"this woman *can't* sue me. I've done nothing to be sued about!"

"Ah now!" Mr. Page, who had been listening intently but with
a kind of imperturbable, unrevealing detachment which said
plainly, 'I hear you, but I grant you nothing,' now straightened
with a jerk and with an air of recognition, and said: "Ah, now I
follow you. I get your point. I see what you're driving at. You
can't be sued, you say, because you've done nothing to be sued
about. My dear boy!" For the first time Mr. Page allowed himself
a smile, a smile tinged with a shade of good humor and forgiving
tolerance, as one who is able to understand and overlook the fond
delusions of youth and immaturity. "My dear boy," Mr. Page repeated, "that has nothing in the world to do with it. Oh, absolutely
nothing!" His manner had changed instantly as he spoke these
words: he shook his round and solid face quickly, grimly, with a
kind of bulldog tenacity that characterized his utterance when he
stated an established fact, one that allowed no further discussion
or debate. "Absolutely nothing!" cried Mr. Page, and shook his
bulldog jaw again. "You say you can't be sued unless you've done
something to be sued about. My dear sir!" — here Mr. Page turned
in his chair and looked grimly at his client with a kind of bulldog
earnestness, pronouncing his words now deliberately and gravely,
with the emphasis of a slowly wagging finger, as if he wanted to
rivet every syllable and atom of his meaning into his client's
brain and memory — "My dear sir," said Mr. Page grimly, "you
are laboring under a grave misapprehension if you think you have
to do something to be sued about. Do not delude yourself. That
has nothing on earth to do with it! Oh, absolutely nothing!" Again
he shook his bulldog jaws. "From this time on," as he spoke, his
words became more slow and positive, and he hammered each
word home with the emphasis of his authoritative finger — "from
this time on, sir, I want you to bear this fact in mind and never
to forget it for a moment, because it may save you much useless
astonishment and chagrin as you go on through life. *Anybody*,
Mr. Spangler," Mr. Page's voice rose strong and solid, "*anybody*
— can sue — *anybody* — about *anything!*" He paused a full

moment after he had uttered these words, in order to let their
full significance sink in; then he said: "Now have you got that
straight? Can you remember it?"

The younger man stared at the attorney with a look of dazed
and baffled stupefaction. Presently he moistened his dry lips and,
as if he still hoped he had not heard correctly, said: "You — you
mean — even if I have not done anything?"

"That has nothing on earth to do with it," said Mr. Page as
before. "Absolutely nothing."

"But suppose — suppose, then, that you do not even know the
person who is suing you — that you have never even heard of
such a person — do you mean to tell me — ?"

"Absolutely!" cried Mr. Page before his visitor could finish.
"It doesn't matter in the slightest whether you've heard of the
person or not! That has nothing to do with it!"

"Good Lord, then," the client cried, as the enormous possibilities
of legal action were revealed to him, "if what you say is true,
then anybody at all — " he exclaimed as the concept burst upon
him in its full power, "why you could be sued, then, by a one-eyed
boy in Bethlehem, Pennsylvania, even if you'd never seen him!"

"Oh absolutely!" Mr. Page responded instantly. "He could
claim," Mr. Page paused a moment and became almost mystically
reflective as juicy possibilities suggested themselves to his legally
fertile mind, "he could claim, for example, that — that, er, one of
your books — hm, now, yes!" — briefly and absently he licked his
lips with an air of relish, as if he himself were now becoming pro-
fessionally interested in the case — "he could claim that one of
your books was printed in such small type that — that — that the
sight of his other eye had been *permanently* impaired!" cried Mr.
Page triumphantly. He settled back in his swivel chair and rocked
back and forth a moment with a look of such satisfaction that it
almost seemed as if he were contemplating the possibility of
taking a hand in the case himself. "Yes! By all means!" cried Mr.
Page, nodding his head in vigorous affirmation. "He might make
out a very good case against you on those grounds. While I
haven't considered carefully all the merits of such a case, I can see

how it might have its points. Hm, now, yes." He cleared his throat reflectively. "It might be very interesting to see what one could do with a case like that."

For a moment the younger man could not speak. He just sat there looking at the lawyer with an air of baffled incredulity. "But — but — " he managed presently to say " — why there's no Justice in the thing!" he burst out indignantly, in his excitement making use of the discredited word again.

"Ah, Justice," said Mr. Page, nodding. "Yes, I see now what you mean. That's quite another matter. But we're not talking of Justice. We're talking of the Law — which brings us to this case of yours." And, reaching out a pudgy hand, he pulled the mass of papers toward him and began to read them.

Such was our pilgrim's introduction to that strange, fantastic world of twist and weave, that labyrinthine cave at the end of which waits that great Minotaur, the Law.

PART II

THE BOOKS

• •

The greatest asset Wolfe had besides the lofty talent with which he was born was the sympathetic understanding of his editors. After Maxwell Perkins came Edward Aswell of Harper and Brothers. It was Aswell who prepared "The Web and the Rock" and "You Can't Go Home Again" for posthumous publication, and it was he who wrote the appreciative essay on Wolfe at the end of "The Hills Beyond." It is Aswell, now, who as the second literary executor supervises the seemingly endless publication and republication of Wolfe's books.

AN INTRODUCTION TO THOMAS WOLFE

by

Edward C. Aswell

In the fall of 1929 two extraordinary events occurred almost simultaneously. One was the crash of the stock market on October 24th, which ushered in the Great Depression. The other was the publication, six days earlier, of a book by an unknown American writer named Thomas Wolfe. It was called *Look Homeward, Angel*.

The two events were not related, yet in a strange way each shed light on the other. The depression represented the disillusionment of a nation, and *Look Homeward, Angel*, some said, represented a corresponding disillusionment in its author. This comparison was false, and was based on a complete misunderstanding of what Thomas Wolfe had meant to do in writing the book. Nevertheless, many people saw it in that light; and in Asheville, North Carolina, Wolfe's home town, misconceptions were heightened by personal factors and a spate of gossip. Some of his former acquaintances read *Look Homeward, Angel* and were outraged. They felt he had betrayed his family, his friends, his town, the South; and they vented their feelings by denouncing him in bitter letters. One wrote that he was "a monster against life." Others threatened to ride him out of town on a rail if he ever came home again.

Looking back on that fantastic time of 1929, we can see clearly how things were then and why the first reactions to *Look Homeward, Angel* were less sympathetic than its author had expected. The boom years of the 1920's had been a period of crazy illusion on a nation-wide scale. To untold millions, the pot of gold at the end of the rainbow seemed almost within grasp. Then, suddenly, the dazzling mirage vanished, and people felt lost and afraid. It took several years for most of them to get their bearings and come down to earth again, and the return to sanity was accompanied by painful disillusionment. But there was no disillusionment in *Look Homeward, Angel*. The book laid bare certain spiritual realities in American life, and did it, as Wolfe later wrote, "in a manner of naked directness . . . that was rather rare in books." That was what caused the trouble. The people who said Wolfe was disillusioned really meant that *they* were disillusioned. He had opened their eyes to things they had not seen before — things they had deliberately avoided looking at.

Disillusionment, the hindsight of the self-deluded and the half-blind, was not one of Thomas Wolfe's qualities. No one ever accused him of being blind in any degree. His fault, if fault it was, was that he saw too much. Till the day he died he retained that luminous gift which all bright children seem to possess up to a certain age: the ability to look at life and see it as it really is, with its many and ever-changing faces, its mystery and wonder, its exhilaration and stark terror, its endless contrasts of beauty and ugliness, its haunting interplay of good and evil, its flashing colors and subtly shifting shadows. Somewhere along the way, as we grow up, most of us lose that gift. There comes a time, some nameless day and hour which we are not aware of, when what passes as education does us in, and, in our hearts, all unknowing, we accept things as we are told they are and learn to conform. From that moment our vision, our precious gift of true seeing, begins to drop away. From then on, for most of us, we are rather like those mules one sees plodding along country roads in the deep South, beasts of burden, shackled, harnessed, and wearing blinders designed to shut out the green grass beside the road by keeping the eyes fixed on the narrow path straight ahead.

Somehow — and just how it happened remains the mystery of genius — Thomas Wolfe acquired an education without acquiring blinders. He went to school in Asheville. He went to college at Chapel Hill. He took a master's degree at Harvard. And then, with his schooling behind him and no blinders to limit his view, he began to write. He wrote about life as he had lived it and observed it. Above all, he wrote about people.

People fascinated him. Every new person he met was a challenge to him. Why is this fellow so shifty-eyed — what is he afraid of? Why do the corners of that one's mouth turn down — what has gone sour in him? Why is A. drinking himself to death — what is he running away from? Why does B. clap you on the back and deafen your ears with hearty nothings every time he meets you — what is the emptiness in him that he must try so desperately to fill it with mere noise and bustle?

Once he had formulated the question that seemed to him the clue to each new personality, Wolfe never rested till he had tracked down the answer, and in so doing he usually managed to piece together a full life history. To Wolfe, nothing was irrelevant. He took all things human for his province. The color of a man's eyes, the way he walked, the intonation of his voice, his opinions and prejudices, his gestures, facial expressions, habits, tastes, often even his name — everything was grist to Wolfe's mill. All of it went in, to help him get at the hidden kernels of character. More often than not all of it came out, too; and sooner or later the friend or acquaintance who had responded to Wolfe's probings, who had expanded in the warmth of his presence and his very obvious interest, sympathy, and understanding, would wake up some morning to find himself a character in a book.

This was Wolfe's method, yet to state it so baldly is to distort it. Brevity may be the soul of wit, but Wolfe knew better than anyone that the wit of which brevity is the soul is usually superficial and only half true. Life is too big to be caught in an epigram. And that fact, more than anything else, explains why Wolfe wrote in the large. He has been much criticized for writing so lengthily, for "making ten words do the work of one." But as a friend of mine once observed: "Wolfe is a much greater writer than the whole crew of much neater writers." If one is to tell the truth about almost anything it needs to be stated, expanded, qualified, fined down, and then restated in such a way that what one means comes through precisely, with all the overtones of possible distortion recognized and eliminated.

So about Wolfe and his friends. What I have written of his method is essentially true, yet anyone reading it might jump to the conclusion that Wolfe spent his life searching for material to put into books, that he approached everyone he met with a coldly calculating eye, appraising him, coaxing him into revealing intimate secrets, and at last pinning him down like a butterfly in a museum cabinet, all to suit his ulterior purposes as a collector of human specimens. That was not true. Life came first with Wolfe; the thought of books came much later. He had an insatiable hunger to find out everything he could about life and all his years were spent in learning. His interest in people was genuine because he loved and pitied mankind and had a profound sense of the glory as well as the inescapable tragedy of human existence. Even strangers recognized that quality in him and that is why they opened up to him as flowers open to the sun.

But Wolfe the man was one thing, and Wolfe the writer was another. Whatever he saw and heard and felt and touched became fixed with photographic exactitude in his phenomenal memory. He thought about it long and earnestly, turning it over and over in his mind, examining it from all sides, infusing the bare facts with poetic imagination, penetrating to the core of them with uncanny insight; and then when he knew what he knew and was ready to write, Wolfe the man did what every great writer must do: as author he played God. He not only numbered "the very hairs of your head," but he also meted out a strict and impartial justice to all who had come before the seat of his judgment. He searched out the chinks in each man's armor, and revealed them. He scorned lies, hypocrisy, and sham, and exposed them. He hated evil, and lashed out at it wherever he found it.

It was not strange, therefore, that Wolfe the man, the friend and brother of all mankind, often brought upon himself violent reactions, including threats against his life, for what Wolfe the writer had written. This puzzled him, and he never really understood it. In this he reminds us of the character in *Princess Ida* who sings:

> "I love my fellow creatures — I do all the good I can —
> Yet everybody says I'm such a disagreeable man!
> And I can't think why!"

The immense difference was that Wolfe's puzzlement was as innocent and naïve as that of a child who has been scolded for speaking of the family skeleton before company.

Something of all this went into the making of *Look Homeward, Angel*. Since it was Wolfe's first book, he had gone back to the beginnings of his life and inevitably he had written about Asheville, though he called it Altamont; about his own strange and wonderful family (aren't all families strange and wonderful?), though he called them Gants; about himself, though he renamed himself Eugene. And just as inevitably as all the rest, some people did not like it. For he wrote with singleness of purpose, trying to catch in words and fix upon the printed page something deep and dark and tortured and twisted in human nature and in the America he loved, the bad of it along with the good of it, the sum of it being — simply the truth of it.

But it was late in 1929 when the book came out. That was a time when people were desperately hoping the false prophets were right who kept saying that prosperity was just around the corner, word magic, which if it meant anything, meant simply that folly was a kind of superior wisdom for which there could be no retribution. The last thing anybody wanted to hear was the truth. So, contrary to an impression which has become quite general, *Look Homeward, Angel* was not an immediate success. In its original edition its sale was disappointing — far less than that of any of the other Wolfe "novels" that followed it.

Time, however, has a way of correcting human errors. The mood of 1929 passed. Little by little, the nation began to face reality. And little by little, *Look Homeward, Angel* became more popular. It was reissued in new editions. It was reprinted again and again. Its author began to be famous, and even the home-folks who had denounced him now changed their minds. The irony of this did not escape Wolfe. Shortly before his death he said to me: "The only people in Asheville who are sore at me now are those who aren't in the book."

And today, after nineteen years, while most books of the period are dead and forgotten, *Look Homeward, Angel* is still being reprinted and its total sales have far exceeded those of most best sellers. Each new generation as it comes along rediscovers it and claims this book for its own. For Wolfe wrote about youth, and he spoke to youth more convincingly than any American writer has ever done. Thousands, reading him for the first time, have found something of themselves suddenly become articulate and universal, and with the joy of recognition have murmured: "Ah, yes, that's the way it is."

Can any writer hope for a greater tribute from his readers?

The critics of 1929 who first reviewed "Look Homeward, Angel"
were understandably not ready for the tremendous task which
awaited them. But even then Wolfe was compared to Rabelais,
to James Joyce. "For sheer dramatic power," said John Chamber-
lain in the Bookman, *"read the death of Ben and then compare*
it with the death of Madame Bovary." The present discussion of
the book, written when the novel had mellowed and American
literature had felt its greatness, is only a part of a chapter on
Wolfe in a volume which also discusses Lardner, Hemingway,
Dos Passos, Faulkner, and Steinbeck. Maxwell Geismar, teacher
and critic, has edited "The Portable Thomas Wolfe" for the
Viking Press.

DIARY OF A PROVINCIAL

by

Maxwell Geismar

"All serious work," Wolfe says in the preface to his first novel,
"is autobiographical," but with him more than conventionally so,
his work is his life. When he attempted in *The Web and the Rock*
to write a more "objective" novel, the Webber hero becomes
progressively more and more Wolfian, and by the last sections the
novel almost abandons the attempt at anonymity. In the recounting of his life, moreover, we are fortunate that Wolfe had few
false reticences. The artist, as Somerset Maugham has noticed so
nicely in *Cakes and Ale*, is the only free man. The treachery of
friends, the departure of his beloved, the unaccountable malice of
acquaintances — these are the grist of the writer's mill. Whatever
blows life deals him, he alone can repay them with profit to his

From *Writers in Crisis* by Maxwell Geismar, published by Houghton Mifflin
Company, 1942. By special permission.

soul, and often indeed to his pocketbook. And if through his writing Wolfe did not always gain this complete artist's freedom (which, by the way, has its ambiguous aspects for the beloved, the friend, and even the acquaintance) he at least achieved a wonderful frankness. Nothing was to Wolfe, but writing made it more so. His novels are the diary, tremendous, often inchoate and very possibly unique in our time, of the artist in America. And more particularly of the writer in our provincial America. Here, indeed, is the local origin of Wolfe's "unspeakable and incommunicable prison," the Pentlands of Wolfe's first novel, in which, enchained, his broken angel looks vainly homeward.

In the old myth, as we know, man himself, as the broken angel, has his memories of an earlier heaven before his fall. We remember Milton's paradise, with its modest claim of

> things unattempted yet in prose or rhyme

— or Eve's garden itself. With our more analytic modern sense we have come to see that the haunting feeling of man's better past derives in part at least from the peace of the womb in the individual's life, and that perhaps of sheer inanimate matter in the race's memory of its existence. How strong a theme this is in our history! So cruelly pointing backward to its ultimate goal of death, and perhaps even so ironically the hidden and despairing cause of all our infinite progress. We find many traces and currents of the theme in European literature, from Plato to the Wordsworthian infant trailing his clouds of glory. And too few traces of it are found in American culture, where this idyllic garden is never in the forsaken and haunting past, but, as we all know, immediately ahead of us: paradise and prosperity right around the corner. No melancholy mysticisms for our pragmatic optimists in a land where work, not recollection, will prove our salvation.

Wolfe is perhaps the only major modern author who has seized upon the theme of the lost paradise for his first novel, and he had his reasons. If we for the moment ignore the soaring rhetoric which marks *Look Homeward, Angel*, we may see in it a very realistic portrait of Wolfe's society. Out of its calculations and pretensions Wolfe has fashioned a sort of heroic scene. But the calculations and pretensions remain. He embellishes the provincial rudeness with poetry, but the ornamentation also accentuates the frame. It is Gant, of course, with his memories of rich meadows, corn, plum trees, and ripe grain, of the old rich pioneer America, who is the exile in the Reconstruction South. It is Gant who recalls the "great, forgotten language, the lost lane-end into Heaven." Why here? O Lost! Lost indeed the Gantian South with its gray and withered Altamonts, its squalid Toytown cities, the "pasteboard pebbledash" hotels. The muddy clay roads. The slattern people. The rows of yokels strung like apes along the fences. The drunken McGuires (the more talented souls of Wolfe's South are the drunkards) and the Pentland dwellers. But is there only the southern idiocy to oppose Gant's northern madness? The Pentlands, Wolfe says, by marriage and intermarriage among their own kin, "could boast of some connections with the great, of some insanity, and a modicum of idiocy" — for once a Wolfian understatement. For Bacchus Pentland, Armageddon was due any day now, and for his family, as a matter of fact, it seems to have arrived. We remember the first reception of Gant by the Pentland clan, this tribe "who saw one another only in times of death, pestilence and terror." The males with their birdlike winks and nods, the children with their lapping idiot grins, the roaring of the wind outside, "remote and demented." Was it a time of joy for the northern Gant, his marriage with the daughter of this clan? It proved in fact a time of death, pestilence, and terror, for it marked his union with them, the prelude to his long and painful conquest by them.

And for the young Eugene of the novel, these Pentlands are the South with variations. There are two characters who stand out in some contrast: the younger brother Ben, whom Wolfe tries unsuccessfully to create as a tragic and lovable person, and the teacher, Margaret Leonard, who is perhaps the only character in the book possessing a genuine warmth. And here, of course, we come upon the major fault of *Look Homeward, Angel.* The writer who is fully himself is certainly the rebel. His nature, his obligation, his essence is the civilizing spirit which evaluates and condemns. In the midst of Utopia the writer, as it were, must protest the divine injustices, and in the context of, as yet, an imperfect and mortal society, he must remain continually sensitive to human abuses. He is at once society's irritant and antiseptic. Yet to become wholly this, to lose the sense of loyalty to one's origins, of devotion to one's land or of faith in one's neighbors, to lose this basic sense of a creative if always skeptical affection for his material, is for the writer and his society equally sterile. The most brilliant satire which has no focus within our human hopes leaves us its victims, perhaps, but not its followers. The writer who in his intelligence forsakes his humanity — an Aldous Huxley, for example, in the manner of *After Many a Summer Dies the Swan* — loses his own purpose as a writer.

It is incorrect to mention Huxley and Wolfe together here, and only as the extreme may illustrate the mean. For Wolfe's entire struggle, as we shall see, becomes the attempt to remedy the emotional deficiencies he felt within himself. But in the range of his first novel, which always arouses our interest, the moments which also compel our sympathy are few. With all Wolfe's marvelous faculty of characterization, he omits the essential of our identification with these people of *Look Homeward, Angel*. We see them brilliantly and we hardly feel them at all. We are the outsiders watching a variety of human specimens operating in their milieu, which should be ours. We recognize Wolfe's Altamont, but we are bound to it by few ties of affection, nor those of mere companionship, common neighborliness, nor by any mutual concern for our collective achievement. We exist in it merely, as it were, by proximity. Just so, Wolfe was born in the South, but he shared with it little except the accident of birth. A strange irony that this writer — so American in his temperament, so filled with the necessity of his belonging to his land in order to fulfill his destiny — should be denied the ordinary heritage of a home, of a place and people to love.

Yet what was there in Wolfe's early life to evoke this obvious loving-kindness, this ordinary and basic attribute of art, the common identification of a writer with his brothers, which the critic is almost ashamed to identify, such is our period, and must speak of with bated breath? If Margaret Leonard is the one person in Wolfe's portrait of his youth who gives out some humanity, who has some interest in Wolfe's hero, Eugene, can we say as much for her fellow teachers? "What is an Epode, Mr. Leonard?" asks Eugene's friend of the drawling, stupid schoolmaster. "Why," said Mr. Leonard reflectively, "it's a form of poetry." "Hell," said the boy, "I knew that before I paid tuition." Is there very much in fact which these boys didn't know before they came to school? The dry and distorted forms of Cicero, Ovid, Lucretius, which John Leonard presented to his adolescent audience, squirming in its seats, projecting petty obscenities to divert itself from such intolerable boredom — what connection have these "classics" with Eugene's actual life? Nor was Leonard an unusually stupid man, Wolfe tells us. He was indeed

an example of that sad liberalism of the village — an advanced thinker among the Methodists, a bearer of the torch at noon, an apologist for the toleration of ideas that have been established for fifty years.

The ludicrous Shakespearian pageant, one of the finest scenes in *Look Homeward, Angel,* and in which Wolfe shows very sharply the satiric gift which was later to constitute his most impressive achievement, is the logical symbol of the false values of Eugene's education. And just so Wolfe himself sums up his impression of the more enlightened thinking of the "university":

The appraisal of personality, like all other appraisal with them was coarse and blunt. They were suspicious of all eminence. . . . The vast champaign of the world stretched out its limitless wonder, but few were seduced away from the fortress of the State, few ever heard the distant reverberation of an idea. They could get no greater glory for themselves than a seat in the Senate, and the way to glory — the way to all power, highness and distinction whatsoever — was through the law, a string tie, and a hat.

Such is the verdict of our hero upon his total provincial education. It is harsh, biased, no doubt, but there is reason for its bias. Even Margaret Leonard, who encourages at least Eugene's avid hunger for knowledge, though without much discipline or discrimination in the sort of knowledge, has perhaps little sense of

Eugene's real needs. His hunger is also for human relationships as well as poetry, for some knowledge also of his own physical and mental development, this hero tormented by his family's disgrace and by his own adolescent sexual fantasies. "She was an inspired sentimentalist," Wolfe writes of Margaret Leonard. "She thought she 'knew boys'" —

In fact, however, she had little knowledge of them. She would have been stricken with horror if she could have known the wild confusion of adolescence, the sexual nightmares of puberty, the grief, the fear, the shame in which a boy broods over the dark world of his desire. She did not know that every boy, caged in from confession by his fear, is to himself a monster.

Yet the "fear" which cages in Eugene is not at all a necessary condition of a boy's education except within the strait limits of the provincial-puritan view of youth. From the insistence, indeed, with which these "sexual nightmares" intrude upon Eugene's life, it might almost seem that his education had in the end only one major function: the stimulation of his prurience. But if Eugene's formal education cannot thus be viewed as highly constructive, what can be said of his sexual education itself?

Only, I am afraid, that it was compounded, in a pattern familiar to our society, of secrecy and salaciousness, and of ignorance which is no bliss. The colored prostitute, Ella Corpening, with her pathetic Kewpie dolls and calendars from the Altamont Coal Company, her moaning, undulating, writhing "Jelly Roll," is in fact an advance for the young Eugene, at least from the class-room obscenities, the sneaking sexualism of his white companions; for Ella's passion, if commercial, is also honest. The little waitress, Louise, may add something further to Eugene's amorous sophistication, but hardly to his sense that often a human relationship may accompany the sexual one. From Louise, the young Eugene moves to Lily Jones in her house in Exeter, Lily Jones with her "coy and frigid modesty" —

She yielded her kisses with the coy and frigid modesty of the provincial harlot, turning her mouth away. . . . She chafed him with rough, embarrassed professionalism. In a moment she rose impatiently. "Let's git started," she said. "Where's my money?"

Is the pursuing of such affection, then, the lost language Wolfe seeks, the lane-end into paradise? If love should be the core of the adolescent's growth, is this to be the love which rewards him? In Eugene, Wolfe writes, the ghost turned grievously away. "The lost bright wonder died." Based on such premises how can Eugene's final affair with Laura James, the climax of *Look Homeward, Angel*, if it attempts to be idyllic, have any genuine substance? It seems, despite all of Wolfe's efforts, artificial and empty; so too is the young Eugene in respect to any previous knowledge of a sound relationship. It is literary, and D. H. Lawrence; what other standard can Eugene create for himself? Certainly not that of reality. And if in it the pornographic again often replaces the passionate, this has been the essence of Eugene's sexual education.

Love like charity begins at home. Of course, Eugene's family should have created the emotional security which might compensate for the terrors of these other areas of his learning, but it is among the members of his family that we find the greatest indifference toward the facts. It is precisely this family, indeed, which contributes most to the sense of shame, fear, disturbance underlying Eugene's youth. Eliza, Eugene's mother, we recall, since her husband is a tombstone cutter, declares that death is not remunerative. "People," she thought, "died too slowly." With Eliza's entrance into real-estate speculation, she gains "a freedom she had never known." But this "freedom" is that of materialist America, of Lardner's U.S.A., the freedom of possession and power which in the end is only a superior sort of bondage. What does Eliza not offer up as human sacrifice to this insensate freedom? — her husband, her children, her home, and, of course, herself. A Rockefeller is reputed, in Matthew Josephson's *Robber Barons*, to have stated the classic American dictum of family life: that he cheated his sons every chance he could. "I want to make 'em sharp. I trade with the boys and skin 'em and I just beat 'em every time I can. I want to make 'em sharp." But to Wolfe's Eliza we cannot even attribute this rather primitive parental concern. Tending her property, she could not also tend to her children. Hoarding old string, empty cans, paper, anything she may retail

at a profit, symbol of the property psychology which a Balzac
flayed in France, she is the twentieth-century version of Shakespeare's "snapper-up of unconsidered trifles." Sometimes she at-
tains a comic dignity, grandly ascribing to her tubercular clients
"a little bronchial trouble." But lacking at last any warmth and
ease of personality, we feel only her increasing sterility, a woman
who lusts only for money. We share with Eugene his gradually
perceptive hatred, first of Eliza's effect on her husband Gant, and
then on the boy Eugene himself:

> He felt, rather than understood, the waste, the confusion, the blind
> cruelty of their lives . . . the conviction that their lives could not be
> more hopelessly distorted, wrenched, mutilated and perverted away
> from all simple comfort, repose, happiness, if they had set themselves
> deliberately to tangle the skein, twist the pattern. . . . He saw plainly
> by this time that their poverty, the threat of the poorhouse, the lurid
> references to the pauper's grave belonged to the insensate mythology of
> hoarding.

And the growing perception of the actual conditions of his
existence, the young Eugene materializes a little later in a perhaps
less rhetorical but more convincing statement to Eliza on Gant's
dying agonies:

> My God, my God, where are we going? What's it all about? He's
> dying — can't you see it? Don't you know it? Look at his life. Look at
> yours. No light, no love, no comfort — nothing. . . . Mama, mama, in
> God's name what is it? What do you want? Are you going to strangle
> and drown us all? Don't you own enough? Do you want more string?
> Do you want more bottles? . . . Do you want the town? What is it?

As though, indeed, all the young men of America were crying
such phrases to certain other industrial Lords of Creation!

Such, then, are the outlines of "the buried life" from which a
Thomas Wolfe slowly and painfully extricated his spirit. If we are
accused of simplifying the picture Wolfe gives us, it is simply
because the grim outlines are softened by the lyric passages of
Look Homeward, Angel. It is precisely this other strain in his first
novel which we must now for a moment examine. The rich
meadows, corn, plum trees, the ripe grain Gant forever mourns,
and for the splendors of which, now forever lost, he may only

substitute the tides of his preposterous rhetoric, a richness of words for the vanished richness of fact — this is Gant's memory of a different America. And Wolfe's long, rich elaborations of food throughout this book and his later novels also, the orgies of tremendous feeding, the hunger for richness not only of food, but of personality, action, knowledge, sensation, of words and life itself — these are Wolfe's desire. Memory and desire: what power resides in these attributes of the human temperament, and especially when they are denied their realization by the facts of our life! Then indeed they rise triumphant to their extremes, and their excesses, just when they are most evidently betrayed by the realities of our existence, to demonstrate beyond doubt the dominance of the wish over the statistic. Wolfe's passion for the sensuous wealth of life, his repeated invocations to black, wet, spermy earth, existence oozing, bursting, with fertility —

huge, frosty apples, whole hogs, smoked bacons, great bins full of flour, dark, recessed shelves groaning with preserved cherries, peaches, plums, quinces, apples, pears. . .

— we must surely establish this as not the truth of his own life, but its hunger; and a hunger based exactly on the material and spiritual poverty of the life he describes in such harsh and condemnatory terms. The excesses of Wolfe's quest for abundance are in short attributable to its absence in his early environment.

We must mention in this respect Wolfe's affinity (which was surely a southern sacrilege) for the Jews of his novels, an affinity which was to lead him to such strange terminating conditions of his life. Like him the Jews are the outcasts of society, the exiles, the strangers. But they often seem also to possess the very qualities denied to Wolfe by his own existence: laughter, ease, a generosity of temperament. Thus the ridiculous and ironic excesses of gaiety and warmth with which Wolfe later endows his New York Jewish friends, and which to a large degree led to catastrophe when Wolfe was faced with facts rather than his romantic and wishful imagination. For the Jews are, as Dorothy Parker noted, just like everybody else, only more so, and even they could not measure up to Wolfe's exorbitant demands. In the meantime, Wolfe was to preserve his special affection for them, those Jewish students of his, as he tells us in *The Story of a Novel*, who stood first even in the accusing circle of his dreams of guilt; the little Jews of *Of Time and the River*, with their swarthy faces, sensuous beings, full of the life and laughter lacking in Wolfe's own. And they also are, as Wolfe is, alone, imprisoned. Like him, alas, they also sought their lost, forgotten language, their lane-end into paradise, strove to escape the unspeakable and incommunicable prison of this earth.

A prison indeed if we may trust Wolfe's portrait of his youth. Early, if somewhat absurdly, echoing Wordsworth's omniscient infant, he saw himself as the sad one, "caged in that little round of skull, imprisoned in that beating and most scared heart," his life forever walking down lonely passages —

He understood that men were forever strangers to one another, that no one ever comes really to know any one, that imprisoned in the dark womb of our mother, we come to life without having seen her face, that we are given to her arms a stranger, and that, caught in the insoluble prison of being, we escape it never, no matter what arms may clasp us, what mouth may kiss us, what heart may warm us.

And if this is perhaps a little prescient for the baby, it is certainly evident to the mature Eugene.

Is it likewise so evident to all the rest of us, the common condition of our existence, the inexorable terms of our own being? If the dominant theme of imprisonment, which is the framework of *Look Homeward, Angel*, certainly is to a large extent the immutable analysis of our worldly activity, it is just as certainly true that the characteristic of the human, as against the brute, spirit lies in the effort to defy it: to break the bars of our savage bondage, to escape from this brutalizing loneliness. To communicate and share, to depend on and support our fellow exiles and prisoners, to fuse through our common experience and effort a communal unity — these are the defiant aims of the progressive forces in humanity. Civilization is the attempt to escape from this prison. And long ago the poet's song reminded us

> Stone walls do not a prison make,
> Nor iron bars a cage.

But what was there in Wolfe's provincial culture to support such a faith? The instruments of our salvation from the Wolfian tomb are precisely those which, as we have seen, were denied to him: family, friends, love, and knowledge. These, like Ariadne's "clue of silk" which rescued ancient Theseus from the labyrinth, are the slender but nevertheless sufficient thread to lead us from the domains of our own modern solitude, but for Wolfe the thread, the clue, was missing.

The pilgrimage of a Thomas Wolfe from this point onward is the attempt, often misdirected, sometimes even lacking consciousness of his problem, and yet in the end with a sure purpose, to solve this enigma for himself and his work. Meanwhile we should notice that Eugene's farewell to his Altamont has, for this prison-pent soul, a certain degree of vigor. Years later, Wolfe tells us, his hero was still afraid of his South. Even —

when he could no longer think of the barren spiritual wilderness, the hostile and murderous entrenchment against all new life — when their cheap mythology, their legend of the charm of their manner, the aristocratic culture of their lives . . . made him writhe — when he could think of no return to their life and its swarming superstitions without weariness and horror, so great was his fear of the legend, his fear of their antagonism, that he still pretended the most fanatic devotion, excusing his Northern residence on grounds of necessity rather than desire.

But finally, Wolfe concludes, it occurred to Eugene that his education, his family, his friends, these people of the South had given him nothing —

that neither their love nor their hatred could injure him, that he owed them nothing, and he determined that he would say so, and repay their insolence with a curse.

The "curse" was, of course, *Look Homeward, Angel,* but what Wolfe owed to the South was not in fact so easily concluded.

The most satisfactory commentaries to read in connection with the second novel, "Of Time and the River" (1935), are Wolfe's own accounts of its writing and reception in "The Story of a Novel" and in "You Can't Go Home Again." With contemporary reviewers, estimates of its worth ranged from the derogatory and the merely disappointed, through the defensive and the pleased, then finally to the extremely enthusiastic. Robert Penn Warren, already in 1935 an associate of the group later to be known as the New Critics, is a poet, novelist, and teacher. Among other books, he has written "All the King's Men" and "World Enough and Time."

THE HAMLET OF THOMAS WOLFE

by

Robert Penn Warren

Thomas Wolfe owns an enormous talent; and chooses to exercise it on an enormous scale. This talent was recognized promptly enough several years ago when his first novel, *Look Homeward, Angel*, came from the press to overwhelm a high percentage of the critics and, in turn, a high percentage of the cash customers. Nor was this sensational success for a first novel undeserved, even if the book was not, as Hugh Walpole suggested, as "near perfect as a novel can be." Now Mr. Wolfe's second novel, *Of Time and the River*, appears, and the enthusiasm of the reception of the first will probably be repeated; though, I venture to predict, on a scale scarcely so magnificent. That remains to be seen; but it may not be too early to attempt a definition of the special excellence

Titled "A Note on the Hamlet of Thomas Wolfe" in the *American Review*, May 1935. Reprinted in *Literary Opinion in America* (1937). By permission of the author.

and the special limitations of the enormous talent that has produced two big books and threatens to produce others in the near future.

If Mr. Wolfe's talent is enormous, his energies are more enormous, and fortunately so. A big book is forbidding, but, at the same time, it carries a challenge in its very pretension. It seems to say, "This is a serious project and demands serious attention from serious minds." There is, of course, a snobbery of the three-decker. Mr. Wolfe is prolific. His publishers assure the public that he has written in the neighborhood of two million words. In his scheme of six novels two are now published (*Look Homeward, Angel*, 1884–1920, and *Of Time and the River*, 1920–1925); two more are already written (*The October Fair*, 1925–1928, and *The Hills Beyond Pentland*, 1838–1926); and two more are projected (*The Death of the Enemy*, 1928–1933, and *Pacific End*, 1791–1884). Presumably, the novels unpublished and unwritten will extend forward and backward the ramifications of the fortunes of the Gant and Pentland families.

Look Homeward, Angel and the present volume are essentially two parts of an autobiography; the pretense of fiction is so thin and slovenly that Mr. Wolfe in referring to the hero writes indifferently "Eugene Gant" or "I" and "me." There may be many modifications, omissions, and additions in character and event, but the impulse and material are fundamentally personal. The story begins in *Look Homeward, Angel* in the latter part of the nineteenth century with the arrival of Gant, the father of the hero, in Altamont, in the State of Old Catawba, which is Asheville, North Carolina. It continues with the marriage to Eliza Pentland, the birth of the various children, the debaucheries and repentance of old Gant, the growth of the village into a flourishing resort, the profitable real-estate speculations of Eliza, her boarding house, the education of Eugene Gant in Altamont and at the State University, the collapse of old Gant's health, and the departure of Eugene for Harvard. *Of Time and the River* resumes on the station platform as Eugene leaves for Harvard, sees him through three years there in the drama school under "Professor Hatcher," presents in full horror of detail the death of old Gant from cancer of the prostate, treats the period in New York when Eugene teaches the Jews in a college there, and takes the hero to Europe, where he reads, writes, and dissipates tremendously. He is left at the point of embarking for America. During this time he is serving his apprenticeship as a writer and trying to come to terms with his own spirit and with America. So much for the bare materials of the two books.

The root of Mr. Wolfe's talent is his ability at portraiture. The figures of Eliza Gant and old Gant, of Ben and Helen, in *Look Homeward, Angel,* are permanent properties of the reader's imagination. Mr. Wolfe has managed to convey the great central vitality of the old man, for whom fires would roar up the chimney and plants would grow, who stormed into his house in the evening laden with food, and whose quality is perpetually heroic, mythical, and symbolic. It is the same with Eliza with her flair for business, her almost animal stupidity, her great, but sometimes aimless, energies, her almost sardonic and defensive love for her son, whom she does not understand, her avarice and her sporadic squandering of money. These two figures dominate both books; even after old Gant is dead the force of his personality, or rather the force of the symbol into which that personality has been elevated, is an active agent, and a point of reference for interpretation.

These two characters, and Ben and Helen in a lesser degree, are triumphs of poetic conception. The uncle in *Of Time and the River,* Bascom Pentland, exhibits likewise some of the family lineaments, the family vitality, and something of the symbolic aspect of the other characters; but the method of presentation is more conventional and straightforward, and the result more static and anecdotal.

Mr. Wolfe's method in presenting these characters, and the special quality of symbol he manages to derive from them, is subject to certain special qualifications. Obviously it would not serve as a routine process for the treatment of character, at least not on the scale on which it is here rendered. The reader of a novel demands something more realistic, less lyrical; he demands an interplay of characters on another and more specific level, a method less dependent on the direct intrusion of the novelist's personal sensibility. As I have said, the figures of the Gant family are powerful and overwhelming as symbols, as an emotional focus for the novel, and as a point of reference. But the method collapses completely when applied to Starwick, a character of equal importance in Mr. Wolfe's scheme.

We amass a great fund of information concerning Francis Starwick. He was born in a town in the Middle West and early rebelled against the crudities and ugliness of his background. At Harvard he assists Professor Hatcher in the drama school and leads the life of a mannered and affected aesthete, foppish in dress, artificial in speech, over-sensitive and sometimes cruel. He becomes the best friend of Eugene at Harvard. Later he appears in Europe in company with two young women of Boston families, somewhat older than he, who are in love with him and who are willing to pay, with their reputations and their purses, for the pleasure of his conversation. With these three Eugene enters a period of debauchery in Paris. Finally he discovers that Starwick is homosexual, and in his undefinable resentment beats him into unconsciousness.

But this body of information is not all that the writer intends. F. Scott Fitzgerald and Ernest Hemingway have been able to use effectively such characters as Starwick and to extract their meaning, because as novelists they were willing to work strictly in terms of character. But in *Of Time and the River* the writer is forever straining to convince the reader of some value in Starwick that is not perceptible, that the writer himself cannot define; he tries, since he is writing an autobiography, to make Starwick a symbol, a kind of *alter ego*, for a certain period of his own experience. The strain is tremendous; and without conviction. The writing about Starwick, as the climax of the relationship approaches, sinks into a slush of poetical bathos and juvenility. And here is the scene of parting:

". . . you had a place in my life that no one else has ever had."
"And what was that?" said Starwick.
"I think it was that you were young — my own age — and that you were my friend. Last night after — after that thing happened," he

went on, his own face flushing with the pain of the memory, "I thought back over all the time since I have known you. And for the first time I realized that you were the first and only person of my own age that I could call my friend. You were my one true friend — the one I always turned to, believed in with unquestioning devotion. You were the only real friend that I ever had. Now something else has happened. You have taken from me something that I wanted, you have taken it without knowing that you took it, and it will always be like this. You were my brother and my friend —"

"And now?" said Starwick quietly.

"You are my mortal enemy. Good-bye."

"Good-bye, Eugene," said Starwick sadly. "But let me tell you this before I go. Whatever it was I took from you, it was something that I did not want or wish to take. And I would give it back again if I could."

"Oh, fortunate and favored Starwick," the other jeered. "To be so rich — to have such gifts and not to know he has them — to be forever victorious, and to be so meek and mild."

"And I will tell you this as well," Starwick continued. "Whatever anguish and suffering this mad hunger, this impossible desire, has caused you, however fortunate or favored you may think I am, I would give my whole life if I could change places with you for an hour — know for an hour an atom of your anguish and your hunger and your hope. . . . Oh, to feel so, suffer so, and live so! — however mistaken you may be! . . . To have come lusty, young, and living into this world . . . not to have come, like me, still-born from your mother's womb — never to know the dead heart and the passionless passion — the cold brain and the cold hopelessness of hope — to be wild, mad, furious, and tormented — but to have belief, to live in anguish, but to live, — and not to die." . . . He turned and opened the door. "I would give all I have and all you think I have, for just one hour of it. You call me fortunate and happy. *You* are the most fortunate and happy man I ever knew. Good-bye, Eugene."

"Good-bye, Frank. Good-bye, my enemy."

"And good-bye, my friend," said Starwick. He went out, and the door closed behind him.

The dialogue, the very rhythms of the sentences, and the scene itself, scream the unreality.

The potency of the figures from the family and the failure with Starwick may derive from the autobiographical nature of Mr. Wolfe's work. Eliza and old Gant come from a more primary level of experience, figures of motherhood and fatherhood that gradually, as the book progresses, assume a wider significance and become at the same time a reference for the hero's personal experience. And the author, knowing them first on that level, has a way of knowing them more intimately and profoundly as people than he ever knows Starwick. Starwick is more artificial, because he is at the same time a social symbol and a symbol for a purely private confusion the roots of which are never clear.

Most of the other characters are treated directly. Mr. Wolfe has an appetite for people and occasionally a faculty of very acute perception. The portrait of Abe Jones, the Jewish student at the college in New York, and those of the people at the Coulson household in Oxford, are evidence enough of this capacity. But his method, or rather methods, of presentation are various and not unvaryingly successful. There are long stretches of stenographic dialogue that has little focus, or no focus whatsoever, for instance the first part of the conversation of the businessmen in the pullman in Book I, of the residents of the hotel in Book IV, of the artistic hangers-on at the Cambridge tea parties, or even of Eugene and his companions in the Paris cafés. Some of this reporting is very scrupulous, and good as reporting, but in its mass, its aimlessness, and its lack of direction it is frequently dull; the momentary interest of recognition is not enough to sustain it, and it bears no precise relation to the intention of the novel. It is conversation for conversation's sake, a loquacity and documentation that testifies to the author's talent but not to his intelligence as an artist. Generally this type of presentation is imitative of Sinclair Lewis's realistic dialogue, but it lacks the meticulous, cautious, and selective quality of the best of Lewis, the controlled malice; it is too random, and in an incidental sense, too heavily pointed.

Further, there are tremendous masses of description and characters. Mr. Wolfe has the habit of developing his own *clichés* for description of character, and of then exhibiting them at irregular intervals. It is as if he realized the bulk of the novel and the difficulty a reader might experience in recognizing a character on reappearance, and so determined to prevent this, if possible, by repetition and insistence. For instance, Starwick and Ann, one of the young women from Boston who is in love with Starwick, have a complete set of tags and labels that are affixed to them time after time during the novel. Mr. Wolfe underrates the memory of the reader; or this may be but another instance of the lack of control that impairs his work.

Only in the section dealing with the Coulson episode does Mr. Wolfe seem to have all his resources for character presentation under control. The men who room in the house, the jaunty Captain Nicholl with his blasted arm and the other two young men from the motor-car factory — these with the Coulsons themselves are very precise to the imagination, and are sketched in with an economy usually foreign to Mr. Wolfe. The Coulson girl, accepting the mysterious ruin that presides over the household, is best drawn and dominates the group. Here Mr. Wolfe has managed to convey an atmosphere and to convince the reader of the reality of his characters without any of his habitual exaggerations of method and style. This section, with slight alterations, originally appeared as a short story; it possesses what is rare enough in *Of Time and the River*, a constant focus.

I have remarked that some of Mr. Wolfe's material is not subordinated to the intention of the book. What is his intention? On what is the mass of material focussed? What is to give it form? His novels are obviously autobiographical. This means that the binding factor should be, at least in part, the personality of the narrator, or since Mr. Wolfe adopts a disguise, of the hero, Eugene Gant. The two books are, in short, an account of the development of a sensibility; obviously something more is intended than the looseness and irresponsibility of pure memoirs or observations. The work demands comparison with such things as Joyce's *Portrait of the Artist as a Young Man* or Lawrence's *Sons and Lovers*; it may even demand comparison with proper autobiographies such as Rousseau's *Confessions* or *The Education of Henry Adams*. But the comparison with these books is not to the advantage of Mr. Wolfe's performance. It has not the artistry of the first two, the constant and dramatic relation of incident to a developing consciousness of the world, nor has it the historical importance of the third, or the philosophical and intellectual interest of the last.

The hero of *Look Homeward, Angel,* though a child and adolescent, is essentially more interesting than the Eugene of *Of Time and the River.* He is more comprehensible, because there is a real (and necessarily conventional) pattern to his developing awareness of the world around him. Further, the life of the Gant household, and even of the community, is patterned with a certain amount of strictness in relation to Eugene: the impress of the vast vitality of old Gant, the lack of understanding on the part of the mother and the perpetual emotional drag of resentment and affection she exerts on her son, the quarrels with Steve, the confusion and pathos of the sexual experiences, the profound attachment between Ben and Eugene, and the climatic and daring scene with Ben's spirit. There is a progress toward maturity, a fairly precise psychological interest. The novel contains much pure baggage and much material that is out of tone, usually in the form of an ironic commentary that violates the point of view; but the book is more of a unit, and is, for that reason perhaps, more exciting and forceful.

In *Of Time and the River* as Eugene in his pullman rides at night across Virginia, going "northward, worldward, towards the secret borders of Virginia, towards the great world cities of his hope, the fable of his childhood legendry," the following passage is interpolated:

Who has seen fury riding in the mountains? Who has known fury striding in the storm? Who has been mad with fury in his youth, given no rest or peace or certitude by fury, driven on across the earth by fury, until the great vine of his heart was broke, the sinews wrenched, the little tenement of bone, blood, marrow, brain, and feeling in which great fury raged, was twisted, wrung, depleted, worn out, and exhausted by the fury which it could not lose or put away? Who has known fury, how it came?

How have we breathed him, drunk him, eaten fury to the core, until we have him in us now and cannot lose him anywhere we go? It is a strange and subtle worm that will. . . .

Now this furious Eugene is scarcely made so comprehensible. The reader amasses a large body of facts about him, as about Starwick, but with something of the same result. He knows that

Eugene is big; that he is a creature of enormous appetites of which he is rather proud; that he has the habit of walking much at night; that he is fascinated by the health and urbanity of his friend Joel and by the personality of Starwick; that he ceases to like Shelley after spending an afternoon in a jail cell; that he reads 20,000 books in ten years; that he is obsessed by the idea of devouring all of life. Then, the reader knows the facts of Eugene's comings and goings, and knows the people he meets and what they say. But the Eugene susceptible to such definition is not the hero of the book, or at least does not function adequately as such. The hero is really that nameless fury that drives Eugene. The book is an effort to name that fury, and perhaps by naming it, to tame it. But the fury goes unnamed and untamed. Since the book is formless otherwise, only a proper emotional reference to such a centre could give it form. Instead, at the centre there is this chaos that steams and bubbles in rhetoric and apocalyptic apostrophe, sometimes grand and sometimes febrile and empty; the centre is a maelstrom, perhaps artificially generated at times; and the other, tangible items are the flotsam and jetsam and dead wood spewed up, iridescent or soggy as the case may be.

It may be objected that other works of literary art, and very great ones at that, have heroes who defy definition and who are merely centres of "fury." For instance, there is Hamlet, or Lear. But a difference may be observed. Those characters may defy the attempt at central definition, but the play hangs together in each case as a structure without such definition; that is, there has been no confusion between the sensibility that produced a play, as an object of art, and the sensibility of a hero in a play. (And the mere fact that *Hamlet* and *Lear* employ verse as a vehicle adds further to the impression of discipline, focus, and control.)

There are two other factors in the character of Eugene that may deserve mention. The hero feels a sense of destiny and direction, the sense of being "chosen" in the midst of a world of defeated, aimless, snobbish, vulgar, depleted, or suicidal people. (This is, apparently, the source of much of the interpolated irony in both books, an irony almost regularly derivative and mechanical.) In real life this conviction of a high calling may be enough to make a "hero" feel that life does have form and meaning; but the mere fact that a hero in a novel professes the high calling and is contrasted in his social contacts with an inferior breed does not, in itself, give the novel form and meaning. The transference of the matter from the actuality of life to the actuality of art cannot be accomplished so easily. Second, at the very end of the novel Eugene, about to embark for America, sees a woman who, according to the somewhat extended lyrical epilogue, makes him "lose" self and so be "found":

After all the blind, tormented wanderings of youth, that woman would become his heart's centre and the target for his life, the image of immortal one-ness that again collected him to one, and hurled the whole collected passion, power, and might of his one life into the blazing certitude, the immortal governance and unity, of love.

Certainly this is what we call fine writing; it may or may not be good writing. And probably, falling in love may make a man "find himself"; but this epilogue scarcely makes the novel find itself.

It is possible sometimes that a novel possessing no structure in the ordinary sense of the word, or not properly dominated by its hero's personality or fortunes, may be given a focus by the concrete incorporation of an idea, or related ideas. Now, *Of Time and the River* has such a leading idea, but an idea insufficient in its operation. The leading symbol of the father, old Gant, gradually assumes another aspect, not purely personal; he becomes, in other words, a kind of symbol of the fatherland, the source, the land of violence, drunkenness, fecundity, beauty, and vigour on which the hero occasionally reflects during his wanderings and to which in the end he returns. But this symbol is not the total expression of the idea, which is worked out more explicitly and at length. There are long series of cinematic flashes of "phases of American life": locomotive drivers, gangsters, pioneers, little towns with the squares deserted at night, evangelists, housewives, rich and suicidal young men, whores on subways, drunk college boys. Or there are more lyrical passages, less effective in pictorial detail, such as the following:

It was the wild, sweet, casual, savage, and incredibly lovely earth of America, and the wilderness, and it haunted them like legends, and pierced them like a sword, and filled them with a wild and swelling prescience of joy that was like sorrow and delight.

This kind of material alternates with the more sedate or realistic progress of the chronicle, a kind of running commentary of patriotic mysticism on the more tangible events and perceptions. For Mr. Wolfe has the mysticism of the American idea that we find in Whitman, Sandburg, Masters, Crane, and Benét, or more recently and frivolously, in Coffin and Paul Engle. He pants for the Word, the union that will clarify all the disparate and confused elements which he enumerates and many of which fill him with revulsion and disgust. He, apparently, has experienced the visionary moment he proclaims, but, like other mystics, he suffers some difficulty when he attempts to prepare it for the consumption of ordinary citizens of the Republic. He must wreak some indignity on the chastity of the vision. This indignity is speech: but he burns, perversely, to speak.

The other promulgators of the American vision have been poets. Mr. Wolfe, in addition to being a poet in instinct, is, as well, the owner on a large scale of many of the gifts of the novelist. He attempts to bolster, or as it were to prove, the mystical and poetic vision by fusing it with a body of everyday experience of which the novelist ordinarily treats. But there is scarcely a fusion or a correlation; rather, an oscillation. On the tangible side, the hero flees from America, where his somewhat quivering sensibilities are frequently tortured, and goes to Europe; in the end, worn out by drinking and late hours, disgusted with his friends, unacquainted with the English or the French, and suffering homesickness, he returns to America. But Mr. Wolfe, more than most novelists, is concerned with the intangible; not so much with the psychological process and interrelation as with the visionary "truth."

The other poets, at least Whitman and Crane, have a certain advantage over the poet in Mr. Wolfe. They overtly consented to be poets; Mr. Wolfe has not consented. Therefore their vision is purer, the illusion of communication (*illusion*, for it is doubtful that they have really communicated with central vision) is more readily palatable, because they never made a serious pretense of proving it autobiographically or otherwise; they were content with the hortatory moment, the fleeting symbol, and the affirmation. (Mr. Benét, of course, did attempt in *John Brown's Body* such a validation, but with a degree of success that does not demand comment here.) It may simply be that the poets were content to be lyric poets, and therefore could more readily attempt the discipline of selection and concentration; in those respects, even Whitman shows more of an instinct for form than does Mr. Wolfe. Mr. Wolfe is astonishingly diffuse, astonishingly loose in his rhetoric — qualities that, for the moment, may provide more praise than blame. That rhetoric is sometimes grand, but probably more often tedious and tinged with hysteria. Because he is officially writing prose and not poetry he has no caution of the *clichés* of phrase or rhythm, and no compunction about pilfering from other poets. His vocabulary itself is worth comment. If the reader will inspect the few passages quoted in the course of this essay he will observe a constant quality of strain, a fancy for the violent word or phrase (but often conventionally poetic as well as violent): "wild, sweet, casual, savage. . . ," "haunted them like legends," "no rest or peace or certitude of fury," "target of his life," "blazing certitude, the immortal governance and unity, of love." Mr. Wolfe often shows very powerfully the poetic instinct, and the praise given by a number of critics to his "sensuousness" and "gusto" is not without justification in the fact; but even more often his prose simply shows the poetic instinct unbuckled on a kind of week-end debauch. He sometimes wants it both ways: the structural irresponsibility of prose and the emotional intensity of poetry. He may overlook the fact that the intensity is rarely to be achieved without a certain rigour in selection and structure.

Further, Mr. Wolfe, we understand from blurbs and reviewers, is attempting a kind of prose epic. American literature has produced one, *Moby Dick*. There is much in common between *Moby Dick* and *Of Time and the River*, but there is one major difference. Melville had a powerful fable, a myth of human destiny, which saved his work from the centrifugal impulses of his genius, and which gave it structure and climax. Its dignity is inherent in the fable itself. No such dignity is inherent in Mr. Wolfe's scheme, if it can properly be termed a scheme. The nearest approach to it is in the character of old Gant, but that is scarcely adequate. And Mr. Wolfe has not been able to compensate for the lack of a fable by all his well-directed and misdirected attempts to endow his subject with a proper dignity, by all his rhetorical insistence, all the clarity and justice of his incidental poetic perceptions, all the hysteria or magnificent hypnosis.

Probably all of these defects, or most of them, are inherent in the autobiographical impulse when the writer attempts to make this special application of it. In the first place, all the impurities and baggage in the book must strike the author as of peculiar and necessary value because they were observed or actually occurred. But he is not writing a strict autobiography in which all observations or experiences, however vague, might conceivably find a justification. He is trying, and this in the second place, to erect the autobiographical material into an epical and symbolic importance, to make of it a fable, a "Legend of Man's Hunger in his Youth." This much is definitely declared by the sub-title.

Mr. Wolfe promises to write some historical novels, and they may well be crucial in the definition of his genius, because he may be required to re-order the use of his powers. What, thus far, he has produced are fine fragments, several brilliant pieces of portraiture, and many sharp observations on men and nature: in other words, a kind of symbol of the fatherland, the source, the a fine novel, or several fine novels, might be written. If he never writes these novels, it may yet be that his books will retain a value as documents of some historical importance and as confused records of an unusual personality. Meanwhile, despite his admirable energies and his powerful literary endowments, his work illustrates once more the limitations, perhaps the necessary limitations, of an attempt to exploit directly and naïvely the personal experience and the self-defined personality in art.

And meanwhile it may be well to recollect that Shakespeare merely wrote *Hamlet*; he was *not* Hamlet.

A second type of discussion of "Of Time and the River" is the one by Henry Seidel Canby, though in critical perception greatly above the average of its kind. Here the book is debated in terms of its contemporaneity. In reading the review, one might remember that Canby, teacher, editor, and sometimes lecturer in English at Yale, is a biographer of Thoreau and Whitman. He is also chairman of the board of editors of the 'Saturday Review' and chairman of the Book-of-the-Month Club board.

THE RIVER OF YOUTH

by

Henry Seidel Canby

There was much laughter when years ago D. H. Lawrence in his *Studies in Classical American Literature* described an Old Indian Devil who was always plaguing the great Americans with sudden flushes of paganism, great resurgences of sex, and obstinate maladjustments between their European souls and their unfenced continent. It is not so funny now, for some devil, Indian, Marxian, or psycho-analytic, has surely been torturing the best American writers of our era. They squirm, they lash, they spit out filth and imprecations, they whine, they defy. They are not at ease in this Zion of our ancestors.

For Thomas Wolfe in his recent novel, *Of Time and the River*, the curse is impotence. There is for him a brooding loneliness in the American landscape which drives the man-mass into a nervous activity of hurrying on trains, motors, subways, airplanes, a restlessness which drives the sensitive writer into an agony of frustration because the towns, the cities, the countryside oppress him with unrealized and inexpressible energy. It is a country that grips the imagination and lets the heart go, a country in which humanity mixed and at the boiling point — black Negro flesh, amber Jewish flesh, dark, light, sanguine — is incited by fierce energies toward no end but movement and frustration, a country where life has sacrificed its mass for its force, and the observer can neither hold on nor let go of a rush of experience that always seems to have, yet never quite achieves, a meaning.

The impotence of America is an impotence of expression. When in Wolfe's novel Gene Gant's train shrieks through the night on his first journey northward, he feels the enormous push of continental energy and can rise to it only by drunken hysteria. When in the last chapter he meets the ocean liner sailing from France, he sees that vast organization of speed and change floating above his tender, and knows that it is America again, clutching at his sensitive spirit. In three hundred years the American soul has not made itself a home.

And hence the strange impulse toward autobiography which has carried so many Americans to the verge of incoherence! — Melville in *Moby Dick* wrestling with transcendental interpretations of his restlessness, or Whitman in the "Song of Myself" blatantly proclaiming his identity with the expansiveness of a continent. They cannot write novels, these rebel Americans, there is nothing stable to write of. They can only proclaim their egos, in defiance of the inhumanity of a continent which the energy of their race has exploited but to which they are not yet assimilated. Hence an impotence which prevents complete expression, and books which are, as the eighteenth century would have said, far more nature than art.

Of Time and the River, time being the time of youth, the river that mysterious current of life which flows under the perplexing surface of America, is the epitome, after so many books, of the troublous and disintegrating years of the Twenties when Mr. Wolfe was young. And those who wish to get in fullest and most impassioned form the spiritual record of those years, or who would see as in a news-reel the typical scenes of that period as youth saw them, will find, if they are persistent, what they want in this book, which is neither fiction nor autobiography, but both.

For although the scene of Mr. Wolfe's long-expected narrative changes from North Carolina to the biting realities and warped romance of New England, from New England to the aloofness of Oxford, from Oxford to the loneliness of an American's France, yet it is a wholly American book, one of the most American books of our time. It is in the direct tradition of those earlier anguished spirits and great seekers on our soil, Thoreau, Melville, Whitman. It is in the tradition, but with a momentous difference for which the break-up of the Twenties and Mr. Wolfe's own idiosyncrasies are responsible. Yet if I should wish to know what these Twenties meant to an American youth still asking the questions asked by his spiritual ancestors, "Why are we here?" "What does this continent mean to us?" "What are we becoming?" I should go to this book. If I fail to give a clear account of Mr. Wolfe's thousand-page story of how a passion-driven youth tried to tear all knowledge from the Harvard library, all experience from America, all wisdom from Europe, and to pluck out, in his twenties, the secret of the loneliness and the fascination of America, forgive me. Have you ever tried to review the *Encyclopaedia Britannica?*

Mr. Wolfe's odd thousand pages are condensed but not adequately described in the paragraphs above. He calls them fiction, and fiction they are of the kind that he put into *Look Homeward, Angel,* but better organized, more poetical where poetical, more sharply realistic when realistic; and they are to be followed by a million words more or less in which the ego which is the raison d'être of them all is to conclude the story. But fiction in the strict sense they are not, nor story, nor drama, but rather spirtual autobiography in which the thousand incidents, many of them trivial, and the dozens of characters, many of them extraordinary, have as their excuse for being that a youth met them on his way. Plot there is none. Structure in the ordinary narrative sense, there is none. It is a picaresque novel with the distraught mind of a poet of the Twenties as *picaro,* and the incidents adventures in seeking a spiritual home.

To be more precise, this book is a study of American dualism and it is this which gives it poignancy. Leaf through it and you will see as in a moving picture successive moments of prose and poetry. Here are the fleshy people of an intensely actual Carolina, of a literal Boston, and of a photographic France. No reporter could have done them more vividly as news, and indeed Wolfe is a great reporter. No one of them is usual, indeed for such a passionate student of humanity no man or woman could be merely usual; most of them are eccentrics, half mad from pain, or love, or greed, or vanity, or frustration; or wholly lost in what is really fantasy, like Starwick the homosexual, or the pathetic collegiate Weaver, or the gross sensualist Flood who is like some mushroom sprung from, yet alien to, the good earth. And between these flashes of intimate, literal humanity from the man-swarm, the novel leaves the literal entirely and in a poetic prose that owes much to Whitman and a little to Joyce,* but has become Wolfe's own, rises into a chorus of anguish, perplexity, and delight, which chants the loneliness and the impotence and the beauty of this America, and struggles to break through to some solution which will satisfy the seeker, who is the youth Gant, the hero, and the excuse for all this profusion of words.

And linking the two worlds is the decaying but still mighty figure of the Father, the old stone cutter who was the center of *Look Homeward, Angel.* Dying (and his death scene is Mr. Wolfe at his best), he still dominates the imagination of the youth, for he in his vast energy and incredible vitality is the old America where man almost became worthy of his continent; and in his cancerous decline, in his frustrated career, and in the immense confusion of his brain, he symbolizes what has happened in a twentieth century in which there seems to be no graspable relation between the prose and the poetry of a continent.

So much for the purpose of this novel. Its achievement is less. With all its richness of detail, its passion, its poetry, and its intense realism of contemporary life, there is an impotence in this book like the impotence Wolfe ascribes to his America.

* Joyce was the favorite novelist of Gene Gant, and this novel has been more influenced by *Ulysses* than by any other recent book. — H.S.C.

In America it is an impotence of wandering men at home wherever wheels carry them yet never strong enough to grip the continent and make it serve their happiness. In this America, "so casual and rich and limitless and free," they become arid or lonely or broken, or have got the "new look" of the machine-ridden masses. With Mr. Wolfe the impotence is exactly equivalent. His imagination has provided him with a great theme and his accurate memory flashes infinite exact detail of the life of which he intends to make his book. But he cannot control the theme or reduce his substance to a medium. He will write neither poetry nor prose, but both. He will not be content with the literal autobiographic description of men and events which his journalistic sense supplies so readily but must intersperse with passages of sheer fantasy or poetical uplift. He will stick neither to fiction nor to fact. Hence the reader never enters into that created world of the real novelist which has its own laws, its own atmosphere, its own people, but goes from here to there in Mr. Wolfe's own life, seeing real people as he saw them, and often recognizing them (as with George Pierce Baker in Professor Hatcher, and many others) not as created characters but as literal transcripts from the life. So that the effect is always of being in two worlds at once, fiction and fact, until curiosity takes the place of that ready acceptance of a homogeneous life in the imagination which a fine novel invariably permits. You are forced to read this book as an autobiography with a poetic accompaniment, and for the first five or six hundred pages the personality of the narrator, this passion-driven youth, is too vague, too unimportant to hold suspense, so that it is for the objective realistic incidents that one reads and these change and succeed one another without relation or real consequence, except that one ego experiences them all. Hence a book that is verbose, and which seems much more verbose, much more repetitive than it is. Not until well past its vast middle is the reader caught up and carried on. Before that he reads either a passage of extravagant but vital poetry (drunken poetry in this quotation) —

Casey Jones! Open the throttle, boy, and let her rip! Boys, I'm a belly-busting bastard from the State of old Catawba — a rootin' tootin' shootin' son-of-a-bitch from Saw Toop Gap in Buncombe — why, God help this lovely bastard of a train — it is the best damned train that ever turned a wheel since Casey Jones's father was a pup — why, you sweet bastard, run! Eat up Virginia!

or he reads a complete realistic episode in which the Pentlands snigger "k, k, k, k, k," pull at their cleft chins, smolder with their hidden fires. Or an aggressive Jew boy pulls out the stopper of young Gant's wrath, and makes a friend for life. Or an attempted seduction. Or a satire on silly young Harvard intellectuals poohing and pahing and saying "Ace" for "Yes." Immense power, immense variety, little control, less continuity, and an almost complete failure to make this true epic of longing youth in a lonely, disintegrated America either drama, fiction, poetry, satire, any *one* thing, *one* medium of expression, into which the imagination of the reader can enter and stay, for more than twenty pages, at home.

I think that this novel, like many other fiery and ambitious American books — like Melville's *Pierre*, like many of Whitman's poems, like the now forgotten romantic-philosophic extravaganzas so common in the magazines of a century ago — is an artistic failure. And Mr. Wolfe's books, as wholes, will continue to be artistic failures until he finds and controls a medium in which the ego is sublimated into an imagination less involved in the immediate circumstances of his life. Yet it is an important book, and Mr. Wolfe is an important writer. He has more material, more vitality, more originality, more gusto than any two contemporary British novelists put together, even though they may be real novelists and he is not. He stands to them as Whitman stood to the wearied *Idylls of the King*. And he entirely escapes the sordid, whining defeatism of so many of his American contemporaries. I am not fool enough to try to teach him how to write. No one can do that. He can write like his own angel now, he can make speech that is a new speech in fiction and yet unmistakably authentic, he can strike off flashing pictures.

In waning light, in faint shadows, far, far away in a great city of the north, the 40,000 small empetaled faces bend forward breathless, waiting — single and strange and beautiful as all life, all living, and man's destiny. There's a man on base, the last flash of the great right arm, the crack of the bat, the streaking white of a clean-hit ball, the wild, sudden, solid roar, a pair of flashing legs have crossed the rubber, and the game is over!

But he has not yet made his book. He has poured out his heart into a mold, over a mold, spilling through a thousand pages. He has tried to be philosopher, poet, journalist-observer, satirist, story-teller, historian, and dreamer, not all at once which is quite possible, but one after the other, which cannot be done in a book, which, like a man, no matter how complex, should be integrated, harmonious, homogeneous, and unmistakably not many but one.

This article, actually a review of Wolfe's "The Story of a Novel,"
has been the banner beneath which the anti-Wolfeans have long
rallied. The pro-Wolfeans, as well as the academicians, have,
as a result of it, continually pointed to Bernard DeVoto as Wolfe's
archenemy. Certainly DeVoto is not one of Wolfe's great ad-
mirers, but in "The World of Fiction" (1950, page 85) he disdains
the "literary folklore" which has developed because of this single
review. DeVoto, teacher, critic, novelist, and historian, is the
present occupant of the Easy Chair for "Harper's Magazine."

GENIUS IS NOT ENOUGH

by

Bernard DeVoto

Some months ago *The Saturday Review* serialized Mr. Thomas
Wolfe's account of the conception, gestation and as yet uncompleted delivery of his Novel, and Scribners are now publishing
the three articles as a book. It is one of the most appealing books
of our time. No one who reads it can doubt Mr. Wolfe's complete
dedication to his job or regard with anything but respect his
attempt to describe the dark and nameless fury of the million-
footed life swarming in his dark and unknown soul. So honest or
so exhaustive an effort at self-analysis in the interest of esthetics
has seldom been made in the history of American literature, and
The Story of a Novel is likely to have a long life as a source-book
for students of literature and for psychologists as well. But also it
brings into the public domain material that has been hitherto out-

From *Forays and Rebuttals* copyright 1936 by Bernard DeVoto, published by
Little, Brown & Company. First appearance in *Saturday Review of Literature*,
25 April 1936. By permission of the author.

side the privilege of criticism. Our first essay must be to examine
it in relation to Mr. Wolfe's novels, to see what continuities and
determinants it may reveal, and to inquire into their bearing on
the art of fiction.

Let us begin with one of many aspects of Mr. Wolfe's novels
that impress the reader, the frequent recurrence of material to
which one must apply the adjective placental. (The birth metaphors are imposed by Mr. Wolfe himself. In *The Story of a Novel*
he finds himself big with first a thunder-cloud and then a river.
The symbolism of waters is obviously important to him, and the
title of his latest novel is to be that of the series as a whole.) A
great part of *Look Homeward, Angel* was just the routine first-
novel of the period which many novelists had published and many
others had suppressed, the story of a sensitive and rebellious
adolescent who was headed toward the writing of novels. The rest
of it was not so easily catalogued. Parts of it showed intuition,
understanding and ecstasy, and an ability to realize all three in
character and scene, whose equal it would have been hard to point
out anywhere in the fiction of the time. These looked like great
talent, and in such passages as the lunchroom scene in the dawn
that Mr. Wolfe called nacreous some fifty times, they seemed to
exist on both a higher and a deeper level of realization than any
of Mr. Wolfe's contemporaries had attained. But also there were
parts that looked very dubious indeed — long, whirling discharges
of words, unabsorbed in the novel, unrelated to the proper business of fiction, badly if not altogether unacceptably written, raw
gobs of emotion, aimless and quite meaningless jabber, claptrap,
belches, grunts and Tarzan-like screams. Their rawness, their unshaped quality must be insisted upon: it was as if the birth of the
novel had been accompanied by a lot of the material that had
nourished its gestation. The material which nature and most
novelists discard when its use has been served. It looked like one
of two things, there was no telling which. It looked like the self-
consciously literary posturing of a novelist too young and too
naïve to have learned his trade. Or, from another point of view, it
looked like a document in psychic disintegration. And one of the
most important questions in contemporary literature was: would

the proportion of fiction to placenta increase or decrease in Mr. Wolfe's next book?

It decreased. If fiction of the quality of that lunchroom scene made up about one-fifth of *Look Homeward, Angel*, it constituted, in *Of Time and the River*, hardly more than a tenth. The placental material had enormously grown and, what was even more ominous, it now had a rationalization. It was as unshaped as before, but it had now been retroactively associated with the dark and nameless heaving of the voiceless and unknown womb of Time, and with the unknown and voiceless fury of the dark and lovely and lost America. There were still passages where Mr. Wolfe was a novelist not only better than most of his contemporaries but altogether out of their class. But they were pushed farther apart and even diluted when they occurred by this dark substance which may have been nameless but was certainly far from voiceless.

Certain other aspects of the new book seemed revealing. For one thing, there was a shocking contempt of the medium. Some passages were not completely translated from the "I" in which they had apparently been written to the "he" of Eugene Gant. Other passages alluded to incidents which had probably appeared in an earlier draft but could not be found in the final one. Others contradictorily reported scenes which had already appeared and at least once a passage that had seen service already was reënlisted for second hitch in a quite different context, apparently with no recollection that it had been used before.

Again, a state of mind that had been appropriate to the puberty of Eugene seemed inappropriate as the boy grew older, and might therefore be significant. I mean the giantism of the characters. Eugene himself, in *Of Time and the River*, was clearly a borderline manic-depressive: he exhibited the classic cycle in his alternation between "fury" and "despair" and the classic accompaniment of obsessional neurosis in the compulsions he was under to read all the books in the world, see all the people in Boston, observe all the lives of the man-swarm and list all the names and places in America. That was simple enough, but practically every other character in the book also suffered from fury and compulsions, and, what was more suggestive, they were all twenty feet tall, spoke with the voice of trumpets and the thunder, ate like Pantagruel, wept like Niobe, laughed like Falstaff and bellowed like the bulls of Bashan. The significant thing was that we were seeing them all through Eugene's eyes. To a child all adults are giants: their voices are thunderous, their actions are portentous and grotesquely magnified, and all their exhibited emotions are seismic. It looked as if part of Eugene's condition was an infantile regression.

This appearance was reinforced by what seemed to be another stigma of infantilism: that all the experiences in *Of Time and the River* were on the same level and had the same value. When Mr. Gant died (of enough cancer to have exterminated an army corps), the reader accepted the accompanying frenzy as proper to the death of a man's father — which is one of the most important events in anyone's life. But when the same frenzy accompanied nearly everything else in the book — a ride on a railroad train, a literary tea-fight, a midnight lunch in the kitchen, a quarrel between friends, a walk at night, the rejection of a play, an automobile trip, a seduction that misfired, the discovery of Eugene's true love — one could only decide that something was dreadfully wrong. If the death of a father comes out even with a ham-on-rye, then the art of fiction is cockeyed.

Well, *The Story of a Novel* puts an end to speculation and supplies some unexpected but very welcome light. To think of these matters as contempt of the medium, regression and infantilism is to be too complex and subtle. The truth shows up in two much simpler facts: that Mr. Wolfe is still astonishingly immature, and that he has mastered neither the psychic material out of which a novel is made nor the technique of writing fiction. He does not seem aware of the first fact, but he acknowledges the second with a frankness and an understanding that are the finest promise to date for his future books. How far either defect is reparable it is idle to speculate. But at least Mr. Wolfe realizes that he is, as yet, by no means a complete novelist.

The most flagrant evidence of his incompleteness is the fact that, so far, one indispensable part of the artist has existed not in Mr. Wolfe but in Maxwell Perkins. Such organizing faculty and such critical intelligence as have been applied to the book have come not from inside the artist, not from the artist's feeling for form and esthetic integrity, but from the office of Charles Scribner's Sons. For five years the artist pours out words "like burning lava from a volcano" — with little or no idea what their purpose is, which book they belong in, what the relation of part to part is, what is organic and what irrelevant, or what emphasis or coloration in the completed work of art is being served by the job at hand. Then Mr. Perkins decides these questions — from without, and by a process to which rumor applies the word "assembly." But works of art cannot be assembled like a carburetor — they must be grown like a plant, or in Mr. Wolfe's favorite simile like an embryo. The artist writes a hundred thousand words about a train: Mr. Perkins decides that the train is worth only five thousand words. But such a decision as this is properly not within Mr. Perkins's power; it must be made by the highly conscious self-criticism of the artist in relation to the pulse of the book itself. Worse still, the artist goes on writing till Mr. Perkins tells him that the novel is finished. But the end of a novel is, properly, dictated by the internal pressure, osmosis, metabolism — what you will — of the novel itself, of which only the novelist can have a first-hand knowledge. There comes a point where the necessities of the book are satisfied, where its organic processes have reached completion. It is hard to see how awareness of that point can manifest itself at an editor's desk — and harder still to trust the integrity of a work of art in which not the artist but the publisher has determined where the true ends and the false begins.

All this is made more ominous by Mr. Wolfe's almost incredibly youthful attitude toward revision. No novel is written till it is revised — the process is organic, it is one of the processes of art. It is, furthermore, the process above all others that requires objectivity, a feeling for form, a knowledge of what the necessities of the book are, a determination that those necessities shall outweigh and dominate everything else. It is, if not the highest functioning of the artistic intelligence, at least a fundamental and culminating one. But the process appears to Mr. Wolfe not one which will free his book from falsity, irrelevance and its private

encumbrances, not one which will justify and so exalt the artist —
but one that makes his spirit quiver "at the bloody execution" and
his soul recoil "from the carnage of so many lovely things." But
superfluous and mistaken things are lovely to only a very young
writer, and the excision of them is bloody carnage only if the artist
has not learned to subdue his ego in favor of his book. And the
same juvenility makes him prowl "the streets of Paris like a maddened animal" because — for God's sake! — the reviewers may not
like the job.

The placental passages are now explained. They consist of
psychic material which the novelist has proved unable to shape
into fiction. The failure may be due either to immature understanding or to insufficient technical skill: probably both causes
operate here and cannot be separated. The principle is very simple.
When Mr. Wolfe gives us his doctors, undertakers and newspaper-
men talking in a lunchroom at dawn, he does his job — magnificently. There they are, and the reader revels in the dynamic presentation of human beings, and in something else as well that
should have the greatest possible significance for Mr. Wolfe. For
while the doctors and undertakers are chaffing one another, the
reader gets that feeling of the glamour and mystery of American
life which Mr. Wolfe elsewhere unsuccessfully labors to evoke in
thousands of rhapsodic words. The novelist makes his point in the
lives of his characters, not in tidal surges of rhetoric.

Is America lost, lonely, nameless and unknown? Maybe, and
maybe not. But if it is, the conditions of the novelist's medium
require him to make it lost and lonely in the lives of his characters,
not in blank verse bombast and apocalyptic delirium. You cannot
represent America by hurling adjectives at it. Do "the rats of death
and age and dark oblivion feed forever at the roots of sleep"? It
sounds like a high school valedictory, but if in fact they do, then
the novelist is constrained to show them feeding so by means of
what his characters do and say and feel in relation to one another,
and not by chasing the ghosts of Whitman and Ezekiel through
fifty pages of disembodied emotion. Such emotion is certainly the
material that fiction works with, but until it is embodied in character and scene it is not fiction — it is only logorrhea. A poem

should not mean but be, Mr. MacLeish tells us, and poetry is always proving that fundamental. In a homelier aphorism Mr. Cohan has expressed the same imperative of the drama: "Don't tell 'em, show 'em." In the art of fiction the *thing* is not only an imperative, it is a primary condition. A novel *is* — it cannot be asserted, ranted or even detonated. A novelist represents life. When he does anything else, no matter how beautiful or furious or ecstatic the way in which he does it, he is not writing fiction. Mr. Wolfe can write fiction — has written some of the finest fiction of our day. But a great part of what he writes is not fiction at all; it is only material with which the novelist has struggled but which has defeated him. The most important question in American fiction to-day, probably, is whether he can win that encounter in his next book. It may be that *The October Fair* and *The Hills Beyond Pentland* will show him winning it, but one remembers the dilution from *Look Homeward, Angel* to *Of Time and the River* and is apprehensive. If he does win it, he must do so inside himself; Mr. Perkins and the assembly-line at Scribners' can do nothing to help him.

That struggle also has another aspect. A novelist utilizes the mechanism of fantasy for the creation of a novel, and there are three kinds of fantasy with which he works. One of them is unconscious fantasy, about which Dr. Kubie was writing in these columns something over a year ago. A novelist is wholly subject to its emphases and can do nothing whatever about them — though when Mr. Wolfe says that the center of all living is reconciliation with one's father he comes close to revealing its pattern in him. There remain two kinds of fantasy which every novelist employs — but which everyone employs in a different ratio. Call them identification and projection, call them automatic and directed, call them proliferating and objectified — the names do not matter. The novelist surrenders himself to the first kind, but dominates and directs the second kind. In the first kind he says, "I am Napoleon," and examines himself to see how he feels. In the second kind, he wonders how Napoleon feels, and instead of identifying himself with him, he tries to discover Napoleon's necessities. If he is excessively endowed with the first kind of fantasy, he is likely to be a genius. But if he learns to utilize the second kind in the manifold interrelationships of a novel he is certain to be an artist. Whatever Mr. Wolfe's future in the wider and looser interest of Literature, his future in the far more rigorous interest of fiction just about comes down to the question of whether he can increase his facility at the second kind of fantasy. People would stop idiotically calling him autobiographical, if he gave us less identification and more understanding. And we could do with a lot less genius, if we got a little more artist.

For the truth is that Mr. Wolfe is presented to us, and to himself, as a genius. There is no more dissent from that judgment in his thinking about himself than in Scribner's publicity. And, what is more, a genius of the good old-fashioned romantic kind — possessed by a demon, driven by the gales of his own fury, helpless before the lava-flood of his own passion, selected and set apart for greatness, his lips touched by a live coal, consequently unable to exercise any control over what he does and in fact likely to be damaged or diminished by any effort at control. Chaos is everything, if you have enough of it in you to make a world. Yes, but what if you don't make a world — what if you just make a noise? There was chaos in Stephen Dedalus's soul, but he thought of that soul not as sufficient in itself but merely as a smithy wherein he might forge his novel. And listen to Mr. Thomas Mann: "When I think of the masterpiece of the twentieth century, I have an idea of something that differs essentially and, in my opinion, with profit from the Wagnerian masterpiece — something exceptionally logical, clear, and well developed in form, something at once austere and serene, with no less intensity of will than his, but of cooler, nobler, even healthier spirituality, something that seeks its greatness not in the colossal, the baroque, and its beauty not in intoxication." Something, in other words, with inescapable form, something which exists as the imposition of order on chaos, something that *is*, not is merely asserted.

One can only respect Mr. Wolfe for his determination to realize himself on the highest level and to be satisfied with nothing short of greatness. But, however useful genius may be in the writing of novels, it is not enough in itself — it never has been enough, in any art, and it never will be. At the very least it must be supported by an ability to impart shape to material, simple competence in the use of tools. Until Mr. Wolfe develops more craftsmanship, he will not be the important novelist he is now widely accepted as being. In order to be a great novelist he must also mature his emotions till he can see more profoundly into character than he now does, and he must learn to put a corset on his prose. Once more: his own smithy is the only possible place for these developments — they cannot occur in the office of any editor whom he will ever know.

The most difficult book ever to come from Wolfe's pen was his first posthumous novel, "The Web and the Rock," the major portion concerning a great love affair. The woman's side of this affair had already been written in "The Journey Down" (1938) by Aline Bernstein, and Wolfe's novel was, in a way, simply a retelling of some of the same episodes. Furthermore, Wolfe's attempt to satisfy some of his critics by displaying more objectivity is noticeable in the first sections, then confused by an almost complete reversion to his lyric style. Clifton Fadiman's review of this strangely perplexing book is a fair one, taking into account its redeeming qualities as well as its complexities.

THE WEB AND THE ROCK*

by

Clifton Fadiman

This novel, then, marks not only a turning away from the books I have written in the past, but a genuine spiritual and artistic change. It is the most objective novel that I have written. . . . I have sought, through free creation, a release of my inventive power.

So wrote Thomas Wolfe in the Author's Note to *The Web and the Rock* four months before his tragic death at Johns Hopkins Hospital on September 15, 1938. How keenly one wishes the novel itself confirmed his brave words! But the gray truth is that *The Web and the Rock*, except for some hundred-odd scattered and magnificent pages, marks no particular advance, either in power or objectivity, over *Of Time and the River*. The central character, though he is called George Webber, is still the Eugene

* From the *New Yorker*, 24 June 1939; copyright 1939 The New Yorker Magazine, Inc. By permission of the author.

Gant of the previous books. One may at last freely and sadly say both George Webber and Eugene Gant are Thomas Wolfe. George Webber is, again, the young writer who wishes to experience everything and is driven to frenzy because he cannot. All the motifs we are used to from the other books repeat themselves here: the attraction-repulsion exerted on the provincial by New York, the voyage-and-return pattern that marked *Of Time and the River*, the sonorous but vague celebration of America, the insistence on man's "aloneness" and on the "strangeness" of "time." You even feel that certain characters are only seemingly new and have their roots in the other books. The style, too, remains unchanged — distended, straining for impossible effects, often capable of high (but never the highest) beauty, often reminiscent of old-time movie-caption prose. No, *The Web and the Rock* does not, it seems to me, mark that "spiritual and artistic change" we were all looking for. It is simply more of the same Wolfe, which is to say more of the most gifted young American writer produced during the last fifteen years. It is not a self-contained novel any more than the others were. It is a cut-off length of the endless experiences of Thomas Wolfe.

We meet George Webber when he is a twelve-year-old boy in the small town of Libya Hill in Old Catawba (read North Carolina). George at twelve is George at twenty-five; his reactions to life have no relation to his age. He lies in the front yard of his uncle's home and muses, "How strange, and plain, and savage, sweet and cruel, lovely, terrible, and mysterious, and how unmistakable and familiar all things are!" It's the same old nonsense; the same unselective excitement; the same tyranny of words; it's Eugene Gant once more.

But it is not George Webber who makes the first sections of the book wonderful — for they are wonderful. It is the townsfolk he describes — seen, it is true, through a very special vision, but seen unforgettably. I should say, for example, that Nebraska Crane, the Cherokee boy, is almost as great a characterization as Huckleberry Finn. The terrible outsize Lampley family comprise the most memorable grotesques in the whole Wolfe gallery. Magnificent, too, is the whole account of Dick Prosser, the gentlemanly Negro who ran amok — a story that, to my mind, brings out more of the underlying violence of the Southern temperament than do all the novels of William Faulkner combined.

Much of this small-town material is magnificent, but not all. The further the event from George's own experience, the more moving it is; the nearer it approaches his own life and mind, the more tedious it becomes — and the harder Wolfe works to prevent it from becoming tedious. Thus, when Wolfe describes a dogfight, you see it before your own eyes, but when young George reflects on the dogfight, unreality sets in. I seem to be in a pathetic minority here, but it seems to me that the one crucial defect of the Wolfe books is that the central character, despite the hundreds of pages devoted to him, despite his endless monologues, despite all the introspection, never quite becomes believable. The most boring pages in Wolfe are the most personal ones; the most fascinating are devoted to people and scenes he remembers vividly, but which he does not incorporate within his gigantic sense of self.

If *The Web and the Rock* had stopped at page 170, it would have been a far finer book. Not that the succeeding 525 pages are without interest, but one must pick and choose among them, wade through overwritten passages, repetitions, and almost incredible naïvetés of thought and feeling. The college sections — though there is some extremely funny if exaggerated satire here — are formless and inferior to those in *Look Homeward, Angel.* Also, the chapters dealing with George's early days in New York are dragged out beyond their natural length. Wolfe remembered with almost painful particularity everything that had happened to him. He committed the fallacy of assuming that the intensity of his memory would naturally awaken an equally intense reaction in the reader. He never seems to have asked himself the simple question: Is this detail worthy of being remembered? He could write fervently about anything, but he never knew what things one ought to be fervent about.

The second half of the book deals almost entirely with a love affair and with George Webber's introduction to the "smart" life of New York. The lady is a successful stage designer, a half-Jewess, very sensitive and lovely, rather older than George, a member of the fashionable world. Her culture is in direct opposition to George's which is primitive, provincial, puritanical. Partly because of this opposition, partly because George "tears up everything he gets his hands on," the affair is bound to end badly, and it does. Not, however, before you have waded through about 400 pages of highly conversational raptures and quarrels. I guess I may as well confess that most of this seemed to me a crashing bore. I'm not sure why. I think it's simply that there's just too much of everything — too much recrimination, too much ecstasy, too many scenes, too many reconciliations. Enough is enough.

The book ends, rather oddly, with a European-travel section, sufficiently interesting in itself but somehow tacked on, superfluous.

What is one to say of this enormous, puzzling, overwhelming, disappointing talent? Wolfe has been called genius by so many shrewd and calm judges that the temptation is strong to join the procession. At times he wrote like one inspired; there is no doubt of it. No one in his generation had his command of language, his passion, his memory, his energy, his sensitivity. Yet his books, I believe, are not great works of art. They do not add up to anything. They do not, in the end, satisfy you. They paint no single vision of life, not even the vision of multiplicity. Wolfe had a primitive, impetuous nature that rejected thought in favor of a set of titanic prejudices. Because he could bring no order into his life, he could bring no order into his prose. And so he was forced to celebrate disorder — to try to forge an epic out of sheer fury. He belongs, in Santayana's phrase, with those who create a literature of barbarism. Such a literature, depending upon the motor values of energy rather than the moral values of truth, may fascinate and overwhelm us for a time, but will it endure? Ossian seemed terrific stuff in his day, but who reads Ossian now? In all the great and almost great novels, even in such dionysian works as *Moby Dick*, there is an intellectual substratum, and this intellectual substratum acts as a quiet preservative against the ravages of time. Rhetoric, however great and however sincere — for Wolfe's rhetoric was sincere — has not the final power to endure.

All the virtues and all the defects of the provincial are in Wolfe.

He had that great innocence of the provincial, the innocence the metropolitan would dearly love to own. He had the energy of the provincial, his boldness, his contempt for pseudo-intellectual conventions. He had the poetry of earth. But, on the other hand, he had the provincial's furious disregard for rationality and order. He had a naïve contempt for people and ideas and traditions he could not understand. If a thing was alien, he either drew away from it in desperate horror or engulfed it in desperate passion. He overestimated New York, and he underestimated it. His aggressiveness, his desire to conquer the city, lent him a certain passion, but at the same time it disoriented and disordered his faculties, making his reactions seem at times like those of a bad-tempered child with a superb flow of language.

It is impossible to say what would have happened to him had he lived, but it is certainly possible to say that this book shows no growth, save an increase in confusion. Perhaps the unpublished novel still remaining — to be called *You Can't Go Home Again* — may bear witness to that "spiritual and artistic change" that Wolfe so earnestly hoped had taken place in him.

It seems inevitable that Wolfe's wanderings, which began in "Look Homeward, Angel," should lead him finally through the mazes of uncertainty into assurance — the assurance of belief which mounts to the closing chapters of "You Can't Go Home Again." The fourth novel in the colossal tetralogy brought conviction to many of those who had felt that Wolfe was hopelessly "lost." The author of "John Brown's Body" needed little persuasion; yet the statement of confidence is here. Stephen Vincent Benét, poet, librettist, short story writer, and novelist, died in 1943.

A TORRENT OF RECOLLECTION

by

Stephen Vincent Benét

This posthumous novel continues and concludes the story of George Webber — the story of Thomas Wolfe — the story of seeking and finding that is at the back of all the work which Wolfe was allowed to do. They were always saying — the well-informed and the critical — that, if he could stand off from himself, be more objective, tame, and order the extravagances of his power — well, well, then he might become the really great novelist, the conscious artist, all that sort of thing.

It was good advice for nine writers out of ten, but his power was not that sort of power. In this book, as in its predecessor, *The Web and the Rock*, it is shown that he came to know himself, his strength and his weaknesses, much more clearly and objectively than was supposed. But that knowledge did not make any differ-

From the *Saturday Review of Literature*, 21 September 1940 under title "Thomas Wolfe's Torrent of Recollection." By special permission.

ence. He had to write as he wrote. He had to draw upon the giant web, the torrent of recollection, the all-feeling explorativeness, for everything in American earth, draw upon it and pour it forth again with shouts and cries, a river of sights, sounds, smells, tastes, feelings, memories, a river deafening the ears and stunning the eyes but not to be forgotten while Mississippi ran. "The forgotten moments and unnumbered hours came back to me with all the enormous cargo of my memory, together with lost voices in the mountains long ago, the voices of the kinsmen dead and never seen, and the houses they had built and died in, and the rutted roads they trod upon and every unrecorded moment."

That is how the work was done. He lacked taste at times, he was often verbose and rhetorical. He was fond of certain rubber stamps of dialect and never got over them. He was so prodigal of talent that he could and did write a thousand passages as good as the one I have quoted above. He was so little self-critical that, when his ear and his genius deserted him momentarily, he could write such appalling English as "Aristocrats of ancient lineage who had always held to a tradition of stiff-necked exclusiveness could be seen chatting familiarly with the plebeian parvenus of the new rich." He committed the errors of a giant — a small man can write bad prose but it takes a Dickens to assassinate Little Nell. And, when all is said and done, he will stand with Melville.

You Can't Go Home Again is the story of a man's pilgrimage, with its successive returns that meet with defeat, its successive reachings out for something that, even when grasped, eludes the hand. George Webber returns to Esther Jack and for a time they resume their old relation. But love is not enough — the two lives are too disparate — and the relation ends. He returns to Libya Hill and the deep roots of his childhood — and finds it in the frenzy of the boom, a city of lost men. He returns to the Germany he loved — and must say farewell to it — it is being delivered over to something old and evil. His first book brings him a brief celebrity and the hatred of his own people of Libya Hill — his second book brings him fame — and he sees through Lloyd McHarg the huge, restless disillusion that comes with fame. You can't go home again — not even to the tried friend, Foxhall Edwards. So stated, the book sounds like a study in disillusion. And is nothing of the sort.

It is written with all Wolfe's furious energy, with his devouring zest for all sorts of different human beings, with his amazing gift for sucking the very last drop of juice out of a character or a scene. It contains some telling, and some very heavy-handed, satire on literary life in New York. It will be read for that and people will babble over the various names. And none of that part is going to matter, in time, except for Piggy Logan's circus at the Jacks' where Wolfe has caught a genuine horror and genuine scorn. The party itself, the sudden irruption of Piggy Logan's senseless young friends and the effect of the monstrous little circus of wire dolls on those who watch it — these are beautifully done. The first that follows is both well done and badly done — very few people could have done it at all and yet it does not quite come off. A good deal of the rest of the satire is a dropping of five-hundred-pound bombs to demolish gnats. The lion-hunters described in the chapter of that name shouldn't, somehow, have mattered as much as they did to George Webber.

They don't, in the end — in the real plan and mass of the book. For, though there are extraneous chapters — though *You Can't Go Home Again* contains some of Wolfe's worst writing as well as much of his best — there is a clear, though winding path through the great forest of words and incidents and memories. There is a line, and a mature line. George Webber does grow up, not merely by fiat. There are such brilliant single incidents as that of Mr. Katamoto and that of the fantastic, believable meeting with Lloyd McHarg. But, more than that, though many things on the way were vanity, George Webber's pilgrimage was not vanity, and we do not feel that it was. The book ends neither in doubt nor in disillusion. It ends, in the remarkable last chapter, with a cry of faith.

I believe that we are lost here in America but I believe we shall be found. . . . I think the life which we have fashioned in America and which has fashioned us — the forms we made, the cells that grew, the honeycomb that was created — was self-destructive in its nature, and must be destroyed. I think these forms are dying and must die just as I know that America and the people in it are deathless, undiscovered, and immortal, and must live.

I think the true discovery of America is before us. I think the true fulfillment of our spirit, of our people, of our mighty and immortal land is yet to come. I think the true discovery of our own democracy is still before us. And I think that all these things are certain as the morning, as inevitable as noon. . . .

The prose mounts to its moving end, with its strange premonition of death.

To lose the earth you know, for greater knowing; to lose the life you have, for greater life; to leave the friends you loved, for greater loving; to find a land more kind than home, more large than earth —

These are great words, greatly spoken. To our loss, they come from the dead; but they speak to the living, and now. Out of passionate belief and faith they speak, and will keep on speaking, through the years, though the great tree is down and the wide and turbulent river sunk back into the ground.

PART III
THE COMMENTATORS

Did Thomas Wolfe write "The Great American Novel"? Have Wolfe's critics been on solid ground in their dictums? How does Wolfe measure up in scope, in greatness, in significance, in form? Was Wolfe a genius? — These are the questions to which Thomas Lyle Collins gives his answer in this omnium-gatherum of the various problems with which the serious reader of Wolfe is often confronted. In a way, it is a rebuttal to those whom Collins sees as Wolfe's imposing detractors, chiefly Robert Penn Warren and Bernard DeVoto, whose articles in question appear previously in this volume.

WOLFE'S GENIUS VS. HIS CRITICS

by

Thomas Lyle Collins

I

Out of the vigorous American renaissance which began in the second decade of this century grew the literary myth of the "Great American Novel." By this was meant a novel which should capture completely the spirit and meaning of this immense and bewildering new society of ours. Half a century before, Walt Whitman had flung a ringing challenge to the future artists of America. In the period during and following the First World War, the new schools of American writers attempted, and with no little success, to meet that challenge. An enormous body of good writing appeared, and quite a bit that deserved even to be called great. But of the novels written during that period, none seemed really deserving of the designation, "The Great American Novel."

Original title in 1942: "Thomas Wolfe." By special permission.

However, of the attempts to capture and immortalize this spirit of twentieth-century America, there have been three which have been of major importance.

In his trilogy, *U.S.A.*, John Dos Passos attempted a literary project of more comprehensive scope than any previous American work. With striking economy and a deft hand, he made sketches of the lives of more than a score of typical Americans who might have lived in the period between 1910 and 1930, and wove and interwove these sketches into an even-textured fictional whole. But these sketches had a certain drabness and colorlessness about them, and Mr. Dos Passos, in order to suggest the melodramatic, tabloid aspect of American life, inserted the "Newsreels" — impressionistic glimpses of contemporaneous newspaper headlines, news stories, popular songs, and so forth. However, there was still lacking the strong lyric strain which is an essential part of the American temper, and so the author also wove in imagistic stream-of-consciousness passages of an autobiographical nature, calling this "The Camera Eye." The result was a novel which looked something like a department store and which, though fascinating and at times even moving, was somehow not great. Probably the chief flaw was the author's failure to synthesize the prosaic, commonplace America and the poetic, lyrical America into an organic artistic whole. Furthermore, Dos Passos cannot be criticized on the grounds of something he was not trying to do, and he would probably be the first to admit that he was not trying to deal with the whole of America, but rather only the American metropolis.

The poetic spirit of the American people was more nearly perfectly expressed by Carl Sandburg, the modern disciple of Whitman, who, after several volumes of mumbling and fumbling, finally burst out into a great American song, *The People, Yes*. But although much more powerful and skillful than his teacher, Sandburg is inflicted with the same blind optimism as Whitman. A further limitation is that, although the book is filled with The People, there are no real people in it — only shifting masses without name or shape. The People, yes, but people, no. One suspects that actually The People do not exist as an entity, that instead they constitute a myth comparable to the much-discussed but mythical American Youth. Needless to say, I am not comparing *U.S.A.* and *The People, Yes*, since the latter is a book of verse; I am merely pointing out that *The People, Yes* contains an element of the American temper which Dos Passos's novel lacks.

In 1929 a virtually unknown young writer named Thomas Wolfe published an autobiographical novel called *Look Homeward, Angel.* Many favorable comments were made by the promiscuously favorable reviewers, the sales were brisk, and a few years later the novel was reprinted in the Modern Library series, a mark of moderate distinction for living writers. In 1935 Wolfe's second novel, *Of Time and the River,* appeared. Again the reviewers cast their superlatives recklessly, again the sales were good. Comments such as the one by Lewis Gannett (reprinted on the book jacket of a later edition) showed that at least Wolfe's style had an amusingly strong influence on impressionable readers: "Thomas Wolfe writes like a mighty, furious Paul Bunyan, with the passionate love of America of a Walt Whitman and the enraged adolescent idealism of a Shelley also pulsing in his veins. . . . The 912 pages . . . tumble, pour, roar, sing with savage joy and fury."

In the meantime excerpts from Wolfe began to appear occasionally in American literature anthologies, and critics began to take notice of him in their surveys of the modern field. Vernon Loggins, for instance, compares him not too unfavorably with Dostoevski, but then adds deprecatingly, "The world in which he [Eugene Gant] moves is so commonplace that it can easily become tedious."

But what no critic seems to have realized is that the appearance of Thomas Wolfe may have been an event of the utmost significance in the history of American literature: certainly, at least, his power of description and narration is unexcelled in the entire range of our literature. There is even a possibility that future generations will come to regard him as the author of The Great American Novel which we have so long awaited. Let us then take this popular phrase, The Great American Novel, as a four-unit yardstick to measure him; for in these four words lie the four main problems which the modern critic encounters in the novel. These four critical problems, in their respective order, are: *the problem of scope, the problem of greatness, the problem of significance,* and *the problem of form.* By this standard perhaps we may be able to decide how nearly Wolfe's novels approach the ideal of The Great American Novel. Since the first of these problems is the one most important to this consideration, it will be treated last.

However, before any positive critical statements about Wolfe can be made, the ground must first be cleared by an examination of the line of critical attack laid down by two representative critics, Bernard DeVoto and Robert Penn Warren.

II

What chiefly troubled Mr. DeVoto about Wolfe were the long lyrical passages of flowing rhetoric — some "dark substance . . . unrelated to the proper business of fiction. . . ." The proper business of fiction, says DeVoto, is dramatic narrative, undiluted by any of this new rhetorical nonsense. "Is America lost, lonely, nameless and unknown? Maybe, and maybe not. But if it is, the condition of the novelist's medium requires him to make it lost and lonely in the lives of his characters, not in blank verse, bombast, and apocalyptic delirium."

Mr. DeVoto here makes a great show of being hard-headed and commonsensical, but better critics than he have failed to survive beyond their time because they adhered to a critical dogmatism which attempts to keep poetry and fiction and comedies and tragedies and ballet and opera set completely apart from each other in neat little compartments. I wonder what Mr. DeVoto would have to say about the chapters of exposition in *The Grapes of Wrath,* the internal monologue in such novels as *Mrs. Dalloway,* or the aforementioned peculiarities of *U.S.A.?* In so restricting "the proper business of fiction," he has bitten off a great deal less than he can chew.

Now if Wolfe *merely told* us that Americans are lost and lonely, there might be a basis for DeVoto's criticism. If Wolfe's "dark substance" had no dramatic backbone, it would be a bore. But it must not be forgotten that Wolfe keeps an unwritten bargain with his reader: he always shows us everything he tells us, each element complementing the other. DeVoto asks for lost and lonely characters: who of the readers of *Of Time and the River* will ever forget the enormously funny and heartbreakingly pathetic little middle-class mother, Mrs. Simpson —

"We want you to feel absolutely at home here," she said brightly. "Make this your headquarters. You will find us simple folk here, without any frills," she continued, with a glance around the living-room, letting her eye rest with brief satisfaction upon the striped tiles of the hearth, the flowered vases of the mantle, the naked doll, tied with a pink sash, on the piano, and the pictures of "The Horse Fair," the lovers flying before the storm, Maxfield Parrish's "Dawn," and Leonardo Da Vinci's "Last Supper," which broke the spaces of the wall, "but if you like a quiet family life, a welcome is always waiting for you here. Oh, yes — every one is for each other here: we keep no secrets from each other in our little family."

And who will forget the simple courage and dignity which arose in the mother when she became conscious that Eugene had made the family the butt of a cruel joke? Or the symphonic passage which closed the episode, a passage which Mr. DeVoto would have us believe is "unrelated to the proper business of fiction" —

He never saw any of them again, but he could not forget them. And as the years went on, the memory of all their folly, falseness, and hypocrisy was curiously altered and subdued and the memory that grew more vivid and dominant was of a little family, one of millions huddled below the immense and timeless skies that bend above us, lost in the darkness of nameless and unnumbered lives upon the lonely wilderness of life that is America, and banked together against these giant antagonists, for comfort, warmth, and love, with a courage and integrity that would not die, and could not be forgotten.

Later Mr. DeVoto quotes from MacLeish, "A poem should not mean but be," and then goes on to say, "A novel *is* — it cannot be asserted, ranted, or even detonated." If DeVoto had read "Ars Poetica" more carefully, he would also have seen these lines —

A poem should be equal to:
Not true

For all the history of grief
An empty doorway and a maple leaf . . .

What Wolfe has done is fill in both sides of this equation — that is, he has given us both the history of grief *and* the empty doorway and the maple leaf. (It is interesting to note that Wolfe's symbols, "a stone, a leaf, an unfound door," are remarkably similar to these employed by MacLeish.) In this manner Wolfe has achieved an effective synthesis of the prosaic and the poetic. And to say that poetry has no business in the novel is just as absurd as to say that poetry has no business in the drama, nor narrative in poetry.

DeVoto continues: "A novelist represents life. When he does anything else, no matter how beautiful or furious or ecstatic the way in which he does it, he is not writing fiction." Even if we should grant this highly questionable limitation of the term fiction, we still have recourse to the vulgar retort, "So what?" For what should chiefly concern us is not whether Wolfe's writing does or does not fit into the technical category of fiction, but rather whether Wolfe's writing is or is not great. If, as many critics agree, it is true that the figures in his novels are blazing triumphs of characterization, if, as even Mr. DeVoto admits may be the case, his writing is "beautiful . . . furious . . . ecstatic," the problem of *genre* is of secondary importance. After we have decided how good or how great Wolfe's writing is, there will be time enough to decide *what* it is.

The other major issue which DeVoto brings to light is the problem of artistic integrity as manifested in a feeling for form. It is generally known that Wolfe wrote too much, was overwhelmed by the welter of words which he poured out into his stacks of ledgers, and that the editorial genius of Maxwell Perkins was mainly responsible for getting Wolfe's novels into publishable shape. And this is Mr. DeVoto's point: "The artist writes a hundred thousand words about a train: Mr. Perkins decides the train is worth only about five thousand words. But such a decision as this is properly

not within Mr. Perkins' power; it must be made by the highly
conscious self-criticism of the artist in relation to the pulse of the
book itself." Now there is a measure of truth in this which cannot
be denied. But there is a fallacy in Mr. DeVoto's critical reasoning
which lies in his confusing structural emphasis and form. Mr.
Perkins' working with Wolfe was, without a doubt, responsible for
a tightening up of the structure of Wolfe's novels; and this is indicative of a grave limitation of Wolfe's artistic powers. But no
editor can, by the wielding of a blue pencil, impart *form* to a work
of art; he can only lay bare the form which is somewhat obscured
by surplus material — and that is what Mr. Perkins has done. If
the novel had not been there in the first place, no editor's pencil
could have brought it to light. Form is an integral part of the work
of art; every dramatic scene, every colorful characterization was
formed by Wolfe, not by his editor. A man wanders the earth,
seeking "a stone, a leaf, an unfound door" — that is the theme
which imparts form to Wolfe's novels, and it is a theme which has
four phases, a natural division for the four novels. When Wolfe
came to the dividing line which marked the end of one phase and
the beginning of another, he was not always aware of it, and this
is to be regretted. But the point is that the dividing line *was* there
and he *did* come to it: it was there because his feeling for the form
which his great theme was to take had put it there, unconsciously
though it may have been.

Mr. DeVoto's most biting accusation is that Wolfe should have
learned to "put a corset on his prose. . . ." This is possibly true
though certainly not to the extent that DeVoto would have us believe. And a corset is often quite a handy device: it keeps the body
looking trim and neat. But it also restricts free movement and
respiration, and is often quite detrimental to the health. It can
never be more than idle speculation to try to determine whether
or not Wolfe's prose would have been better had it been corseted;
but corseted or uncorseted, there is a certain statuesque quality
about his style which, by comparison, makes the pale prose of the
lesser American novelists seem to be suffering from malnutrition.

Robert Penn Warren, in his article, "The Hamlet of Thomas
Wolfe," more or less follows the critical line laid down by DeVoto

— he worries about Wolfe's straining to make his characters seem significant, about Wolfe's constant repetition of his own "clichés" (a man named Homer used to be fond of that sort of thing), about Wolfe's seeming lack of discipline, "focus," and control.

In addition, Warren raises a new problem — that of objectivity in the autobiographical novel. This is best expressed by his parting shot: "And meanwhile it may be well to recollect that Shakespeare merely wrote *Hamlet*; he was *not* Hamlet." Mr. Warren's objection is that Wolfe not only wrote about Eugene Gant, but that his own personality and feelings became identical with those of that character. The critical dictum by which Mr. Warren makes this accusation is this: that there must be no confusion between the sensibility that produces a dramatic narrative and the sensibility of the hero in that narrative. This would be a valid criticism save that one feels that Mr. Warren's sequence of thought is from the novelist to the novel, rather than *vice versa*. That is to say, he is not keeping his eye on the critical object, which is the work of art. *Hamlet*, as a play, would be no less great if Shakespeare actually had been a prince of Denmark whose father had been murdered by his uncle. We must look to the art, not to the artist. No valid criticism can come from the comparison, explicit or implicit, of the characters of Thomas Wolfe and Eugene Gant.

It seems to me that there are two circumstances in a novel in which a charge of lack of objectivity might be justified: when the author places his own sentiments in the mouth of a character incapable of such sentiments; and when the author places himself in his novel without first objectifying his own sentiments to the extent that he can see and present himself clearly and vividly. As to the first charge, it is true that many of Wolfe's characters are "Wolfian," but this is true in varying degree for all novelists. That is to say, all characters by one novelist have something of the same quality, because all are given life by the same moving spirit.

As to the second charge, Wolfe has objectified his own character with commendable vividness and clarity. Eugene Gant–Monk Webber is one of the immortal autobiographical characters of fiction. Certainly it required an exercise of his powers of objectification for Wolfe to laugh at himself the way he did, such as in the scene in *Look Homeward, Angel* where the Acting Dean of Pulpit Hill advises Eugene not to go Over There but to stay and Do His Bit —

"Yes," said Eugene, with a pale tortured face, "I know. . . . But oh, sir, — when I think of those murderous beasts, when I think of how they have menaced All that we Hold Dear, when I think of Little Belgium, and then of My Own Mother, My Own Sister — " He turned away, clenching his hands, madly in love with himself.

"Yes, yes," said the Acting Dean gently, "for boys with a spirit like yours it's not easy."

"Oh sir, it's hard!" cried Eugene passionately. "I tell you it's hard."

"We must endure," said the Dean quietly. "We must be tempered in the fire. The Future of Mankind hangs in the balance."

Deeply stirred they stood together for a moment, drenched in the radiant beauty of their heroic souls.

I cannot repeat too often that it is true that Wolfe has many faults, that he wrote many bad passages. But these faults are the flaws in greatness, not the limitations of talent.

In short, Mr. DeVoto and Mr. Warren are trying to make a molehill out of a mountain.

III

The Problem of Greatness: True greatness, in the strictest sense of the word, always implies a certain transcendency, an ability to rise above the particular circumstance or experience to its more universal implications. This is precisely the quality which distinguishes Wolfe from his lesser contemporaries. This is precisely why the sentimental Mr. Steinbeck, although he is a more disciplined craftsman, is a less great novelist. Wolfe had a sort of super-vision which enabled him to see people in their several artistic dimensions. He found some people, such as the Simpsons, tremendously funny, and he shared with us his belly-laugh over them — but then he penetrated beyond the comic surface to the pathetic essence. He found the Pierces to be quite wonderful — for a while he thought he had discovered the "lane-end into heaven" — but then, rising above them, he saw beyond the cloud of glory which hid them and looked upon the weariness and decay which possessed them. He was completely taken in by the magic of Starwick's glamour, but he eventually saw through it. He was enraptured by Paris "sophistication," but he eventually saw through it. This is the key to Wolfe's genius, this ability to transcend his own experiences, and once having done so, to look back upon it all and write of it with power and clarity, flooding the scene with the rich light of his own personality.

That many readers do not seem to understand fully Wolfe's use of symbols is indicated by the two critical essays mentioned above. DeVoto could not see why Eugene was so preoccupied with the death of his father, and Warren failed to understand the significance of his relation with Starwick or the importance of his falling in love. Therefore it might be wise to make a thorough examination of Wolfe's theme as embodied in his symbols.

Wolfe's general theme is somewhat reminiscent of Wordsworth's *Ode on the Intimations of Immortality* in that it is suggestive of the passage containing the line "trailing clouds of glory do we come." On the title-page of *Look Homeward, Angel* Wolfe quotes this sentence from Tarr and McMurry — "At one time the earth was probably a white-hot sphere like the sun." Then the prefatory poem which follows explains in a measure both the quotation and the theme of the book —

. . . a stone, a leaf, an unfound door; of a stone, a leaf, a door. And of all the forgotten faces.

Naked and alone we came into exile. In her dark womb we did not know our mother's face; from the prison of her flesh have we come into the unspeakable and incommunicable prison of this earth.

Which of us has known his brother? Which of us has looked into his father's heart? Which of us has not remained forever prison-pent? Which of us is not forever a stranger and alone?

O waste of loss, in the hot mazes, lost, among bright stars on this most weary unbright cinder, lost! Remembering speechlessly we seek the great forgotten language, the lost lane-end into heaven, a stone, a leaf, an unfound door. Where? When?

O lost, and by the wind grieved, ghost, come back again.

From this we may extract a brutally prosaic statement of Wolfe's theme: all through life we are searching for some sign — "a stone, a leaf, a door" — which will open up to us the universe of perfection and enchantment which we feel vaguely to have left behind us when we were born. The implication is that our souls have been torn from this enchanted heaven and imprisoned in corporeal frames here on earth. A spiritually necessary unity is wanting, for we are unable to communicate with our fellow-prisoners. Monads have no windows: "we seek the great forgotten language . . ."

Or: Wolfe notes a discrepancy between the ideal world and the real, the former figuratively represented by the sun, the latter by "this most weary unbright cinder," the earth.

Or: Wolfe believes, in a non-Christian sense, in Original Sin. We are born into the damnation of spiritual isolation, and must achieve grace by ending that isolation.

Perhaps this essential and ever-present theme may be best described by a passage from *The Web and the Rock*, a passage of some more of Mr. DeVoto's "dark substance" —

We are small grope-things crying for the light and love by which we might be saved, and which, like us, is dying in the darkness a hand's breadth off from us if we could touch it. We are like blind sucks and sea-valves and the eyeless crawls that grope along the forest of the sea's great floor, and we die alone in the darkness, a second away from hope, a moment from ecstasy and fulfillment, a little half an hour from love.

At the heart of Wolfe's novels is an essential paradox which does not become apparent until Eugene's visit to England: it is that there is a door, there is a way to feel at home on the earth, there is a secret room — but though when you're outside you want in, when you're inside you want out! Traditionless America is on the outside and wants in; traditional England is on the inside and wants out. This is clearly illustrated by the following passages concerning England —

Yes, they had found a way, a door, a room to enter, and there were walls about them now, and the way was theirs. The mark of dark time and the architecture of unnumbered centuries of years were on them, and had made them what they were; and what they were, they were, and would not change.

All his life Eugene had been seeking "an unfound door." The English had found a door; had they found *the* door? He found the answer when, upon his departure, Edith Coulson told him —

"We shall remember you . . . And I hope you think of us some-time — back here, buried, lost, in all the fog and rain and ruin of England. How good it must be to know that you are young in a very young country — where nothing that you did yesterday matters very much. How wonderful it must be to know that none of the failure of the past can pull you down — that there will always be another day for you — a new beginning. I wonder if you Americans will ever know how fortunate you are. . . ."

The answer is, then, that life without meaning is far better than and preferable to life with certainty and security, for the latter results in death-in-life, which Wolfe views with abhorrence in all his novels.

This paradox of man accounts for Eugene's fascination with Jewish people. Wolfe bestows upon them a symbolic rôle because they alone were at home on the earth without being enmeshed by it. They are not beset by death-in-life because their certainty is the true one — the certainty of Ecclesiastes, the certainty of pain and folly and useless endeavor. It was almost inevitable that he should fall in love with a Jewish woman.

But the two principal symbols are love and death, for they are the only things that will end the spiritual isolation of the soul. In the great poem which prefaces *Of Time and the River*, these symbols are presented, symbols which are expanded throughout the novel:

Whoever needs the earth shall have the earth: he shall be still upon it, he shall rest within a little place, he shall dwell in one small room forever.

O flower of love whose strong lips drink us downward into death, in all things far and fleeting, enchantress of our twenty thousand days, the brain will madden and the heart be twisted, broken by her kiss, but glory, glory, glory, she remains: Immortal love, alone and aching in the wilderness, we cried to you: You were not absent from our loneliness.

The other symbols now unfold to us with greater ease. Gant's father stands for his spiritual, certain past, a past to which he can never return for certainty. This symbol may have been derived from the Bloom-Dedalus relationship in James Joyce's *Ulysses*, particularly since Wolfe is self-admittedly indebted to Joyce. His brother Ben is the symbol for all men who cannot speak or give a sign of brotherhood. The Simpsons are the millions of lonely families in America "huddled below immense and timeless skies." In Starwick, Eugene found the unfound door: Francis could order a spaghetti dinner and make it sound like a royal banquet — thus the great shock when Eugene's illusions about Starwick crumbled. Eugene's mad desire to read all the books ever written is due to his hunger to see out over the walls of his soul into the outside world. The trains rushing through America are symbols of America itself — violent, splendid, powerful, blindly rushing through the night. The night is also symbolic of America, and the lonely men who huddle about the street-lamps and in the lighted lunch-rooms late at night take on a transcendent meaning.

It is this unity of the soul and the body of Wolfe's novels, this synthesis of the universal and the particular, which is the chief contributor to his greatness. The worlds of great artists are always complete. Homer's world was complete, as was Dante's, Shakespeare's, Goethe's. In other words, to put it crudely, they have an answer for everything. These artists, although they never lost sight of men, looked beyond and saw a vision of Man, eternal and immutable. Wolfe's *Weltanschauung* displays this same combination of completeness and accuracy, and therefore, in many ways, ranks him accordingly.

IV

The Problem of Significance: The American reading public, made acutely self-critical by Mr. Mencken *et al.* during the twenties, is very message-conscious in their reading of novels. What is the author's theme? What suggestion does he have to make in his novel for the political, economic, sociological, or cultural improvement of the nation? Is Main Street stifling the finer instincts? Are we suffering from mass inhibition? Did the World War leave the American doughboy maladjusted to society? This was the sort of question the novelist was asking, and it has been by the soundness and pertinency of his thesis that we have been inclined to judge the worth of his novel. I think this accounts in part, at least, for the hesitant reception of Wolfe's novels by the American critics. For Wolfe seemed much more concerned with his own personal problems than with the problems of America. This is why *You Can't Go Home Again* was greeted with such sighs of satisfaction, for at last Wolfe had become "significant."

I have already spoken of Wolfe's central theme of spiritual isolation. Its universal nature is apparent. Its particular application is that while it is true in varying degree for men of all time and place, it is most true for Americans of the present day. We *are* "like blind sucks and sea-valves and the eyeless crawls that grope along the forests of the sea's great floor. . . ." Our poverty of tradition, our blind materialism, our barrenness of middle-class life could not be described better. One does not have to read *You Can't Go Home Again* to find "significance." There is significance a-plenty in Wolfe's first three novels if one will but read carefully some of the passages of "dark substance" therein.

And Wolfe for the most part avoids the sentimental fallacy of ascribing our evils to institutions. With a dim but perceptible certainty he sees that the fault lies not outside but inside, deep within the heart of man.

In *You Can't Go Home Again* this implied belief becomes explicit. In his conclusion, called "Credo," he says "I think the enemy is single selfishness and compulsive greed." In the chapters called "Boom Town" and "The Company" he lashes out viciously at this single selfishness and compulsive greed. And in the chapter, "Piggy Logan's Circus," he achieves an effect of strange and gripping horror of a decadent aristocracy which will watch for hours the morbidly pointless antics of a giggling moron.

In regard to Wolfe's position in our national literature, I think it is safe to say that he stands, and will stand, very close to the top. For in his novels he caught that strange and unique combination of brilliant hope and black despair which is the quintessence of the American spirit.

v

The Problem of Form: The form of Wolfe's novels is enough
to give any critic a nightmare. At first reading they seem to be
little more than miscellaneous collections of autobiographical
anecdotes and personal observations. But after complete reading
and thoughtful contemplation, the nature of his literary form begins to emerge in one's mind.

First, however, a satisfactory definition of form must be found.
Reading between the lines, I infer that Mr. DeVoto's idea of the
form of a novel is that the novel should present a relevant and
closely associated sequence of dramatic incidents, each incident
carrying the reader closer to the final climactic scene. This was
the original form of the novel, and it served more than adequately.
But it is foolish and unprofitable to view this as a fixed and immutable *genre*. The use of *genres* should be for description, not
judgment. If Wolfe's works cannot be squeezed into the requirements for a novel, it is no matter of great concern.

And it is indeed doubtful if they do fit the requirements. There
is quite a gulf between *Pride and Prejudice* and *Of Time and the
River*.

Kenneth Burke has a practical and useful definition of form
which will serve in this case. He says that "form is the creation of
an appetite in the mind of the auditor, and the adequate satisfying
of the appetite."

Applying this definition to Wolfe's works, I find three basic and
interdependent forms. They are, in the order of excellence, the
episode, the complete work, and the novel.

Sometimes these episodes, such as the one about the Simpsons,
are very short. Sometimes, as in "The Child by Tiger" in *The Web
and the Rock* and "The World That Jack Built" in *You Can't Go
Home Again*, they are as long as a short novel. In the latter instance, they are subdivided into sub-episodes, and sub-sub-epi-
sodes, each one creating an appetite in the mind of the reader,
and satisfying that appetite adequately; each one having a
surprising singleness and intensity of effect. The sub-episodes
which go to make up a complete episode do not always observe

a time or place sequence; instead, Wolfe sketches in a detail here, makes a few strokes there, until finally the whole picture is completed.

A typical episode is the one in *The Web and the Rock* describing muscular, tweedy, pipe-smoking Preacher Reed, the Episcopal minister who made a tremendous hit with the boys of Pine Rock College by taking part in their bull sessions and comparing Christ to the quarterback of a football team. This episode is a part of a larger division, a chapter describing the intellectual leader of the campus, Jerry Alsop, and owes its presence to the fact that Alsop considers Preacher Reed the third greatest man since Jesus Christ. Wolfe concludes his bitingly ironic description of a bull session with this passage —

And as Alsop would himself say later, when the last reluctant footsteps died away, and there were the last "good nights" upon the campus, and he stood there in the now deserted room, polishing his misty glasses, and a little husky in the throat:

". . . It was puffectly delightful! Puffectly God-damned delightful! Yes, suh! That's the only word for it!"

And it was.

This is typical of Wolfe's method of rounding off an episode with a neat and delightful shock. The artistry of this method is apparent. In those three, small, modest words, "And it was," Wolfe polishes off Preacher Reed and Jerry Alsop at one fell blow. To say that Wolfe has satisfied our appetite adequately is putting it mildly.

The second basic form, Wolfe's complete work of four novels, contains a spiritual evolution in which may be found the beginning of a conflict, the body of a conflict, and the resolution, elements of a form which should satisfy the most reactionary of critics. The beginning of the conflict is contained in *Look Homeward, Angel*, in which a boy of energy and ambition finds himself buried in a world of pettiness and animosity and meaninglessness, and determines to escape into the outside world, where he may seek glory and love in meaning. The climactic incident is the one in which, after a violent quarrel with his family, Eugene cries triumphantly,

". . . I shall get me some beauty, I shall get me some order out of this jungle of my life: I shall find my way out of it yet, though it take me twenty years more — alone."

"Alone?" said Eliza, with the old suspicion. "Where are you going?"

"Ah," he said, "you were not looking, were you? I've gone."

Of Time and the River and *The Web and the Rock* constitute the body of the conflict. In the first he escapes into the world, and his interests and passions diverge in a thousand different directions in his Faustian search for glory and love and meaning. In the latter his passion strikes a lens and is focused and concentrated in his love for Esther Jack. The lens is then shattered, and the last volume, *You Can't Go Home Again,* contains a desperate race between death and meaning. The last lines he wrote present his premonition of death and his triumphant re-affirmation of a spiritual idealism —

Something has spoken to me in the night, burning the tapers of the waning years; something has spoken in the night, and told me I shall die, I know not where. Saying:

"To lose the earth you know, for greater knowing; to lose the life you have, for greater life; to leave the friends you loved, for greater loving; to find a land more kind than home, more large than earth —

"— Whereon the pillars of this earth are founded, toward which the conscience of the world is tending — a wind is rising, and the rivers flow."

The form of each novel, then, since it is so loose, is only important as a phase of Gant-Webber's spiritual evolution, and as a frame for Wolfe's episodic structure; it has no inherent and self-sufficient form to speak of. But Thomas Wolfe, genius that he was, had that inevitable instinct for form which served him twice where it failed him once.

VI

The Problem of Scope: Wolfe wrote *great* American novels, he wrote great *American* novels, and, loosely speaking, he wrote great American *novels*. But he fails to measure up in the fourth respect: he did not write *the* great American novel. Contained in the phrase is the implication that the novel should summarize and epitomize the promise of America's becoming one of the great ages of man, just as Homer's *Iliad* epitomizes the heroic age of Greece, Dante's *Divine Comedy* the medieval age, and Shakespeare's plays the English Renaissance. This is virtually impossible. There are so many forces of disunity and skepticism present in present-day America that a novel, or even a series of novels, could not bring them all together into a coherent and comprehensible pattern. Homer and Shakespeare and Dante stand far above us because they stand at the peak of a high and mighty structure erected by men of great talent and culture, all working together. There was little in the modern world for Wolfe to stand on.

Also, Wolfe was not of the artistic temper to write such a work. The author of The Great American Novel must be dramatic and omnipresent; Thomas Wolfe was lyrical and uni-present. For him there was only one world and he was at the center of it.

But his third and gravest limitation was his genius: it was the tragic flaw, a flaw of which he was only too conscious. "Genius is not enough," sneers Mr. DeVoto. On the contrary, the genius of Thomas Wolfe was too much. He was driven by a restlessness which kept him from achieving that cool perfection which often comes easy to lesser men.

In a reference to Coleridge in *The Web and the Rock*, Wolfe described better than any critic has ever done his own tragic and irreparable fault: "For genius such as his, unless its owner learns the way to use it, will turn and rend him like a tiger: it can bring death to men as surely as it brings them life."

Wolfe's discovery of America, its heritage, and its meaning was a gradual one. In this essay Professor Burgum makes clear its final revelation to Wolfe by tracing the theme in the novels as it is disclosed through symbolic interpretation. Burgum and Wolfe were colleagues at New York University. But they knew each other only casually, Burgum says, and "observed each other more or less at a distance . . . and so I was surprised to discover from his novels (after he had left the college) that he had watched me closely enough to put me into two paragraphs of his book. . . ."

WOLFE'S DISCOVERY OF AMERICA

by

Edwin Berry Burgum

The career of Thomas Wolfe is the spectacle of a novelist who began with the sole concern to transfer to others his fascination with his own family as material for fiction, who turned thereafter in the same simplicity of intention to his own relationships with persons outside of his family, but who found pouring into these relationships all the disorders of the contemporary world until he was forced at the end to attempt their solution in a letter to his editor on his social views, in which his work as a writer culminated and, it may be said, his life concluded.

The bridge between the personal and the social was the discovery that his own personality was a microcosm of the state of society. It was not quite a conscious discovery. Wolfe was not only the least intellectual of novelists; he was altogether incapable of writing well unless deeply moved by the personal contact. The

From the *Virginia Quarterly Review*, Summer 1946. By permission of the author.

transformation was therefore a gradual and almost automatic broadening of his interests until he had passed from one of the most subjective of novelists at the beginning to one of the most objective at the end. Having exhausted his relationship with his family (which was virtually a part of himself), and then his relationships with friends and lovers, as he groped in his isolation for new ties, he discovered his fellow men. Through the projection of sympathy alone, and not any actual awareness of the parallel between his situation and theirs, his imagination turned to the social scene. But his new attitude of sympathy for human misery in general took the form of his break with his one remaining friend.

Perhaps also, for his readers as well as himself, consciousness of these facts has been clouded by the spirit of gusto that seemed to dominate his first book, *Look Homeward, Angel*. We have gained a mind set from first contact with that book which we have carried over into his later ones. Different readers have reacted in different ways. But we have all made some extravagant emotional response to some extravagant emotional assault this book has made upon us. Those who dislike extravagant emotion altogether have escaped into a distaste for the unevenness of its style, the lifeless prose of passages in which Wolfe's emotions were not involved, the adolescent rhetoric into which his emotion too often evaporated, the overwritten formlessness of the whole. Others, younger or less sophisticated, intoxicated by the gusto, accepted it at its face value. They found something epic in its exaggeration, something tonic and awesome about their participation in its emotional excess. And so they called it the transfer into fiction of the spirit of Paul Bunyan, forgetful of the careless ease, the robust self-assurance with which Bunyan acted, whereas in Wolfe the utterance is explosive, the strength illusory, the action destructive, as he seeks in vain to free his tortured spirit, madly to break through the inner conflicts that reduce him to impotence. Or they were reminded by his style of the Teutonic humor of Carlyle, its earthy vulgarity transfigured by the lightning flash of the Valkyries, though they then forgot that there is no humor in *Look Homeward, Angel*, only a hypnotic identification with the violence of despair. Or they thought of Whitman, sensing some small cry for warmth and understanding, lost in the impulsive clamor of Wolfe's egotism. But they then forgot that he was a Whitman disillusioned, a Prometheus forced back into his chains.

More accurate certainly, since the imitation of his style betrayed Wolfe's awareness of the parallel, was the echo of what has been called the Rabelaisian spirit in James Joyce. But since almost everyone misinterpreted Joyce on this point, failing to sense the pessimism beneath the burly façade of humor, the comparison only strengthened the delusion about Wolfe. Nevertheless, those who liked this novel were more sound in their reactions (if not in their reasons) than those who rejected it on grounds that missed its main intention. Better than Hemingway (who represented the minority of the sophisticated), better than Dos Passos (who could only describe the appearance of things), Wolfe was the novelist of the average American youth of the postwar period, the small-town boy who confused his restlessness with ambition, who thought himself a profound optimist when actually inhibited by inner doubt, and who was sustained chiefly by an illusory identification with the grandiose.

What is taken for gusto in *Look Homeward, Angel*, then, is actually a grandiose illusion expressing itself in random and futile violence of word and action. And this dubious gusto belongs to the father rather than the son. It is under the spell of his father's spirit that the young Gant falls, until it seems to become his own and the reader's. Later on, in the false and doubtful maturity of the son in later volumes, this imaginative identification will become real, and the son will succeed his father. For the time being, the father's spirit is sublimated by the inexperience of youth into those justifiable inevitable dreams of adolescence, which reach out for the life that lies ahead in an ecstasy of escape and self-fulfillment. But even vision cannot be kept steady and uncorrupted. The youth recoils from it, looking homeward, until his leap into the future for a security he has never known degenerates into an ambiguous nostalgia. "O lost, and by the wind grieved, ghost, come back again." Specifically, the ghost is the spirit of his dead brother Ben. But since only through friendship with this brother had he known love and the security of home, the ghost symbolizes these qualities, and the plea for his return becomes a restatement of the novel's title. "Come back" means "look homeward," means "come back to secure for me what should be mine, the sense of being at home in my family and in that larger family which is Altamont." But such a homecoming of the spirit is impossible on the level of reality. Though almost drowned out by the theme of identification with the father, a second theme finds its origin in this dilemma. Eugene's helplessness takes refuge in the substitute paternity of friendship with this older brother, though this tenuous intermittent substitution is soon broken by Ben's death. In the strong somber elegy of Ben's dying the identification changes, and the second melody succeeds in dominating the book. Ben having died, what made home endurable has been withdrawn. But in the moving hallucination of the return of his spirit as Eugene stands in front of his father's shop at midnight, Ben counsels his younger brother more fully and more intimately than ever in life, leaving Eugene "like a man who stands upon a hill above the town he has left, yet does not say 'The town is near,' but turns his eyes upon the distant soaring ranges." For the time being the dilemma has been resolved by the restoration of adolescent optimism, and the possibility of a home is the hope of a future elsewhere.

Life there, when he gets to know it, will only repeat the same patterns. Indeed, they are already emerging in equivocal form in *Look Homeward, Angel*. The tenderness of Ben and Eugene for each other, born out of their mutual loneliness, must seep through an appearance of gruff detachment on the part of the elder son and a timid inarticulate assent on the part of the younger. Their great need for each other makes this surface unimportant to them. But in other relationships the negative emotion is not a façade, easily ignored, but an active ingredient corrupting the superficial optimism in which Eugene takes confidence. He is scarcely aware of how much contamination from the family pattern is already present in his dreams of the future. The town he has left is nearer than he thinks.

Ah [he says in the easy assertion of reverie after he has left Alta-
mont], I'll tell you why you laugh; you are afraid of me because I am
not like the others. You hate me because I do not belong. You see that
I am finer and greater than any one you know; you cannot reach me
and you hate me. That's it. The ethereal (yet manly) beauty of my
features, my boyish charm (for I am Just a Boy) blended with the
tragic wisdom of my eyes (as old as life and filled with the brooding
tragedy of the ages), the sensitive and delicate flicker of my mouth, and
my marvellous dark face blooming inward of strange loveliness like a
flower — all this you want to kill because you cannot touch it. . . .
Ah, but she will know. . . . Proudly with misty eyes, he saw her
standing beside him against the rabble; her small elegant head, wound
with a bracelet of bright hair, against his shoulder, and with two
splendid pearls in her ears. Dearest! dearest! We stand here on a star!
We are beyond them now. Behold! They shrink, they fade, they pass
— victorious, enduring, marvellous love, my dearest, we remain.

This is the essence of his youthful vision, and his vision expresses the subjective state of his most enthusiastic audience, the
youth of the early depression years. Wolfe could no more have
spoken thus frankly in actual life than the youth he represents.
But this is the way they both felt with an intensity that varied
only with the differing pressures of their individual potentialities.
Most of them, having less promise than Wolfe, doubtless experienced a less intense conflict, and it was easy for the observer to
recognize the inertia, the lassitude, and hopelessness in which the
conflict ended. But the youth himself, no more than Eugene Gant,
recognized the stalemate; instead he festered in his inner rebelliousness, supported by its justification in lack of opportunity, and
willed the happy ending in fantasy when he could not in fact.
His was as false an affirmation as that with which Joyce's *Ulysses*
ends.

But I must not press too far this comparison between Wolfe and
the average American boy. The differences of potentialities in
them produced a difference in the degree of assertiveness. Where
Wolfe's rebelliousness differed from the ordinary (where it proved
perhaps that he was a production of the postwar generation rather
than the depression) was that it remained purely personal at first,
and uninterested in politics. As we read this first volume, if we
are not intoxicated by its rhetoric, we recognize how much need to

compensate for frustration and wounded feeling by an attempt at domination of other individuals lurks behind the affirmation of mutual love just quoted. His egoism buoyantly reasserts itself, whatever the obstacles, and always in a demand for the individual contact. And it is, I believe, in this reaction of buoyancy that his unique, his specifically American, contribution to the contemporary novel is to be found. The inability to make friendships, the predominance of rejection, the sense of everybody's being hostile or indifferent, I have elsewhere described as the theme of Joyce's *Ulysses* and much of our better fiction. Most authors have been resigned to the situation they depict. The characteristic contribution of Wolfe is that he both presents characters in rebellion against their isolation and shares himself the optimism implied in the mere positiveness of their demand.

In the portrait of his father (who is not typical of an older generation), the rebellion is certainly a futile one, and the warmth of spirit which might attract a response has all but died within. His is the failure the son must avoid. Actually this parent, who has so bound his sons to himself, has very little to do with them.

But in later novels, in which the focus shifts from father to son, and in which I have said the son takes over his father's personality, an important modification appears. The father's personality in the son proffers a constructive aspect. When the young novelist turns to explore his own difficult attempts at friendship, if attachments are eventually broken, it is not from perversity alone. The valid evidence of optimism in Wolfe, the justification for thinking of him as a belated successor to Whitman rather than an American version of Proust's or Joyce's despair, is that his break of a relationship is always bound up with an obscure kind of growth. He reacts from a friendship partly because he has discovered an imperfection in it he can no longer tolerate. He learns something from every new experience, as he passes from a provincial boyhood where a lust for money has corrupted the quality of the folk inheritance, through the social contacts of a college education in which only the voracious reading of literature counted, into restless travelling that gave him a cosmopolitan knowledge of the world. Under these circumstances, each new friendship starts on a higher level than the last, and has stimulated a superior sense of human values.

Thus, I imagine, the cold precepts of his mother, which she never practiced, got written the more indelibly into his unconscious precisely because (in contrast to his father's expletives) they carried so shy an emotive content. After a bitter quarrel, instigated by the father, in which for all her stubborn self-assurance she played as usual a passive role, when left alone with her son, "Poor child! Poor child!" the mother whispered faintly. "We must try to love one another." Such remarks must have become convictions buried deeper than thought, buried so deep that they may seem scarcely to influence conduct at all, yet hibernating within to rise into authority once the process of living gave them any verification. Never systematized into a philosophy, set in the context of American history, they brought him against the grain of the surface into the tradition of Whitman, causing him to scorn the cant of our Puritanism and our democracy since these ideals were too precious for lip service. They remained deeper than the apparent belligerency, at the very basis of his personality, where they could order his experiences the more and more openly as life allowed.

Once we escape the irrelevant details of the particular novel and see the series together as his life's tale, we become aware of the grandeur of the forming pattern. A modern Promctheus, because he recognized he was in chains, and sought with a terrible sense of isolation to wrest himself free, he discovered, towards the end of his short life, that he was not alone. When the shock of the depression revealed to him that his problem was common to Americans generally, he had found allies in deprivation, and the reality of this sympathy of kinship reawakened a confidence in the principle of kinship as the fundamental directive of American life.

When we read Wolfe with a sense of the cumulative power of this unfolding pattern, the important passages are those in which the tensions of intimate relationships are conveyed with all the vividness of an actual experience in Wolfe's life. The changes he made in the external details of his experience appear unimportant.

What arouses the impression of distortion differs on different occasions, but it is always instigated by the quality of his subjective response. When it verges on the magnification of the grotesque in the portrait of his father, its blending of terror, awe, and helplessness is characteristic of the traumatic events of childhood. And the reaction of outrage at his helplessness fixes upon the traditional victims; he becomes surly with hatred for Jews and Negroes and foreigners and the vast masses of the underprivileged like himself. If later passages appear less distorted, it is that maturity enables the youth to cope with a situation on terms of approximate equality with the other participants, and the irrelevant compensation of race hatred, becoming less necessary, loses its intensity. The final style is altogether lacking in distortion, is as sustained objective writing as one could wish, in which the actions can carry their meanings by themselves because the author has attained the serenity of perspective to recognize their presence; and it is in this work that race hatred changes to contempt for the overprivileged. That Wolfe had some awareness of what was taking place within him seems denoted by his shift of hero in midstream. Eugene Gant, who is associated with the events most illustrative of distortion, gives way to George ("Monk") Webber in the two posthumous novels of his later transformation. But the development was actually a gradual one, and may be represented by four episodes in the novels, each of which denotes a new stage by its change of tone.

The first influence upon him was his English teacher at Pine Rock College who later came to New York and was his colleague at The School for Utility Cultures. He is a Southern version of that phenomenon of American college life, the popular instructor. Doubtless such teachers are desirable members of faculties. They take the naïve student at his own level of appreciation, and, without frightening him by a violation of his own predilections, lead him on to make the best of them through their own intoxication with the superficial values of great literature or the self-evident pleasures of minor. The rock upon which our hero's discipleship floundered was Dostoevski, who, to this Southerner of the slow drawl, the portly figure, and sloppy garb, was unknown, foreign, and, the more Wolfe said about him, immoral. But Wolfe, remembering his father, sensed the affinity, and discovered his greatness. Such a victory was easy, even in adolescence; and the tone of the telling is a tranquil drollery of exposure.

More complex was the friendship with Starwick, whom Wolfe met as Professor Baker's assistant in the interim before he went to New York. To Starwick, Wolfe, a little awed by Harvard besides, was attracted by a veritable superiority of knowledge and sophistication. He accepted Starwick's guidance because it seemed to give the provincial boy the benefits of a cosmopolitan experience. But he soon found that his innocence had involved him in a situation which had other aspects than the purely cultural. Even this situation is typical of the American college, where the youth of literary promise, attracted to a personality finer than his own at the moment, sometimes discovers to his amazement a homosexual element. Because Wolfe writes with power only when his own emotions are deeply and directly affected, the tone of this long episode is hardly more moving than the narrative of Jerry Alsop. But the quiet banter of the first episode loses its complacency. In its place is an uneasy tension, in which a mild alarm merges with curiosity. The suspense with which he awaits the next revelation of eccentricity in his friend is somewhat tinctured by the fear that it may suddenly veer to affect himself.

Perhaps the affair with Mrs. Jack, the scenic designer, is not so different as would appear on the surface. It is essentially the same kind of relationship, but infinitely more intense, since it is clandestine and consummated, and more acceptable since it is not homosexual. Indeed, since Wolfe as usual forces the reader to share its intensity, we may forget that it is only an American version of a well-known Romantic literary tradition. It traces to the episode of Julien and Mathilda in Stendhal's *The Red and the Black*. Our awareness of the tradition is weakened by the greater urgency of its contemporaneity, since it defines what is probably the prevalent abnormality in relationships of love in our own country at the present time. The man who needs the support of affection and the steadying influence of a mother's care must hate himself for wanting it and project his hatred upon the one who gives it; while the woman who must serve advice as well as meals gets a sense of indispensable superiority which demands constant satisfaction and will endure any rebuff to secure it. The competence of the writing is shown by the fact that, though these quarrels and reconciliations follow the same pattern, the vividness of the conversation prevents an impression of repetition and each scene becomes more violent than the last. Feeling suffocated by her constant attention and self-sacrifice, George Webber turns upon Mrs. Jack with completely irrational, unjustifiable abuse, projecting his sense of blame upon his jealousy of her affairs with imaginary lovers. But it is all useless; either he seeks her out or she returns to haunt him. He can break away only by leaving for Europe. But once more, associated with the cruelty of his attacks upon her is the learning process. Mrs. Jack had introduced the young author to the fashionable literary society of New York. He found there another version of the fraudulence he had discovered in Starwick, and when he becomes aware how completely Mrs. Jack accepts its praise and its standards, his rebellion against her love gains a plausible justification. He rejects Mrs. Jack because his conception of art cannot be limited to the tastes and interests of the Broadway audience of the well-to-do.

The next episode, like all the others, involves his response to the advances of another person whom he values as superior. By this time he had become famous himself, partly through the enthusiasm of the famous American novelist, Mr. Lloyd McHarg. So, when McHarg insists upon his accompanying him on a weekend visit in England, he accepts only to discover that the state of the great man's personality is worse than his own. That strident, virile attack upon life which had made McHarg so magnetic as a novelist now turns out to have its unpublicized obverse of drunken prostration. The parallel was probably as reassuring to his own troubled spirit as the dominating immediate contact was dangerous to his ego; and Wolfe withdrew too quickly for a quarrel to develop. But the incident had its larger aspect also. Through it he learned the limitations of fame; and the lesson was possible since he had already become famous himself.

Meanwhile, Wolfe had been learning from the countless observations he made everywhere. Following the American practice of Sinclair Lewis and the later Dreiser, Wolfe crowds his novels with excessive detail. Nevertheless, there is respect for a very individual sense of form behind it. Wolfe's interest in detail is always subject to the authority of his own inner needs. In a general sense his styles of writing represent the mood of the moment bruising the facts of observation in the violence of its embrace. He sublimates his torment in various ways which almost run the gamut of possible emotive reactions and their analogues in the great literary styles of the past. And the sublimation is the uneasy one which tends to repeated shift in the type of equilibrium. When the equilibrium is more stable the whole episode gains a unity of tone and style. When it is less, the changes of mood may appear even within the individual sentence with the fickle charm of stormy summer days. And these moods pass not only from an irony directed now against himself, now against the outer world, into a bitter cynicism poured consistently outward, but indeed into a state of exhaustion in which he seems to continue to write automatically, repeating platitudes of fact or reflection to an extent rarely found in an author of similar talent. These shifts are not confined to mood or style. There are also the changes from observation, however colored, to commentary. Like the great divines of that other troubled period, the seventeenth century in England, Wolfe takes refuge in the poetic homily upon the nature of life. Indeed, his rebellion against the predominant tendencies of his own time is best measured by his finding the most congenial style (where action does not dominate the narrative) in this reversal of the whole modern trend in prose, back, even beyond Shelley, to the periodic sentences and the consolation of abstract statement in Jeremy Taylor and Thomas Browne. In such passages indubitably Wolfe becomes one of the great stylists in the English language, submitting the undisciplined cadences of Whitman to the control of an ear and a mind working in complete harmony to achieve a subtle unity of tone and idea.

And yet he thought that no Spring ever came more sweetly or more gloriously to any man than that one came to him. The sense of ruin, the conviction that he was lost, the horrible fear that all the power and music in his life, like the flying remnants of a routed army, had been blown apart into the fragments of a ghastly dissolution so that they would never come back to him, never again the good times, the golden times, the nights his spirit prowled with the vast stealth and joy of a tiger across the fields of sleep, and the days when his power leaped on from strength to strength, from dream to dream, to the inevitable and sustained accomplishment of a great, exultant labor — the sense of having lost all this forever, so far from making him hate the Spring and the life he saw around him, made him love it more dearly and more passionately than he had ever done before.

Now it is worth noting that these fine passages are found most often in the later books as commentaries upon his most objective writing in those episodes of action I have been stressing. His growth of mastery of style accompanies his growing perception of the world outside himself. The writing in his first novel is the most uneven; out of reaction to its favorable reception, *Of Time and the River* takes on for the most part a monotony of Biblical unction with lengthy sentences of similar construction strung together by initial connectives. It is in the two latest volumes of the tetralogy that he hits his stride.

At the same time, it should be noted that, amid all these variations, two opposite tendencies persist. The one is familiar to all readers and the source of a great deal of his popularity, his escape into the consolation of ambiguity. "O death in life that turns our men to stone! O change that levels down our gods! If only one lives yet, above the cinders of the consuming years, shall not this dust awaken, shall not dead faith revive, shall we not see God again, as once in morning, on the mountain?" Hope here oscillates with despair. But the second tendency is for observations of the miseries of the poor, quite specific in content, to accumulate in the later volumes into political enlightenment. They reappear in the midst of the narrative like faint sounds which gather volume as they draw nearer. These observations which seem cursory, perhaps irrelevant, when they first appear, flash forth symbolic meanings of what is to come. When he rides all night in the subway and finds himself on the surface in a poverty-stricken section of Brooklyn, his own inner misery becomes one with that which he observes around him. A more indelible impression must have

been made upon him by two casual images of the depression because they are repeated at least once in the course of the story.
He stumbles over men sleeping wrapped in newspapers on the
steps of the urinal at the City Hall in New York, and he finds the
subway platform at 33rd Street crowded with sleeping vagrants,
who have sought to escape there the bombing of the depression.

Such images sank deep within him, where with the aid of
those slumbering aphorisms from his mother's lips, they made
contact with his deep sense of himself always having been an
outcast. Community with the unloved brought love into his
world, took him out of himself, afforded his ego the legitimate
stimulus of sympathy. At length, these free floating impressions
coalesce into a positive conviction in the description of the
marionette show at Mrs. Jack's apartment in the final volume,
You Can't Go Home Again. Here at last the facts are allowed to
carry themselves. There is no distortion set up by the author's
inability to adjust to the outward circumstances, since he is no
longer tempted to do so. Now capable of holding himself aloof
from a distasteful situation, he can use the method of contrasting
panels of narrative familiar in contemporary objective prose. As
this absurd exhibition of polite society's sensational pursuit of
any new artistic experiment draws to a close, the guests are
thrilled by the unexpected sensation of a fire in the huge Park
Avenue apartment house. Descending by the novel inconvenience
of the staircases, on the street they mingle in a mock democracy,
meet neighbors for the first time in the geniality of temporary
deprivation. Later they return to their apartments neither knowing nor in a mood to care that two elevator boys have lost their
lives. For Wolfe this was the final lesson in human values and
their proper relationship to art; and it forced his reluctant final
break with the man who had been editor and foster-father to
him.

The long letter with which the series of novels ends is not
fiction. It is the credo to which Wolfe attained through the
method of fiction. What it has to say of democracy and the common man is commonplace today. What counts is the process of
utilizing experience that has brought it into the awareness of ex-

pression. For we forget that all functioning truth is ideationally platitude, and that what is important is that the platitude be true and functioning. The "proof" in fiction, as it is essentially in life, is not to be found in logic but in the perception of order in the sum total of a man's experience. It is in default, at best in clarification, of this order that argument needs to enter. But for Wolfe the clarification had come already in his last trip to Germany under Hitler. He had gone there with his aroused human sympathy still uncrystallized into political conviction. Always an admirer of things German, he accepts the immediate surface impression as usual. But the more he sees of his friends, the more he comes to know that the surface is a façade, beneath which their real emotional state is one of agony at the fate of relatives and a paralyzing terror as they face their own. A similar affectation of gaiety, he sees now, concealed in his Park Avenue friends an indifference to the larger social issues, and had promoted the advent of Fascism in Germany. His political lesson, as usual, is knit up with a literary one. Never having permitted the sham of the façade in his own personality, he refuses to rest in appearances when he becomes absorbed in the world about him. He returned home not only convinced that Fascism was possible in his own country, but realizing also that a novelist could not be content with the narrowly personal concerns of men and women. He must go deeper into their emotional life, and when he does, he finds them indissolubly mingled with social and political issues. The only doubt remaining is that his new conviction is not shared in his most stable and profitable friendship. He is left with the dilemma that his editor's stability of character, so admirable in his family life and personal contacts, seemed purchased at the price of a stoic retreat from these larger problems, from which, Wolfe now sees, retreat is in the long view impossible. His friend will not act in any public capacity. He sticks to his last, living within the framework of each day as it passes. More serious still, he advises Wolfe to do the same, to continue writing within the subjective perspective of his earlier novels. Wolfe does not expect that his letter will enlighten his friend; but its tone of tact and clarity betrays his desire to part without a rupture of his

respect. The side of him that will always require a father surro-
gate cannot be crippled too openly; and yet it is the side of him
that has faced life with a resolute and desperate demand to
fathom its secret that has now the upper hand.

The vision is there. But the competence to pursue it friendless
and alone is wanting. Wolfe's dilemma cannot be broken so
easily by either word or action. It still exists as a cleavage of his
personality between the opposite needs for a very personal dependence and a rebellion against it. Such a dilemma cannot be
broken within the area of life. Wolfe temporarily assuaged it by
transference into an imagined future.

Dear Fox, old friend [he ends his letter], thus we have come to the
end of the road that we were to go together. My tale is finished — and
so farewell.

But before I go, I have just one more thing to tell you: something
has spoken to me in the night, burning the tapers of the waning year;
something has spoken in the night, and told me I shall die, I know not
where. Saying:

"To lose the earth you know, for greater knowing; to lose the life you
have, for greater life; to leave the friends you loved, for greater loving;
to find a land more kind than home, more large than earth —

"Whereon the pillars of this earth are founded, towards which the
conscience of the world is tending — a wind is rising, and the rivers
flow."

With the aid of the mysticism of Christ and Shelley and Whitman, Wolfe sought finally to will a fantasy in defiance of the
actual world about him, just as he had earlier imagined his
lover and himself together against its hostility. Only now his lover
is justice and the rights of man; and he turns his eyes from the
hostility of the world, impatient to leap beyond present difficulties with which he cannot cope into the ideal of a better world
to come. For he was so constituted that he must fight alone. Beneath the show of optimism, beneath the apparent ecstasy with
which he called upon the great styles of past literature to aid his
present purpose, there remained a sense of personal inadequacy.
In his floundering between an awareness of the tragic choice
facing his country and his own incompetence as an isolated individual to promote the right one, he differed from the ordinary

American only in his violent will to reach a decision, and his capacity as a man of letters to draw comfort from the long literary tradition of reconciliation with despair.

In the backyard of the old brick house in which he lived, one of those small, fenced backyards of a New York house, a minute part in the checkered pattern of a block, there was, out of the old and worn earth, a patch of tender grass, and a single tree was growing there. That April, day by day, he watched the swift coming of that tree into its glory of young green leaf again. And then one day he looked into its heart of sudden and magical green and saw the trembling lights that came and went in it . . . and it was so real, so vivid, so intense that it made a magic and a mystery, evoking the whole poignant dream of time and of man's life upon the earth, and instantly it seemed to Monk, the tree became coherent with his destiny, and his life was one with all its brevity from birth to death.

But what by contrast was not so fleeting a revelation of changing beauty leading but to death, he had since come to learn, was his trust in a man's ever more successful pursuit of the security of friendship, even though he found himself cut off from the sharing.

Wolfe's insistent admiration of the English Romantic poets, especially Coleridge, is here extended to an interpretation of the novels based on the Romantic-Platonic theory of existence. Monroe M. Stearns finds many of Wolfe's symbols in the less familiar works of Coleridge and Wordsworth. His discussion of Wolfe's genesis, in the terms of modern psychology, provides reasonable basis for the novelist's absorption in the ideas propounded by the Romantic poets. Monroe M. Stearns is the head of the English Department at Berkshire School, Sheffield, Massachusetts.

THE METAPHYSICS OF THOMAS WOLFE

by

Monroe M. Stearns

.

When into the world there come those *reine kinder Gottes*, as Goethe called individuals of genius, the greatest wonder is in what field they will exhibit their heavenly gift. Psychology provides an answer, and from a study of many cases it may be inferred that if the man of genius finds it difficult to adjust his personality to the world and discover therein an easy spiritual survival, it is an artist that he becomes. On the other hand, if such an adjustment is — or is made — easy for him, he becomes a scientist and regards the world as a passive victim rather than as an active enemy. Be he artist or scientist, however, he has but one aim, namely, to benefit the world as he finds it; as the one to interpret its spiritual abstractions; as the other to solve its physical enigmas.

From *College English*, January 1945. By special permission of the author and publisher.

The creative artist is necessarily subjective and egocentric. Since he feels rather than reasons, expression is necessary to him as the release of a tension occasioned by his sense of enmity with the world; and the stronger this hostility, the more violently it is released. Furthermore, because his mission of interpretation requires the medium of his own personality, he states things as they appear to him, realizing that truth among abstractions is a matter of opinion, and consequently he both consciously and unconsciously identifies himself with any hero-character he may create.

This identification of himself with his hero is the key to the personality problem of the most recent of geniuses in America, Thomas Wolfe. So many of Wolfe's characters, settings, and incidents can be identified with actual ones in his own life that it is safe to say there is no figure, place, or action in his works that had not its living analogue. Wolfe's egocentricity supersaturates his novels and his short stories. Facing him was the problem of some kind of sublimation, since he had chosen fiction as his medium of release. In search of a guide or a model for this sublimation he turned to the founders of English Romantic poetry, the metaphysical Coleridge and Wordsworth; but the process was not so simple as that. Its causes were long and obscure.

There are three stages through which the artist passes on his journey toward personal adjustment to the world. The first is his idea of God as a void, especially conspicuous in America because of the prevalence of the old frontier attitude toward any of the forms of art. The second stage is the idea of God as the enemy. The first produces in the artist the sense of being an orphan and an outcast; the second produces the sense of being a rebel. Wolfe gives signs of having reached the second stage only at the close of his career. The third stage, that of God the friend, representing complete assimilation into the world and adjustment with it, he never attained.

Deep-seated in the hypersensitive organism of the artist is his relationship with his mother. Perhaps in the process of Wolfe's growth no period was so hazardous to the child's emotional stability as the period of weaning. This is the point at which the physical relationship of the child with his mother is severed and lost. Within the womb the child has found shelter and nourishment. After the exclusion from this magic circle of protection the nursing period equals the sustenance and seclusion of the womb. Then comes the painfulness of consciousness and of establishing a communication with the world by language, gesture, and every other articulate or inarticulate means. Alone in a world he never made, the child struggles to gain his emotional equilibrium, even as he struggles to get his balance when learning to walk. If the weaning period is tactfully and intelligently managed, the shock of having to sustain himself is lessened for the infant; but, should the opposite obtain, the child experiences a frantic sense of rejection and abandonment.

In the case of Thomas Wolfe, his accurately autobiographical novels, his letters, and his mother's own words serve as indisputable evidence of this experience. Wolfe's descriptions of his mother are perfect. In real life she has the same pursing lips, the same gestures, and the same speech. Her attitude to a visitor is that he does not exist, so absorbed is she in her own businesses and in her own talk. She is a hoarder, her house full of ugly objects. In *Look Homeward, Angel* she is represented as so engrossed in her speculations with real estate and money-making that her family become a nuisance and a hindrance rather than a vital concern. Not only would this attitude produce a psychological feeling of rejection in her youngest child through her lack of motherly empathy and her inability to see the world from the child's point of view, but the fact that she refused to wean Thomas until he was three and a half years old would make that process far more difficult than if it had been accomplished when the child was an infant. It caused a spiritual wound from which he never recovered. The petting which Mrs. Wolfe bestowed on her youngest son in the presence of others was to his sensitive nature but a show of affection. "Naked and alone we came into exile. In her dark womb we did not know our mother's face; from the prison of her flesh have we come into the unspeakable and incommunicable prison of this earth." So Wolfe introduces his story of a buried life.

The hopeless rejection of Wolfe by his mother caused him later to regard all the women he was to love as food-producers. In real life, for example, Elinor in *Of Time and the River* is an experienced and accomplished cook who studied cookery in France with a leading chef. Esther Jack, of the last two novels, also holds her power over George Webber-Wolfe by her succulent dishes. Her prototype is a women so fond of cooking that her idea of relaxation is to go into her kitchen and prepare Sunday lunch for twenty of thirty guests. Food and its consumption figure in Wolfe's novels more often than any other pleasure.

After this rejection, what next can the child do? Gathering its energies into itself, it loves itself. In normal cases, however, this solution is unsatisfactory, and a counterreaction takes place. Having rejected its mother, the child now rejects itself. The possibility remains, nevertheless, of a relationship with the father, who in the home and the family symbolizes God in the universe.

Between Wolfe and his father there were several similarities. Both were gargantuan individuals, devoted to excess in their uses of food, liquor, and women; both were hampered by the petty, irritating conventions of smaller people, conceiving of themselves as Gullivers among Lilliputians. The experience of having had such a father was a great factor in the development of Wolfe's personality. Like William James, Wolfe was the son of a talkative father but was himself a confused talker. The torrent of the father's words leads the son on to find out what he is talking about and to make some order out of his father's thought philosophically or artistically.

Whereas Wolfe, like any child, had first sought for a mother and all the connotations of that word, now he sought for a father. He thought of himself as searching for one. "The deepest search in life, it seemed to me," he wrote in *The Story of a Novel*, "the thing that in one way or another was central to all living was man's search to find a father . . . the image of a strength and wisdom external to his need and superior to his hunger, to which the belief and power of his own life could be united." The search for security is now directed to the male figure, a father-substitute. William Oliver Wolfe, however, was a socially irresponsible man, both actually and as he is represented in the novels of his son. He was a semioutcast, and Thomas Wolfe's identification of himself with him tended to make the author even more of an outcast than he had already felt himself to be. The introductory paragraphs of *Look Homeward, Angel* already quoted are primarily concerned with the mother, but the intention includes the father and the search for him as well.

The Ishmaelitish character of Wolfe's personality derives also from his revulsion at the environment of his childhood. There is little reason to suppose that Mrs. Wolfe's house now is very different from what it was in the early years of the century, when Wolfe was young. His birthplace near the railroad track is small, grayish, and dirty. The tiny plot of land around it has a run-down look. The trees are meager, the whole scale ungenerous. With no respect for or love of nature shown, it narrowly misses squalor. The boarding-house, about four minutes' walk away, though larger than the birthplace, is nevertheless small, and its corridors and rooms are small. It is hemmed in by other houses. Within there is no sense of order or tidiness. Everywhere the accumulation of dust makes it dingy and smelly, and ugly bric-a-brac of the Pullman period renders it far from charming. Asheville itself is a horrid town in a setting of great natural beauty. Commercial interests have cheapened and vulgarized it. On the mind of Wolfe a fundamental disgust at this lack of physical beauty around him produced a revulsion which intensified the orphan outcast in his soul. "It has taken me 27 [*sic*] years," he wrote in 1927, "to rise above the bitterness and hatred of my childhood."

The rejection of the child by his family and the repulsion caused by his environment are likely to release themselves in a story that takes the form of a pilgrimage or odyssey. It is thus no coincidence that one of the chapters in *Of Time and the River* is entitled "Telemachus," and another, "Jason's Voyage." This is perhaps the simplest of Wolfe's symbols.

Long before Wolfe had embarked on his semifictionalized autobiography, he had found the secret of releasing his feelings of rejection and revulsion, and he had found it in the metaphysical Wordsworth and Coleridge. "I would rather listen to Coleridge," he said, "who comes to me sometimes in dreams, shadowy in a darkened room, sitting at a piano, looking at me — *and like me.*" Again he speaks of his love for "all weird fable and wild invention" and of "Samuel Taylor Coleridge, the chief prince of the moon and magic." *The Ancient Mariner* was to become his favorite poem, and from it he was to quote directly countless times or weave its words among his own. What is *The Ancient Mariner* but voyage — odyssey — literature — the journey of an outcast soul to find its salvation through tortuous atonement? In 1931 Wolfe wrote to his colleague at New York University, Henry Volkening, that his next book was to be called "Penance More." The mariner Wolfe had done penance for living thus long, and telling the further chronicle of his life was to be a punishment for him like the expiration of the crime of Coleridge's mariner.

> And till my ghastly tale is told
> This heart within me burns.

In Coleridge, Wolfe found the means of expression by which he could sublimate his feelings. The subjective writer finds a perfect model in the figure of the Romantic genius, and out of the books in which he finds him he remembers and uses that material which also exists in himself and which relates to his own problems.

The Romantic attitude which Wolfe took toward his own life is so similar to Coleridge's in parts that the question might arise as to how much Wolfe is being sincere and how much he is deliberately imitating Coleridge. Both were the youngest of large families. Coleridge describes himself as his mother's darling, a precocious and imaginative boy, taking no pleasure in boyish sports but reading incessantly, especially in imaginative literature. Wolfe's account of his own childhood is almost identical.

There is a passage in *Look Homeward, Angel* in which the young Eugene Gant-Wolfe looked up misty-eyed in the growing dark from the last page of a sensational novel and concluded: "Yes, this was as it should be. This was what he would have done." Later, during the first World War, he read Hankey's *A Student in Arms,* and he became a member of this legion of chivalry — young Galahad-Eugene — a spearhead of righteousness. . . . With glistening eyes he read his own epilogue, enjoyed his post-mortem glory, as his last words were recorded and explained by his editor. Then, witness of his own martyrdom, he dropped two smoking tears upon his young slain body.

The escape from reality which the child enjoyed was the seed of the power Wolfe possessed of making himself one with whatever person he was reading or writing about. Furthermore, both boys were petted by one of their brothers: Coleridge, by his brother George; Wolfe, by the famous Ben. Both apotheosized this brother. Coleridge, for instance, writes "To the Rev. George Coleridge":

> Yet at times
> My soul is sad that I have roamed through life
> Still most a stranger, most with naked heart
> At mine own home and birthplace: chiefly then
> When I remember thee, my earliest friend
>
> . . . .
> He who counts alone
> The beatings of the solitary heart,
> That Being knows, how I have loved thee ever,
> Loved as a brother, as a son revered thee.

Wolfe wrote to his mother in 1927: "Strangers we were born alone into a strange world. We live in it, as Ben did alone and strange, and we are without ever knowing anyone." In 1926 he had written: "In our family Ben was the stranger until his death — I suppose I'm the other one." The dithyrambic rhapsodies of Eugene over Ben in Wolfe's novel expand these statements and raise them into poetry of a higher order than these lines of Coleridge. Coleridge taught Wolfe how to see and how to feel and how to express what he saw and felt. "I have not discovered for myself . . . any obscure poet with the genius of Samuel Taylor Coleridge," he wrote in *Of Time and the River*. "To me he is not one of the great English poets. He is The Poet."

The Platonic doctrines of the pre-existence of the soul and the realm of the absolutes were what haunted Wordsworth, and Coleridge flew even further into the other world with his ab-

sorption of the Neo-Platonists, Plotinus and Iamblichus. Wordsworth expresses his faith most definitely in "My Heart Leaps Up"
and in the "Ode on the Intimations of Immortality," but he soon
passed into the third stage of artistic development and became
reconciled with his world. This Coleridge never managed to
accomplish, and his entire output — both prose and poetry — is
the record of his sublimation of a life of physical and mental
torture in the Plotinean "flight of the alone to the alone."

Wolfe became acquainted with the two poets in the little
private school to which he devotes many pages and much tribute
in *Look Homeward, Angel.* Mrs. Leonard (Mrs. Roberts) there
taught him English literature. "The shorter Wordsworth pieces
he had read at grammar school . . . but Margaret [Leonard-
Roberts] read him the sonnets and made him commit 'The
World is too much with us' to memory." Twenty years later he
could explode in uninhibited conversation about the "getting and
spending" of America. It was through this early familiarity with
Wordsworth that Wolfe found one path to his escape. A thorough
familiarity it was, and another identification of himself with his
author-model. When in Book III of *The Prelude* Wordsworth
writes of his eye

> Which, from a tree, a stone, a withered leaf,
> To the broad ocean and the azure heavens
> Spangled with kindred multitudes of stars
> Could find no surface where its power might sleep;

Wolfe recognized the similarity of the poet's emotion to his own
and appropriated Wordsworth's phrase for his own motto of "a
stone, a leaf, a door," by which he could express the psychological
pains of birth. The loss of relationship with his protector-mother
is symbolized for Wolfe in Wordsworth's nostalgia for that spiritual home whence comes the soul trailing its clouds of glory.
Life thus became to Wolfe a penance for the sin of having been
born and having left that apocalyptic world of Plato, Plotinus,
Wordsworth, and Coleridge, in which the soul knows its true
nature and is free.

When Wolfe was to continue the tale of his life, Wordsworth

also helped him. Again Wolfe shows his intimacy with the poet's less familiar lines, and the key to *Of Time and the River* is the last of Wordsworth's sonnet sequence, *The River Duddon*. At the beginning of the "Telemachus" section of this novel Wolfe writes of himself: "His father was dead and now it seemed to him that he had never found him. His father was dead and yet he sought him everywhere." And the rest of the novel has as its theme these lines of Wordsworth:

AFTER-THOUGHT

I thought of Thee, my partner and my guide,
As being past away. Vain sympathies!
For, backward, Duddon! as I cast my eyes,
I see what was, and is, and will abide;
Still glides the Stream, and shall for ever glide;
The Form remains, the Function never dies;
While we, the brave, the mighty, and the wise,
We Men, who in our morn of youth defied
The elements, must vanish; — be it so!
Enough, if something from our hands have power
To live, and act, and serve the future hour;
And if, as toward the silent tomb we go,
Through love, through hope, and faith's transcendent dower,
We feel that we are greater than we know.

The point of view of the professional metaphysician is different from that of the artist; the artist treats metaphysics as being helpful to life. Thus the definite subjectivity of Wolfe's personality brought the other world away from a distinct existence into one continually interwoven with his own. The very use that he makes of physical metaphors demonstrates his willingness to see this world on a physical level. He accepts the symbolism of the world and nature as Wordsworth and Coleridge did. He does not — and perhaps cannot — impersonalize his problems, as might a Catholic writer, through priest or character sublimation.

Without a knowledge of the total environment of an author, his intention cannot be completely understoood, nor can the entire meaning of his communications be perceived. The terms Wolfe uses in recurring refrains are symbols of other things than their direct referents. Thus "home" is not only the Asheville boarding-house of Wolfe's childhood or a prenatal uterine existence; the word is also used in the Wordsworthian sense for God. The search for a father becomes, as well, a search for God. The "door" is the entrance both back to the protective maternal womb and to the heaven from which, in the Platonic doctrine, we in our essence come. The "stone, leaf, door" refrain symbolizes not only the pain of birth but also those tokens (like Wordsworth's rain-bow, rose, tree, and pansy) which remind the mortal of his im-mortal nature. The "lost, and by the wind grieved, ghost" corre-sponds to the sense of the pre-existence of the soul, which vanishes as the individual advances in material time down the river of corporeal existence.

It is significant in this connection that Wordsworth, too, had a brother, symbolizing for him, as Ben did for Wolfe, man's brotherhood with man, and that John Wordsworth died during the period that elapsed between the composition of the first fifty-seven lines of the "Ode on the Intimations of Immortality" and the lines which begin "Our birth is but a sleep and a for-getting," which Wolfe took as the interpretation and meaning of his own life.

The events and the spirit of Wolfe's own lifetime correspond rather closely to those of the period of Wordsworth and Cole-ridge. As they lamented the materialism, the skepticism, the regi-mentation, and the conservatism of their day, and put their faith in the elemental goodness and spiritual inheritance of the indi-vidual man, so Wolfe's higher purpose is to lead America out of the confusion and disillusionment of the years following the out-break of the first World War. His father-search becomes univer-salized in the common quest for a substitute for the autocratic character of the home — with the father as autocrat — which was then disappearing. Motivated by the same complexes, Wolfe uses the same methods that his poets did in rescuing his generation from the futility of its existence. As they were a link between an old world and a new one, so Wolfe, in following them, becomes a bridge from our world of the past to a new future, and thus he takes his place in the great stream of Anglo-Saxon thought and literature, which has stressed democracy since the time of *Beowulf*.

Thomas Wolfe preaches a return to the natural man, exalts the dignity and beauty of human nature, reaffirms man's divinity and purpose, and restores to his readers thereby a sense of their own value and importance. Like all tragedy, the tragedy of Wolfe's life as he records it purifies and restores the ideals of his readers which else would languish for want of sufficient illustration.

The autobiographical nature of Wolfe's writings has been a concern, at least partially, of most of the commentators about the novelist. Edward K. Brown accepts the initial assumption that Wolfe did use materials from his life and then charts the autobiography from its metamorphosis into realistic fiction and finally onto the level of imaginative symbolism. Professor Brown was at the University of Toronto when this article was written. He was a member of the English Department of the University of Chicago when he died in 1951.

THOMAS WOLFE: REALIST AND SYMBOLIST

by

E. K. Brown

I

When two years ago last September Thomas Wolfe died at the age of thirty-eight, writers and readers of his generation felt a grief that most of our elders have been unable to understand. The reason for our sense of loss was not simply a very real enthusiasm for what Wolfe had written, or even a conviction that he had within him many unwritten books such as no one else could write. It was, most of all, the curiously emblematic position Wolfe had come to hold and in which his death served to confirm him. He died of being Thomas Wolfe — the news reports spoke of pneumonia — of having lived, perceived, reflected, and composed with an intensity which would have killed most men ten times over. He had carried one mode of approaching the universe to the absolute.

From the *University of Toronto Quarterly*, January 1941. By permission.

One may put it in more matter-of-fact terms and say that it was his idea of the novel that killed him. The enormous books he published are but epitomes of those manuscripts with which he filled the office-ledgers which alone seemed to him capacious enough for his works. In his eerie essay *The Story of a Novel* he has told us that he wished to begin one of his novels with a sketch of a train-journey across Virginia; its function, he went on to say, was no more than "to introduce some of the chief characters, to indicate a central situation, to give something of the background from which the book proceeds, and perhaps through the movement of the train across the stillness of the earth to establish a certain beat, evoke a certain emotion which is inherent to the nature of the book." Here is what he intended his train-journey to do; in his ledgers it spread out to a length notably greater than an average novel's. Mr. Whit Burnett malignantly remarks that "Wolfe rode up to his publisher's office in a truck with the manuscript of *Of Time and the River* . . . ; a couple of months later, after the ms. was cut he rode away in a much more nearly normal-sized taxicab." The reason for the truck myth was the unique fullness with which Wolfe presented his material; and the fullness derived from his peculiar theory of knowledge. To know anything about an object one must know everything about it, and knowing everything about it supposed knowing everything about its relationships. One experience to which he often returned seems at first very limited and simple. "Some quiet steps that came and passed along a leafy night-time street in summer in a little town down South long years ago; a woman's voice, her sudden burst of low and tender laughter; then the voices and the footsteps going, silence, and the leafy rustle of trees." This incident — if one may call it so much as an incident — recurs in three of his four novels; to the end he is persuaded that he has not fathomed it. To do so would suppose fathoming the nature of that woman and her companions, of the town, of the wounded South, of the entire nation thirty years ago. . . . Nothing less would appease the curiosity of Wolfe. Hence the ledgers, hence the truck, hence death at thirty-eight. A novelist could not hold such a conception of knowledge and live.

The fall of 1940 has brought the second and last of his post-humous novels, *You Can't Go Home Again*. Significant in many ways, it shows that Wolfe had clearly seen, at the end, that his formula for fiction was not viable. In all his earlier novels he tried to present life as a continuous process, the slave of time and memory; at the end he was willing to be representative, although he could never be brief. He would show the reef of love by a single party — it occupies almost half as many words as make up an average novel; two or three instances, varied in stress, set before the reader with immense detail, would show the reef of fame. As design the book may dissatisfy: it is rough and above all it is lumpy. Still it has a workable formula, and its roughness and lumpiness are accidental, and might well have disappeared in a second attempt.

Whatever may have been wrong with the formula on which his earlier novels were constructed — and it is on them, not on *You Can't Go Home Again*, that his reputation will chiefly rest — they had a fusion of qualities never even juxtaposed by any other American novelist of his time. Wolfe had the realist's regard for the particularity of a shape or a color, a glance or a voice. His novels are thick with description. Set side by side Lewis's Gopher Prairie as Carol Kennicott finds it on her arrival from Minneapolis, and Altamont as Mr. Gant finds it on his return from California; and one will perceive how much sharper is Wolfe's eye for appearances. He joined with this perceptive and devouring eye of the master-realist the imaginative symbolist's regard for relationships, occult and profound. In each generation he sought to uncover the qualities of those before and those to come; all civilization he regarded as a natural unity to whose base he was always trying to dig. The main characters he drew were at once richly complicated human individuals who attracted the realist in him and also typical figures, often indeed gigantic symbols, of American life. His central character in the first two novels, Mr. Gant, as well as having a variety of strongly marked simple aspects — those of the sordid drunkard, the master of invective, the wild foiled seeker after the meaning of his life — has the symbolic significance of nothing less than America itself. Wolfe often ran the gamut within a page or two from the accurate description of the slant of a roof, or the tone of a voice, to some desperate evocation of the meaning of a whole continent's life. Realism and imaginative symbolism he brought together within the roomy formula of autobiographical fiction. His conception of the novel led him to make his autobiographical presentation highly imaginative, to shape the progress of his book not by particular facts but by essential meanings. In such imaginative autobiography there was a place for all the instances of his sensitivity to appearances, and nevertheless the limits of realism could be transcended.

Most of Wolfe's achievements will come under view if one pauses over the three notions: realism, symbolism, roomy autobiography.

II

Wolfe writhed when he was called an autobiographical novelist, unless the term was applied in that most general (and meaningless) sense in which, as he thought, it might be applied to any creator. His dislike of the term had its taproot in the fear that the notion of autobiography would upset the delicate balance between realism and imaginative symbolism he sought to maintain and communicate.

He was astounded by the furore *Look Homeward, Angel* caused in his old home, Asheville, in North Carolina. "I had thought," he says, "there might be a hundred people in that town who would read the book, but if there were a hundred people outside the negro population, the blind, and the positively illiterate who did not read it, I do not know who they are." Asheville was indignant and "seethed with a fury of resentment which I had not believed possible." The clergy denounced it; the tea-parties buzzed with horror and complaint; members of Wolfe's own family took to bed. The writer was threatened with immediate death if he were ever to return to the town; and one old woman whom he had known all his life wrote to warn him she

would not lift a finger to prevent a mob from hauling his "big
overgrown karkus" across the main square.

In Asheville's view the book was autobiography, cunningly
spiced with lies. To support his claim that much of it was the
fruit of a creative imagination, Wolfe points out that some of the
incidents most boldly identified as records, or wilful distortions,
of fact, had no source outside his imagination. Any reader of the
novel will remember that the keeper of a local brothel bought the
stone angel which for forty years had stood outside Mr. Gant's
shop, to set it at the head of a prostitute's grave. In the town's
cemetery there was a statue of an angel, photographed when the
novel came out, and widely circulated in the press. This angel
stood over the grave of a pious church-working woman — and
Wolfe had never seen it. Many of the facts which local readers of
the novel related to the town's history were, Wolfe insists, as
fully the creation of his imagination as the episode of the stone
angel.

Such a disclaimer we may accept without surrendering a belief
that the novels are essentially autobiographical. We know that
his father was a stone-cutter; that Wolfe's life developed in the
same fashion as that of the hero of the first two novels, Eugene
Gant, and that of the hero of the two later, George Webber. But
the main reason for accounting the novels autobiographical is
something that we know of the temper of Wolfe's mind.

He had a very strong and very acute equipment for sense-
experience. Like Webber he had "a good eye, a splendid nose,
and the memory of an elephant." One of his habits, in preparing
to write a novel, was to draw up "gigantic and staggering lists of
the towns, cities, counties, states and countries I had been in,
minutely thorough, desperately evocative descriptions of the
under carriage, the springs, wheels, flanges, axle-rods, color,
weight and quality of the day coach of an American railway
train . . . , lists of the rooms and houses in which I had lived
. . . with the most accurate and evocative descriptions of those
rooms that I could write — their size, their shape, the color and
design of the wallpaper, the way a towel hung down, the way a
chair creaked, a streak of water-rust upon the ceiling."

The magnificent result of such a preoccupation with sense-experience is shown in this passage which tells of the food at the Gant table:

In the morning they rose in a house pungent with breakfast cookery, and they sat at a smoking table loaded with brains and eggs, ham, hot biscuit, fried apples seething in their gummed syrups, honey, golden butter, fried steak, scalding coffee. Or there were stacked batter cakes, rum-colored molasses, fragrant brown sausages, a bowl of wet cherries, plums, fat juicy bacon, jam. At the mid-day meal they ate heavily: a huge hot roast of beef, fat buttered lima beans, tender corn smoking on the cob, thick red slabs of sliced tomatoes, rough savory spinach, hot yellow corn bread, flaky biscuits, a deep-dish peach and apple cobbler spiced with cinnamon, tender cabbage, deep glass dishes piled with preserved fruits, — cherries, pears, peaches. At night they might eat fried steak, hot squares of grits, fried in egg and butter, pork chops, fish, young fried chicken.

Clearly the author of this passage has a need to recall the whole of his sensuous experience — he can be content with no typical representation. Nor can he be content with a dry catalogue: he must recall not only the objects of his experience, but also its quality in all its rich complexity. The power of so recalling experience is one of Wolfe's chief powers. It is also proof of the autobiographical tendency of Wolfe's mind. That food appeared on the Wolfe table in his childhood — who could doubt it?

III

The character who bestrides *Look Homeward, Angel* and a large part of its sequel is undoubtedly Wolfe's own father, put before us with all the resources of a realist. But Mr. Gant is not only a remembered character, he is also the creation of a powerful symbolic imagination. The central idea of the sequel, *Of Time and the River*, Wolfe has himself described: "The deepest search in life, it seemed to me, the thing that in one way or another was central to all living, was man's search to find a father, not merely the father of his flesh, the lost father of his youth, but the image of a strength and wisdom external to his need and superior to his hunger, to which the belief and power of his own life could be united." Several elements in Wolfe's experience combined to lead him towards the father-image as the formative idea of his fiction. The power of atavism, with which he came to associate the father-image, impressed him more and more as he matured; and he has given the closing chapters of his last work to an examination of its role in his own life, in that of the contemporary world, and in that of humanity as a whole. In some of the earlier novels important hints had been given: the enormous impact of the character of Wolfe's own father, the power over Wolfe's imagination of Joyce's exhibition of the father-image in *Ulysses*, long one of Wolfe's enthusiasms, but one which he was later to call in question. Still, it is in *You Can't Go Home Again*, sickened by the corruption of Germany under the Nazi régime, that he says his fullest and clearest say. Of the many significances that his title bears the deepest is the warning against atavism, man's greatest peril and one in which Wolfe thinks he was caught until he escaped in the last months of his writing life.

In Mr. Gant, the perfect expression of the demonic in man, the realist and the symbolist have worked together within the formula of imaginative autobiography to reveal the whole force of Wolfe's characterizing power. The realist has a delighted awareness of the comic quality in his tirades of invective. At first glance such an outburst as this, which has to do with his wife's setting up a boarding-house, is the utterance of a spirit wounded beyond endurance: "Woman, you have deserted my bed and board, you have made a laughing stock of me before the world, and left your children to perish. Fiend that you are, there is nothing that you would not do to torture, humiliate and degrade me. You have deserted me in my old age; you have left me to die alone. Ah Lord, it was a bitter day for us all when your gloating eyes first fell upon this damnable, this murderous and bloody Barn. There is no ignominy to which you will not stoop if you think it will put a nickel in your pocket. You have fallen so low not even your own brothers will come near you. 'Nor beast nor man hath fallen so far.' " In the pantries and through the dining-room door the rich voices of the negresses chuckled, and one could hear them agreeing, "Dat man sho' can tawk!" Mr. Gant knows he can talk; and when he is launched on such a tirade there is a nervous grin about his mouth; he enjoys delivering it, knows that his audience enjoys, and even expects it, regarding it as ritual, integral to the day's routine as much as breakfast or dinner. In his anger he is always self-conscious.

His tirades are not, however, wholly comic: they are his means of expressing his frustration and his resentments, his awareness of his tragic failure as a person. The tragic aspect of his tirades Wolfe's imagination seizes as a symbol of fury. Fury is one of the central conceptions in his theory of the universe, and singularly difficult to define. Wolfe does not attempt a definition: instead he writes page on page of wild and whirling words which disengage a strange music and from which emerges a fusion of the abstract idea of fury and the symbol of fury — Mr. Gant. When Mr. Gant is at the point of death, pitifully weak, pathetically shrunk, Eugene appreciates what he is about to lose:

> Oh, to hear him prowling like a weakened lion below, the stertorous hoarse frenzy of his furious breath; to hear the ominous muttering mounting to faint howls as with infuriated relish he prepared the roaring invective of the morning's tirade, to hear him muttering as the coal went rattling out upon the fire, to hear him growling as savagely the flame shot up the trembling chimney-throat, to hear him muttering back and forth now like a raging beast, finally to hear his giant stride racing through the house prepared now, storming to the charge, and the well-remembered howl of his awakened fury as springing to the door-way of the back-room stairs he flung it open, yelling at them to awake. Was it in such a way, one time as he awoke, and heard below his father's lion-ramp of morning that fury came?

Fury came to Wolfe from many sources: but from none other so powerfully as from his father.

Mr. Gant was cast in a huge mould, physically, emotionally, and in an elemental sense spiritually. Over the town of Altamont, in which he was forever a stranger, he cast a shadow. His howls and curses, his vast gestures and mercurial movements, his sprees, and his savage moulding of statues, impressed upon his townsmen the idea of "something strange and proud and glorious." Over his wife he also cast a shadow: when love and hate had both died down between them, what she felt was that beyond his cruelty and his folly there lay something glorious, in "the enormous beating color of his life and the lost and stricken thing in him which he would never find." Even in her dulled and miserly being "fear and a speechless pity rose when at times she saw the small uneasy eyes grow still and darken with the foiled and groping hunger of old frustration." Frustration in the central quest of his life is the key to Mr. Gant's fury which at once sets him apart from his fellow-townsmen and gives them an imperfect awareness of a hidden affinity — of something in Mr. Gant which is going beyond them on a path that they too ideally would follow.

By his intense emotionalism, his wild energies, his inarticulate awareness of a meaning in life which he cannot fathom, Mr. Gant is raised into a symbol of the American adventure. Wolfe believed that there was a peculiar American tragedy, that on this continent life made specially heavy demands which man was specially inadequate to meet. At the end of *The Story of a Novel*, addressing himself in particular to artists, he tries to make plain the difficulty of American life. He repudiates the idea with which, as a contemporary of the "lost generation," he had once toyed: that the chief difficulty of the American artists lies in the national philistinism "which contends against the artist's life and which prevents his growth." He admits that in America more than anywhere else the artist assumes the heavy load of translating "the enormous space and energy of life" into "the structure of his own design," with but little help from any tradition or "antecedent scheme." Not even this load, heavy as it is, ranks as the American artist's chief impediment: that is the "labor of a complete and whole articulation, the discovery of an entire universe, and of a complete language." These are rather vague words and require close examination.

IV

About the problem of *language* but one observation need be made: the complete language desiderated will be simply the instrument for recording and communicating the universe discovered and the articulation achieved.

What is the *universe* the American artist is called upon to discover? It is the universe Mr. Gant is straining to know, the universe Wolfe wore himself out in exploring.

What it is is most clearly suggested in the presentation of Eugene Gant's attitude towards his uncle Bascom Pentland. Bascom is, after Mr. Gant, the most demonic male figure in the novels, but when he comes before us, even for the first time, he is in senile decay, and it is impossible to feel about him, as one feels about Mr. Gant, that his personality is heroic. His function is to invite Eugene to recapture the past: in his senilities there are certainties of a past greatness of being and experience. As Eugene looks at him he has a "sense of union with the past"; but this sense is soon seen to be spurious, for in men like Bascom the past is dead: "they poured into our hands a handful of dry dust and ashes." It was torture to Eugene to know that if one could rekindle in a man like Bascom Pentland the flame that had gone out forever one might reach to experiences otherwise as impossible to have as if they occurred only on the other side of the moon. Bascom was ten years old when the Civil War ended — the whole of the Reconstruction in Carolina was locked away in that mind: "he had heard the desolate and stricken voices in the South long, long ago, the quiet and casual voices of lost men, a million vanished footsteps in the streets of life." The man who would understand America, the American artist, undergoes his greatest tortures when he sits across from a Bascom Pentland and realizes the huge bulk of secrets slowly mouldering away to nothing within the old mind.

Wolfe had to endure torture of the same kind whenever he forgot an experience of his own and sought in vain to recapture its shapes and colors; and in Eugene's sense of frustration in revisiting Altamont this torture is exemplified. To his brother Ben he says in agony: "I have forgotten the old faces. Where are they, Ben? What were their names? I forget the names of people I knew for years. I get their faces mixed. I get their heads stuck on other people's bodies. I think one man has said what another said. There is something I have lost and forgotten." The need to hold all one's experiences fresh and complete in one's self at all times, the need to open communications with scores and thousands of other minds in order that their whole store of experience fresh and complete may become one's own also — these are kindred needs. They point to a mind which supposed that the way to explore the entire universe lay through an accumulation of infinite fact, infinite experience, actual or vicarious.

All personal relationships Wolfe brought to one major test: what had the other person experienced and how much of his experience could he communicate? In *The Web and the Rock* he puts love itself to that test. In the earlier novels his treatment of love had been episodic, fumbling, and extremely shabby. The reader of *The Web and the Rock* knows why. Wolfe could love — in fact or in imagination — only when a woman could add to his store of vicarious experience as he had hoped that Bascom Pentland would add. None of the women in the earlier novels could do so. It is significant that his first striking portrait of a loved woman — Esther Jack, whom he sets beside his hero in *The Web* — is a person much older than the man, much more travelled, more cultivated and involved in a criss-cross of intimate relationships with half the most interesting people in New York, where he is a stranger.

Before he knew Esther Jack, New York had been a daily torture to him. He had been appalled by "those terrible streets that had neither pause nor curve, nor any door that he could open." About him there were millions of faces, each of which revealed, or half-concealed, a consciousness, a multitude of experiences from which he was utterly excluded. Among a thousand alluring "images of glory, love, and power," he beat against the thin but immovable barriers, aware that he was "only a hand's breadth off from love, if he could span it, only a moment away from friendship if he knew it, only an inch, a door, a word away from all the glory of the earth, if he only knew the way." Esther Jack was the way; "the woman had come to represent the city to him. To him she was the city he had longed to know."

Her great fascination was the intensity with which she experienced the thousand particulars of her crowded New York life and the vivid fullness with which she reported them. What she told her lover he knew as if he had experienced it himself. He did not need to look about for the streets which still kept something of the appearance New York had had in her youth: through her he experienced the nineties. He did not need to dine with Morgans or Barrymores: she had done so and could tell him everything that was said, everything that was eaten or drunk, everything that was looked, in the course of those dinners. Through her miraculous precision and completeness in communication, her lover's quest of a full knowledge of America took its longest forward step. She helped him, more than anyone else he had ever known, to weave the web of illuminating experience: to put it brutally, she saved him time.

The relation between Esther and Webber had developed over more than a year before its undoing began. Her range of experience had been so rich, her hold on it was so firm, that Webber, absorbing that body of experience, was confronted with something stronger than he was. He became uncentred. "It seemed that he would never get her out of him again, never look out on life again with his own proper vision, never again distil out of his flesh and spirit the terrible invasions of love which rob men of . . . the soaring music of their isolation." To preserve "his own proper vision" he breaks with Esther; the recognition that another's range of experience could be so rich and could be communicated so fully that it became a peril, not simply an opportunity, this was the most smashing blow that a man of Wolfe's temper could meet. He was so appalled by the proof of his weakness that he cursed his make-up because it could not perform "the inhuman task he set for it, hated it because its hunger could not match his hunger, which was for the earth and all things living in it." He had now to live with the knowledge that he must accept the limitations imposed upon him by the flaws and strains in his individual nature. He could console himself — but it was inadequate — in the assurance that "he had done all with his hunger and his flesh that one man could. And he knew also, although his bleared and battered face might seem to be the visage of a madman, the spirit that dwelt behind this ruined mask now looked calmly and sanely forth upon the earth for the

first time in ten years." Such a recognition is the psychological
end of *The Web and the Rock.*

The year 1940 has brought its sequel, telling what a man does
when he has bought such bitter knowledge. Wolfe redefines the
will's role in the individual's life. One cannot assimilate all: the
will must be trained (and trusted) to determine what one shall
try to assimilate. One must not be a blotter: the good life is one
of conflict, in the service of loyalties chosen by the will. It had
been Wolfe's belief that art could not properly be representative:
the full record of one experience, he had thought, could not
stand for a dozen distinct experiences, no matter how similar
they might have been. Wolfe, at the end, recognized that his
temperamental repudiation of the representative had been at the
root of his difficulties as artist, and as person. He could admit it,
but the tendency — the strongest if not the finest in his nature —
was too strong to be dominated.

Still he did come to see quite early that if he could not describe
America without reaching out for experience on all sides of his
life and into all the lives he could touch, nevertheless the heaping
up of experience brought one but a short way toward that "door"
into the chamber of perfect awareness, of which, like Mr. Gant,
he was in quest.

It could bring one but a short way because the exploration of
the universe through specific experiences, even in great number,
leads only to fragmentary knowledge, and not to the *articulation*
which is the second phase in the artist's quest. The person with
fragmentary knowledge will suffer from loneliness, the philosophical loneliness which a man may feel in the presence, or
under the weight, of an unexplained universe. Such loneliness is
in Wolfe's view specially the destiny of the American; and the
frame of mind I am attempting to describe he has set forth in a
meditation at the end of a passage in *Of Time and the River*
where he has sought to record his knowledge of America: "And
always America is the place of the deathless and enraptured
moments, the eye that looked, the mouth that smiled and vanished, and the word; the stone, the leaf, the door we never found
and never have forgotten. And these are the things that we

remember of America, for we have known all her thousand lights and weathers, and we walk the streets, we walk the streets forever, we walk the streets of life alone." In this passage in which Wolfe records the loneliness so movingly, he points to the escape from it, the way to articulation. Throughout the first three novels, at least, as a refrain come the references, usually grouped as here, to "the stone, the leaf, the door."

v

These are three central symbols for the nature of life. And at this moment one turns wholly away from the realistic method, the method of faithfully recording experiences, to the method of the imaginative symbolist.

The *stone* is the angel which dominates not only the title but the text of the first novel. In his youth Mr. Gant had seen in a Baltimore stone-cutter's shop a big marble angel, imported from Italy; and in "a cold and nameless excitement" decided that more than anything else he wished "to wreak something dark and unspeakable in him into cold stone." The carving in stone of an angel's head came to represent for him the full realization of the possibilities of life. He never learned to carve an angel's head: the big statue was sold to become a prostitute's memorial; and Mr. Gant's energies waned until of all that huge and muscular body only the hands preserved their strength. When Eugene recalled his father, "he could remember nothing clearly except the powerful sculptured weight and symmetry of his tremendous hands as they lay folded on his body in the coffin." So completely is Mr. Gant's quest of meanings symbolized in his carving that for his son those huge hands "seemed to rest there upon . . . the corpse with a kind of terrible reality as if there really is, in death, some energy of life that will not die, some element of man's life that must persist, and that resumes into a single feature of his life the core and essence of his character." For Mr. Gant the medium of stone which he had chosen for his grapple with the meaning of the universe was too resistant: the faculty within him on which he had staked all was too clumsy.

"All of our lives is written in the twisting of a leaf upon a
bough, a door that opened, a stone." The symbol of the *leaf*,
rather than any other of October's victims in the annual recurrence of death, presented itself to Wolfe through the poet whom
beyond all others he admired. Coleridge, Eugene remarks in his
Paris note-book, "is not one of the great English poets. He is
The Poet." Elsewhere Wolfe quotes the image, already weighed
with tragic meaning in Coleridge's use of it, of the leaf,

> The one red leaf, the last of its clan,
> That dances as often as dance it can,
> Hanging so light and hanging so high,
> On the topmost twig that looks up at the sky.

The leaf is allied with the constant reference to October which,
as *Of Time and the River* proceeds, becomes a mighty chorus:
October when life dries up even in Mr. Gant, whose vitality for
so long seemed inexhaustible.

The *door*, the chief of the three symbols, is the thin barrier
between personalities. It is to be remembered that for Wolfe
personalities mattered not because of what they might in themselves be (it is doubtful if for him the conception of a personality
as something in itself bore any clear sense) but because of the
range of experience which they had undergone, and might communicate. An individual is confined to a fragment of space and a
moment of time: his continual need is to make at least a momentary escape through one of the doors that surround him. If he
cannot go through all these doors — and ideally he would — he
can perhaps go through the few which are most important for
him, as the door leading to Esther Jack was for Webber, or the
door leading to Bascom Pentland for Eugene.

We cannot often pass beyond such doors; the stone is too re-
sistent for us to mould; the leaf dies too soon. Yet if we could
know the content of many minds, if we could hold in all its freshness and completeness the whole of our experience, mould the
stone, keep the ichor of life flowing through the leaf, we could
reach the doors, and they would open at our touch.

The use of such symbols, not spasmodically but throughout his fiction, enabled Wolfe to rise above the inadequate apprehensions of the universe open to him as a faithful realist. Through them he was often able to illuminate places which to the realist in him remained impenetrable. These symbols are securely rooted in his sensuous experience: they are not imposed from the intelligence, but impressed upon the perceptions. The reader of his novels knows that they abound in sharp experiences of sculpture, trees, and entrances. What Wolfe was unable to clarify, either for himself or for his readers, was the exact mode in which he passed from the level of faithful realism to the higher, dimmer level of imaginative symbolism. His struggle towards clarification, both in the analysis of his own nature and in the presentation of relationships, is central to *You Can't Go Home Again*; but the success — and it is not complete — is bought at the cost of great emotional and sensuous impoverishment. He could not even then make the round of his own being. His loss is irreparable if one believes, as I do, that with time he could have achieved perfect clarification without important impoverishment. He would then have been the model — he is already the pioneer — of a profounder kind of fiction than America has yet had.

In this essay Frohock places Wolfe squarely against the background of his time. From the two kinds of worlds in which Wolfe found himself came the conflicts, isolations, and frustrations of himself and his outsize characters. "Wolfe and Dos Passos were the last great exploiters of the theme of time's erosion," writes Frohock elsewhere in "The Novel of Violence in America." In his comparison of Wolfe with Dos Passos, the critic has centered his attention on the two contemporary novelists who have been most consciously "American" in their outlooks. W. M. Frohock is now a professor of French at Columbia University.

OF TIME AND NEUROSIS

by

W. M. Frohock

Tom Wolfe's great poem rises out of our national neurosis, and his characteristic anxiety state is one that most of us have experienced in some measure. Much of America is still rural. Most Americans feel that they have rural origins. Yet our centers of education and culture, through which in the process of our growth we naturally pass, are as a rule urban in spirit and sensitive to the metropolitan influence. Thus in the case history of the educated American there is a record of the emotional adjustment by which the two cultures — urban and rural — were more or less successfully brought to terms. The city is always moving ahead and the country always catching up, so that the young man coming out of the country to the city crosses not only a gap of

From *Southwest Review*, Autumn 1948; revised for *The Novel of Violence in America*, University Press in Dallas, 1950. By permission of author and publisher.

miles but also a gap of years. We live as if in two centuries at once and belong entirely to neither; and the boy who comes from the back-eddy of Maine and arrives on the campus of a New England university wearing his first "College Cut" suit knows as well, by instinct, what Wolfe is talking about as if he had been born in the hills of North Carolina.

Home is the place where you were once and where you really belonged, even though as you remember it you were not always happy there; a part of you which should have been permanent, a place to which you could return after a long stay somewhere else. But it turns out not to be the place where, as Frost says, when you return they have to take you in. It is not in their power to take you in. You have been away, having gone with the premonition that you could not come back, and when you try to return the place has changed and you have changed (O Lost!) and nothing is as it has been. You are, in many senses, the victim of time.

If you are from the South, the feeling may be so much the stronger because you are more aware of the differences. (To find a southerner who is not conscious of being a southerner is rare, whereas your Yankee, for instance, has to migrate from New England to discover that the whole world is not populated by people like himself!) And Wolfe was from North Carolina. Yet the difference was one of degree and not of kind. The breath-taking titles themselves — *Look Homeward, Angel*; *Of Time and the River*; *You Can't Go Home Again* — point to the vast predicament in which a man finds himself trapped and frustrated because everything ebbs, flows, shifts, and refuses to be seen whole; even *The Web and the Rock* juxtaposes an image of permanence with an image of change. And however much his being from the South dramatized this predicament for Wolfe, the predicament is general. It is a paradox that a nation with as short a history as ours should be as obsessed as we are with the flight of time.

Wolfe himself saw the predicament as both general and at the same time extremely personal. The major part of his effort as an artist went into trying to fix the illusory shiftings of memory before they should become lost. Again and again he spoke of his purpose as being to set down, in the time he had, his vision of life. Now, after all the years of controversy since *Look Homeward, Angel* precipitated the sterile debate which centered so often about such questions as whether Wolfe was "magnificently abundant" or "merely garrulous," the scope of his vision remains the central question about him. As he wrote to his old teacher, Mrs. Roberts, he had the Dantesque ambition to create a universe; he did not dodge the question, nor can the serious reader evade it. Every writer of course creates a universe, in the sense, at least, of having to give his characters a world in which to breathe and live. But Wolfe was self-conscious about doing it. He had ready at hand the characters to people his universe. His concern was to give them a habitation, and this habitation is central to his vision.

One might say that he should have written of his ambition to *re*-create a universe. This would have described more accurately the process of recording a vision of the past as viewed through the distorting lens of violent and tortured temperament. "This world I create," he wrote to Mrs. Roberts, ". . . is always inside me." In another connection he wrote that the process of writing a novel was very much as if a great black cloud had gathered inside him and suddenly burst. He never hid — how could he? — the very evident fact that he was writing about himself; the unnecessary little foreword to *Look Homeward, Angel*, in which he defends his method on the somewhat preposterous grounds that there is much of Swift in *Gulliver*, serves only to show how well Wolfe knew what he was doing and how apprehensive he was, as he would always be apprehensive, of what the critics might say. His material was his own experience, as every new fact we learn about him, every new letter published, every anecdote, drives home. Under the name of Eugene Gant or George Webber, the figure of Tom Wolfe always stands in the center of his vision.

How completely different from Dos Passos, who was writing at about the same time and, to a great extent, about the same America! Dos Passos' great strength in *U.S.A.* is his ability to maintain his own detachment. As the result of a discipline which can be traced through his earlier books, Dos Passos can give his reader the feeling that the events which make up his fiction would have taken place just as surely if there had been no novelist at hand to note them down. His ability to establish his perspective — which he finally achieves by the device of presenting his autobiography as a sort of comment on the fiction — has a great deal to do with the success of his great trilogy. Wolfe is the diametrical opposite. The events of his story derive their meaning entirely from their effect upon the central, autobiographical character.

As Dos Passos depends essentially on a discipline which originated in France during the middle years of the nineteenth century, Wolfe seems to go back all the way to the English Romantics. Given the nature of his talent, it is probably just as well that he grew up out of reach of literary modes, that he read more of Virgil than of the little magazines at Asheville, that no one made him give up Melville for Henry James, that he went to the state university and that he reached the literary hotframe of Harvard only after he was a man grown. He seems never to have played the sedulous ape or to have submitted himself to the current literary disciplines or to have acquired the writer's suspicion of himself, of the accuracy of his own senses, or of the validity of his report on them, which marks so much of the literature of our time. He never acquired the constraining awareness of the importance of technique which has conditioned men like Dos Passos. Literary sophistication simply was not his line: who else could have written, with anything like Wolfe's unawareness of the ludicrous side of what he was doing, his endless variations on lines from Shakespeare? One of his major sources of strength was that he was so completely and miraculously out of date. "I began life," he wrote, again to Mrs. Roberts, "as a lyric writer." He ended life as nothing else.

Romantic lyric poetry — and we are agreed that Wolfe's poem is romantic in many ways, including the way of revolt — is the poetry of youth. The greatest praise we give to a poet who in mature years writes lyrics of freshness and originality is that he "seems so young." This strikes me as one of the most helpful keys to Wolfe; his vision of life and the world in which he makes his characters live are the vision and the world of a very young man.

He felt himself so wretchedly, so miserably and so magnificently alone. Despite all his use of the second person plural, Eugene Gant

and George Webber never escape the feeling that their enter-
prises are personal and special, their cases unique. There is a
story about Wolfe, that once when he was riding downtown after
a baseball game he suddenly alarmed a subway car by screaming,
"The bastards are ambushing me!" According to this story —
which for all I know is apocryphal — Wolfe had been talking to
a friend about literary critics, but the world's series crowd on the
subway did not know this, did not know Wolfe and probably had
not read his books, so that his outburst occasioned no little sur-
prise. Now no one who has read his Wolfe faithfully would, or
should, have been surprised in the least. The point is that we were
all bastards — there was Tom Wolfe and then there were all the
other people who were not Tom Wolfe and they were aliens. He
went alone.

If his great feeling of loneliness was not pathological, it was at
least exaggerated. He hated many things because they were not
himself: Negroes (much of the time) and Irish Catholics (or at
least the Boston Irish) and Brahmins and Jews. Eugene Gant and
George Webber are repelled, immediately or eventually, by most
of the people with whom they come in contact. The record of the
autobiographical character's inability to establish satisfactory
communication with other human beings suggests a fundamental
difficulty, a failure to understand and to be understood, which may
in turn be related to the state of compulsive frenzy in which Wolfe
appears to have done much of his writing. With Wolfe, as with
Céline, the other novelist of our time who approaches Wolfe in
this matter of being repelled by people, one cannot help feeling
that the drive to write, and to keep on writing at whatever cost
in prolixity and reiteration, is tied up with some sort of despair
of ever being fully understood.

Yet the exaggeration, painful as its results may be at times both
to Wolfe and his reader, seems only the magnification of one
aspect of the time-neurosis which so generally affects Wolfe's
vision and which indeed afflicts so many of the rest of us. We live,
by circumstances of our birth and culture, in two periods at once
and are completely at home in neither. If we do not, as Eugene
Gant did, envy the English family which appears in *Of Time and*

the River simply because for all their stuffiness they were so thoroughly at home where they were, or if we do not envy a man like Morison who is so sure of being understood that he converses always in ejaculations and fragments of sentences, the hero's underlying feeling of isolation, which makes him envy them, is certainly not foreign to us: transplantation implies that for a long time the plant will not take root firmly. Wolfe comes by the feeling of isolation very honestly indeed.

We have come, of late, to feel that the presence of this theme of isolation makes the mood of a novel tragic. In Wolfe's case, however, it seems clear that the exaggerated feeling of man's loneliness which permeates his work, and which conditions his whole somewhat neurotic vision of life, prevents that vision from being a truly tragic one. At this point, a comparison with the work of André Malraux becomes almost inevitable.

Wolfe and Malraux, better than any other contemporaries who come to mind, have caught up and made their own the feeling of man's solitude. Malraux's early jungle tale, *The Royal Way*, is full of this great loneliness which is accompanied, as it is also in Wolfe, by an almost overwhelming awareness of the imminence of death. In Malraux's other novels (*The Conquerors, Man's Fate*) the principal characters are beset by the problem of breaking through this loneliness into a feeling of community with their fellows. In the act of killing by stealth, Tchen, in *Man's Fate*, is somewhat less bothered by the fact of murder than by the solitude which terrifies him as he commits it. Most of the other characters in the book experience something similar. But certain of them, at least, overcome this feeling of isolation. They go down, but they go in the knowledge that their fate is *man's* fate. And this is precisely the book which made European critics so aware of the possibilities of the tragic novel. Malraux proceeded, in *Days of Wrath*, to write a novel — little known in America — which in its mood, its highly compact and concentrated form, its insistence on struggle, its atmosphere of violence, comes as near to being pure tragedy, I believe, as a novel can come. This is the story of a man imprisoned by the Nazis, whose strength to undergo imprisonment and torture and finally to escape comes from his discovering that even in the solitude of a Nazi prison no man is ever completely alone. In a preface to the book, Malraux insists that man's loneliness and man's essential solidarity are equally important; they may not be separated.

Malraux's mature awareness of the two faces to the medal is what Wolfe seems to me never to have attained. He never convinced himself that no man is an island. Wolfe's feeling of solitude — together with his awareness of the erosions of time and the imminent presence of death — appears, in comparison with Malraux's later work, as a badge of immaturity. Not that this condemns him; many writers as great as and greater than Wolfe have been immature in this sense. But their achievement has nothing to do with tragedy; and neither has his. The feeling of loneliness, and of the individual's being so bafflingly penned within himself, prevents it. The first person singular, as has often been remarked, is not the appropriate pronoun for tragedy.

It would be pointless, of course, to worry such a question unless in the process we got a fresh view of what Wolfe was and of what he did. It is very likely that his chronic immaturity — moral and aesthetic — warped his vision of life.

For all the lore about Wolfe — and many strange yarns are abroad about him — we really know little about him as a private person. Most of his published letters have been literary and, in a way, formal. The Wolfe legend is doubtless as undependable as it is picturesque; he probably was never so colossally incapable of telling the unembellished truth about himself as many stories (such as the one about his persistent complaint that he was starving like Chatterton in a garret, when actually he lived where he did only from inertia) made him seem. In his books he sounds like one of the people — Stendhal was another — who spend their lives trying to see themselves as they are without ever quite penetrating the thick wall of self-delusion.

His ability to make incredible things seem credible is itself almost incredible. It is only when one goes back to *Look Homeward, Angel* that the Aeschylean family of the early book shows itself for what it is and the whole Pentland-Gant clan becomes implausible if not preposterous. W. O. Gant as Agamemnon home

from the wars to die, Eliza as Clytemnestra (her refusal to admit
that there is anything wrong with the old man being a kind of
murder), Helen as Electra when she is not doubling as Cassan-
dra, Eugene as the wretched Orestes . . . one feels that Wolfe
cannot really have intended these things, and yet, vaguely, there
they are! The people, if hardly the setting, of an *Oresteia*. The
family taint on which Eliza and Helen dwell is the Curse upon
the House. And on first reading, or if one has read *Look Homeward, Angel* and no more, one accepts these things unthinkingly;
the Gant-Pentland tribe seems plausible indeed when taken by
itself.

But when one gets out of Altamont into the wider world of *Of
Time and the River*, he begins to see that too many people are
like the Gants and the Pentlands; there are simply too many queer
ducks. Robert Weaver, drinking himself to pieces and already
showing marks of the insanity "that will destroy him"; Francis
Starwick, prey of a diabolical absence of passion; George Thornton, in the quiet depths of whose eyes "the fatal madness which
would destroy him was already legible"; Bascom Pentland, the
crazy uncle in Boston married to the crazy wife; the inordinately
vulgar John T. Brill — with such people around it is impossible
not to feel that we have strayed into some gallery of eccentrics.
At times it seems as if everyone Wolfe writes about is abnormal,
or else downright insane. And after we have seen these people
we look back at Altamont and are much less impressed by the
extraordinary population of *Look Homeward, Angel*; the Aeschylean family now appears as only the first in a long succession of
crackpot figures. There is small doubt that something in Wolfe's
vision has warped them. All of them are a little like the policemen
who pick up Eugene and his friends for drunken driving in a little
South Carolina town.

And these huge creatures evoked for Eugene a whole history if this
earth and people, monstrous, savage, and unutterable — a congruent and
unspeakable legend which he knew, and all of them knew, down to
the roots, and which he could not speak about and had to speak about,
somehow, or die. For in these men there was evident not only the
savage and mindless energy of the earth itself, with all that was wild,
sensual, fecund, cruel and good-natured — the whole weather of life —

but there was also evident the fear, the shame, the horror that had crushed them beneath its ocean weight of nameless and cowering dread, and broken or destroyed their souls.

Applied to a squad of country cops, this is evidently and clumsily out of proportion, but the fact is that Wolfe saw most of his characters in some such light. And because of this extravagance which works to prevent the appearance of any group of reasonably life-size characters in his books by which to measure the outsize of the others, those others, the important ones, lose something of their stature, even in *Look Homeward, Angel* and *You Can't Go Home Again.*

I had better open an apologetic parenthesis here to explain that, to my taste, *Look Homeward, Angel* and *You Can't Go Home Again* are by far the best parts of Wolfe's long novel. In spite of what I have been saying about them, these two books, describing the preparation of Eugene's departure, and the later discovery that, as he had suspected before leaving, true return was impossible, haunt me as no other books written in America have ever done. But the other two, the story of what happened to Gant-Webber between the departure and the attempted return, seem to me less important. Possibly this is because what happens in the first and last books of the series is what happens, in some degree, to every American, whereas what happens in the middle volumes is more special; much that occurs in *The Web and the Rock* could happen only to a rising American novelist. Possibly there is another reason: it is also true that *Look Homeward, Angel* was the work of an unknown on whom the editor could exert the authority of experience, and *You Can't Go Home Again* was edited after Wolfe's death left the editor with a relatively free hand, whereas the middle volumes were products of years when Wolfe had become extremely sensitive on the subject of editing. But whatever the reason, the second and third books are spotty. Pick up any copy of *Of Time and the River* and hold the page-edges to the light; the darkened sections are sure signs that the book has been read as if it were an anthology. After the first time, one does not voluntarily read his way through the 900-odd pages of this book again. One goes directly to certain parts — some of the best writing

Wolfe ever did — like the death of Eugene's father, the race between the trains, the station stop in Troy, the visit to Joel Pierce's
icebox. As novels, that is to say *as wholes,* the middle books do not
seem to me to stand with the other two.

Reading *Of Time and the River* directly after *Look Homeward,
Angel* throws a revealing light on the people of the latter book.
The Gants and Pentlands become not tragic but queer; not
people working out their destiny, but frustrate victims of time.
Their violence, instead of being the inevitable result of forces
which drive them in a given direction, is merely the inevitable
result of frazzled nerves. A typical case of this, perhaps the most
eloquent that Wolfe ever invented, is the struggle between Eugene
and his brother Luke, which takes place in their mother's living
room. There is no point to the fight, nothing is at stake; doing
physical damage to each other will accomplish no more than the
temporary relief of the exasperation. This is violence without
significance. Compare it with the fighting in *The Grapes of Wrath*
or with the last chapter of *For Whom the Bell Tolls* and the distinction is clear. These are eccentrics clawing at each other; they
are frustrated even in the attempt to do lasting harm; and this
is the best proof possible that the people Wolfe sees, as he sees
them, are not tragic figures.

Straightway we also doubt the reality of the places where Wolfe
makes them move. Originally we accepted Altamont without
question, but just as we suspect that the people are distorted as
soon as we leave Altamont for Cambridge, so we also suspect
Altamont itself as soon as we can put it in the new perspective.
Wolfe's New England makes Altamont a never-never land.

. . . New England, with its harsh and stony soil, and its tragic and
lonely beauty; its desolate rocky coasts and its swarming fisheries, the
white, piled, frozen bleakness of its winters with the magnificent
jewelry of stars, the dark firwoods, and the warm little white houses
at which it is impossible to look without thinking of groaning bins,
hung bacon, hard cider, succulent bastings and love's warm, white,
and opulent flesh.

Harsh New England certainly is and there is no exaggerating
the stoniness of its soil. Its beauty is lonely and can be tragic if

you want it to be. And so forth. But New England is above all the homeland of shortage and worry, of industries that move out and of young people who emigrate because New England cannot support the children it spawns, and of old people who stay on to grub what living they can from the farms and — along the main roads — from the tourists. There is indeed a school of New England romanticists who write stuff of the "succulent bastings" sort, and there are apparently readers for it, but the difference between Wolfe's New England and the New England of people like Professor Robert P. T. Coffin is that Wolfe seems actually to believe that his New England exists. It doesn't. Here where the wind is always north-northeast, as Robinson says, care is the rule — not plenty and not sensuousness. Those cozy little white houses have but one warm room in them during the winter and upstairs the chamber-pots are frozen before morning; the succulent bastings are in the writer's mind; and love's flesh is rough with goose-pimples.

Wolfe's New York is probably better. New York is at least so various that nothing said of it can be convicted of falsehood. But here again, as Wolfe watches the gray-faced, hostile millions stream through the subways, he is an outsider. There is always something about him that suggests that he is again looking in at the cozy little white houses. The intimate sentiment of New York, which Dos Passos has in spite of all the Sandburg-Millay romanticism of the big city permeating *Manhattan Transfer*, is not in Wolfe.

It is in the nature of his talent that he should see things from the outside only, and be forced always to guess what is inside them; his vision is the vision of the outsider; and this again is a part of the national neurosis out of which, I am arguing, his vision rises and which warps it. Thus the question naturally arises, after we have finished looking at his middle books, whether his view of Altamont is not the vision of an outsider also. Did this youth of sixteen ever read all the books Wolfe talks about, or are these the reading experiences of a mature man, garnered at the University of North Carolina and at Harvard and thrown back in memory to be associated with the wrong age? And did the still younger lad, delivering papers in Altamont's Niggertown, experience all its alien mystery then, or are these also the emotions of a later age thrown back upon adolescence? All these things in *Look Homeward, Angel* sound much more like a relatively older person, deep in his first work at the age of twenty-four, when he has left Altamont far behind him — as if they were a confused reconstruction of memories. No growing youth was ever quite so full of literature, never felt anything with quite such transcendent keenness, any more than the Gant-Pentland family was ever quite so monstrous as Wolfe makes it look. The reconstruction of the past is a notoriously tricky enterprise and Wolfe has been tricked in it.

Thus, to the earlier remark that the first person singular is not the appropriate pronoun for tragedy, we must add that the perfect is not the appropriate tense. Recollection of tragic events does not make tragedy. To get the full force of the tragic situation we need to feel contemporaneous with it; the author has to show the action as it takes place, not as it is rebuilt in retrospect. And so Wolfe's novels are not tragic, not only because they are so exclusively personal but because his attitude toward his material, with special respect to time, is not a tragic attitude. It is dominantly emotion recollected.

But not emotion recollected in tranquillity. Wolfe's poetry is not calmly and quietly intense; his main theme is the theme of being lost in America, and it is treated by a poet who is still lost. His perspective of America itself is out of joint: distances and spaces are magnified, a trip from New York to North Carolina becomes a journey "down the continent"; much of his America is an abstraction. He has some of the naturalistic pantheism, the feeling that man and the soil are intimately bound together in essence, which marks so much Western literature since Zola and which makes him sound occasionally like Jean Giono, just as he shows at times some of the enthusiasm for being American, if not for the faith democratic, of Walt Whitman. Now and again he reveals a feeling for, though not much knowledge of, the history of our people — the feeling that this land is something apart because the dust of his ancestors is mixed with its dust. But mostly his complaint is that these things do not mean more to him than they do, that he really has no place and "no door where he can enter," and that meanwhile he is being swept along by the stream of time. The answer to his eternal question is not the answer of Whitman and Crane and Paul Engle. The one thing that he can be sure of, the one door that must open for him, is death.

Wolfe is the writer of our century who has written most eloquently about death — the death of Grover, the death of Ben, of old Gant; and of the overwhelming imminence of death everywhere. As each individual submerges beneath the river of time, something of Wolfe himself is lost; each was a parcel of his consciousness. More surely than anything else the thought of death looses that remarkable flow of his language — the unearthly torrent of words which has always been the delight of some of his critics and the bane of the rest — and also the extraordinary resources of his rhetoric.

The rhetoric is essential. One reads much more about Wolfe's breadth of vocabulary and his obviously sensuous pleasure in words, and of what someone has called his multitudinous garrulity, than about the way he used his gift. He has the distinction of being the one writer of his generation who truly dared pull out all the stops. Dos Passos cannot compete with him in this respect, because Dos Passos' method of seeing and recording impressions calls for finding the perfectly right word, and the perfectly right word is obscured if associated with a half-dozen approximately right words; and besides, the completely successful word for Dos Passos needs the least possible rhetorical support: where each word stands completely for an impression the only real linkage needed is that of consciousness, proximity to the word which denotes the preceding impression in the series. Hemingway cannot compete because his instinctive emotional key, subdued and uneloquent, will not permit, and because his favorite characters are frequently talkative but rarely eloquent people.

Wolfe and his characters, on the other hand, have the native eloquence of an old-time political orator. He needs every resource of rhetorical structure to support the great weight of his enormous enumerations, which are as heavy as Dreiser's. It is extraordinary how often the rhetoric of his own sentences is identical with the drunken rhetoric which he puts in the sonorous mouth of the old man Gant, the great difference of course being that Gant has the rhetorical structure he needs, but not the words to go with it; whereas Wolfe has the words.

The hands had given to the interminable protraction of his living death a kind of concrete horror that it otherwise would not have had. For as his powerful gaunt figure waned and wasted under the ravages of the cancer that was consuming him until he had become only the enfeebled shadow of his former self, his gaunt hands, on which there was so little which death could consume, lost none of their former rock-like heaviness, strength and shapely power. Thus, even when the giant figure of the man had become nothing but a spectral remnant of itself, sunk in a sorrow of time, awaiting death, those great, still-living hands of power and strength hung incredibly, horribly, from that spectral form of death to which they were attached.

The words are here. And so also are most of the faults against which the manuals of English continually warn: prolixity, punning, cliché, repetitiousness and the rest. What saves it? It seems to me that in passages like this Wolfe skates determinedly around the edges of the hackneyed, rescuing himself each time through the presence of the particular word which redeems the rest and keeps the phrase from being irremediable cliché: in the first sentence "interminable protraction" saves the hackneyed "living death"; in the second, the appearance of the verb "waned" — entirely unexpected and acquiring from its context a meaning it never quite had before — stands in relation to the other verb, "wasted," as "enfeebled" stands to the rest of what would otherwise be the deadly cliché, "shadow of his former self." Such rhetorical repetitions as "spectral remnant," which picks up the earlier "shadow," and "spectral form" which in turn picks up "spectral remnant," are the sources of a freshness which is all the more perceptible because on analysis we are convinced that it comes from reviving what, except in the hands of Thomas Wolfe, would be entirely beyond hope of resuscitation.

All of this is related to Wolfe's habit of taking up some of the most familiar lines of the literary heritage and making them new and strange by the changing of a word or so: "It was unbelievable

that an old cancer-riddled spectre of a man should have so much
blood in him." I can remember offhand three separate places
where he plays variations on the old man with so much blood in
him. Despite our awareness that Wolfe abuses this device — as
for that matter he abuses, sooner or later, most other rhetorical
devices — its value to him is palpable. The essence of this we find
in Shakespeare himself, in such lines as

>   . . . the feet
> That fourteen hundred years ago were nailed
> For our advantage to the bitter cross

wherein a word like "bitter," common as dirt itself, of its own
strength lifts an ordinary prose discourse into poetry. Wolfe's
gift is of the same kind. The result is the sort of boldness which
allows him to get away with the obvious — note the repeated pun
on Gant's name in the passage above, and the association of "rock-
like heaviness" with the hands of a man who has always been a
stonecutter. This is the kind of eloquence that Wolfe brings to the
themes of time and of death, time's child.

It is impossible to read Wolfe and like him without becoming
something of an anthologist. And since each reader of Wolfe has
his own favorite selections, I am offering here at least one example
of his poetry of time:

> . . . it is not the slow, the punctual sanded drip of the unnumbered
> days that we remember best, the ash of time; nor is it the huge mono-
> tone of the lost years, the unswerving schedules of the lost life and the
> well-known faces, that we remember best. . .

This is the poetry of a theme on which John Dos Passos, with a
poet's discipline turned to his special uses, was writing the prose.

There is no point in denying that often Wolfe let go to print
much that should never have gone. Those of us who like him believe that there was a god in him, but a very unruly god who gave
him no peace and at times went away without warning, as people
sometimes go away and leave a radio with the switch turned on
playing in an empty tenement. He was an enthusiast who had,
as old Gant had, "a tragic consciousness of time," and of death.
Like the people in *Look Homeward, Angel* he was a fanatic, and

time and death were his obsessions. Consequently, in those moments when the god is absent he sounds like a hysterical woman
who insists on feeling unloved, while life slips away without anything really stable appearing amid the flow of existence — a
hysterical woman whose life is a great conspiracy to frustrate her.

Much that he wrote proves that the critics who were hell-
bent to show what really needed no demonstration, i.e., that he
did not know how to compose, were right, and is evidence of the
compulsive frenzy in which he wrote. It was often more important
to him to finish saying something and get on to saying something
else, than to take care for the nicety of the saying. Edward Aswell has done his best to dispel the legend that Wolfe never
rewrote, and other critics who have examined Wolfe's style closely
have found a change appearing in the later work; but there remains abundant proof he did not rewrite enough. Words obsess
him, and rhetoric sweeps him away. Such things as Francis Starwick's having a "rather womanish" voice almost *ad infinitum*, the
appearance of words like "octopal" in and out of acceptable context on so many occasions, the inability to stop ringing the changes
on lines like the one about the old man with all the blood in him,
the multiple repetitions of such an intuition as that Uncle Bascom's head is like Emerson's — and so on indefinitely — simply
mar his work. They also testify to the great truth of Wolfe's own
remark that at times when he wrote it felt as if a great black cloud
had discharged itself inside him. Wolfe knew his weakness; he
was haunted by the example of Flaubert, and grateful to Maxwell
Perkins for assuring him that it was not necessary to be "the
Flaubert kind of writer." He finally changed from Scribner to
Harper in order to prove to his detractors that he, and not Maxwell Perkins, was the one who put the books together. Our criticism of him will become more cogent as we give over arguing
about this incontrovertible weakness and go on to define, as precisely as we can, Wolfe's great strength.

A long time ago the French philosopher Diderot, busy with a
discussion on institutions among the savages of the South Seas,
paused a moment to remark how contrary to common sense it
seems, in a world where time is always at work and change is the

rule, to base marriage on the assumption that love is eternal. Years later his countryman, Musset, picked up the theme in a famous poem, *Le Souvenir*, in which he added a new ingredient: how sad and how poignant that the eternity of the love we swear is, of necessity, an illusion. The difference between the two points of view is probably the essential difference between the eighteenth century and the nineteenth; Diderot's reflection was prompted merely by the fact that he was having a certain amount of trouble with his wife — a situation which he managed somehow to take pretty much in stride — whereas Musset, frustrated in his various attempts to realize a completely satisfactory love, generalizes his predicament into an essential aspect of man's fate. This mood is Wolfe's, leaving out love or substituting for it the whole complex of man's emotions. It puts him in the tradition of Proust . . . and of Dos Passos, a very central and important tradition since it reflects in literature the great discovery of the relativity of all things which is our inheritance from the nineteenth century. But the tradition itself does not need to be eternal, and the feeling we have that after Proust and Dos Passos and Wolfe there was left, *circa* 1930, very little to be said about it, is probably the best indication we have that by that date the nineteenth century was over.

Wolfe's complex notions of time are apparent even to the casual reader. Many of the prose-poetic passages are extensive treatises on the problem. As the title of this essay indicates, Albrecht argues that the feeling of time provides an integration for the tetralogy. W. P. Albrecht, an associate professor of English at the University of New Mexico, has written criticism also on Shelley, Hazlitt, and Conrad Aiken. In the March 1950 issue of "Modern Language Notes" appeared a further Wolfe study, "The Titles of Look Homeward, Angel: A Story of the Buried Life."

TIME AS UNITY IN THOMAS WOLFE

by

W. P. Albrecht

Attempting a form to correspond with his perception of reality, the modern novelist frequently has abandoned the framework of time and space familiar in the nineteenth-century novel. As the novelist tries to convey his own sense of the passing and duration of time, he is likely to link moments of time not by succession but by the continuity of personality, feeling, or development. And, especially if clock or calendar time seems hostile to a desired permanence or security, the novelist may look for a time pattern, or metaphor, more compatible with his desires.

It is largely through his effort to find permanence in flux that the novels of Thomas Wolfe may be considered "modern" in their treatment of time. In Wolfe's novels time becomes a rushing, all-erosive river, which, nevertheless, may be arrested or turned back

From the *New Mexico Quarterly Review*, Autumn 1949. By permission of author and publisher.

by the memory. Like Proust, Wolfe seeks to recapture the past through memory, including unconscious memory, and to show the sensations and moods that recollections of the past evoke in the present. Or again, like Joyce in *Finnegans Wake*, he opposes a linear concept of time with a cyclical one, wherein the eternal is repeated through apparent change.

In Wolfe's novels, however, the recollection of the past is clearly labeled as such and is not, as in Joyce or Virginia Woolf, fused almost indistinguishably with the present. Of course some scenes, like the cross-sectioning of Altamont through glimpses of simultaneous actions, show the influence of *Ulysses*, but unlike Joyce, Wolfe almost always orients the reader in time and space. In itself, the cross-sectioning technique does not make these scenes any more clearly part of the recaptured past than the more traditionally handled scenes; it does not provide a solution to Wolfe's time problem.

Wolfe's metaphor of time, therefore, is not a refocusing that sharpens the meaning or relevance of past and present actions while blurring the usual co-ordinates of time and space. The kind of unity that such refocusing gives the action of *Ulysses*, for instance, is lacking in Wolfe's novels. Nevertheless, the feeling of time — of flux and permanence — unifies each of the completed novels and the four novels considered as one. This is clearly not the temporal logic of *A Farewell to Arms* or even a unity of character development as found in *Of Human Bondage* or *Portrait of the Artist as a Young Man*, but a relating of action to time through image, myth, and symbol.

Wolfe was concerned, first, with the individual and, later, with society in relation to time. His first problem was that of the individual seeking stability in an ever-flowing river of time. This problem he temporarily solved through creativeness, which in a sense recaptured Eugene's past, made Eugene aware of growth, and gave his life direction. But creativeness was not enough. Eugene still faced the problem of his relations with other people. Neither as a man nor as an artist, he discovers in *Of Time and the River*, could he really escape behind the wall of creative solitude that he was building in *Look Homeward, Angel*. His relations with other people once more involved the time problem: time stood in the way of the relationships he desired; it did not let him gain from people all the love, pleasure, knowledge, significance that he wanted. But Eugene and, even more definitely, George Webber discovered, partly through the creative process, that certain human experiences are typical of all human experiences, that identification with the archetypical could bring a man something of the stability he desired. George could never achieve a sustained love for any individual, but sympathy with and understanding of many people enabled him to feel, at the close of *The Web and the Rock*, that he belonged to the great family of earth, no longer isolated in time and space.

Yet neither Eugene nor George, in recapturing the past through creativeness or identifying himself with the buried life of all men, could make time stand still. The forms of life — plant, animal, social — die when they cease to grow. Only growth with time permits life. At the end of *Look Homeward, Angel* Eugene realizes that he can go home to the past only for the materials of his memory, not for his old ideas, his old loves, his old self. At the end of *You Can't Go Home Again* George knows that neither he nor the democracy of which he is a part can go home to its past, but can live only by flowing onward with the river of time.

In *Look Homeward, Angel*, to dramatize the individual lost and then found in relation to time, Wolfe uses the myth of preexistence-and-return, and with it the usual Platonic contrasts of dark and light, many and one, isolation and union, imprisonment and freedom, shadow and reality. The images of loss or transience are dark, and in relation to lost or passing time man is only a "ghost" or "phantom," a "stranger" isolated from others and even his own true self. "Memory" links Eugene with a better time — a time of security and certitude suggested by the "golden" abundance of Gant's Pennsylvania. (Similarly, in George Webber's memory the "warmth and radiance" of his father's North has been woven with the "darkness" of the Joyner's South.) But even while "imprisoned in the dark womb" of his mother, Eugene began to lose the "communications of eternity." Those better times, like any past time, are in themselves irrecoverable, and in his loss

Eugene becomes a "stranger" in the "insoluble prison of being," a "phantom" destined to wander homeless and friendless in a darkened world.

Lostness in relation to past time cannot, of course, be completely separated from lostness in relation to what Wolfe, in *The Story of a Novel,* calls "time immutable"; for it is the latter that sweeps away past, present, and future. In *Of Time and the River* and *The Web and the Rock* time immutable is symbolized by the river. The river of time suggests both transience and permanence. Time passes, and with it man's life. But time is also eternal in its flow, so that it becomes the immutable background for mutable life. In either sense it is usually dark, like the darkening or fading past, like the tragedy of man's strangeness and evanescence. It is a "dark eternal river" in which man is a "phantom flare of grieved desire."

In *Look Homeward, Angel,* and less completely in *Of Time and the River,* permanence in flux and reintegration with the past are achieved through the act of literary creation. Wolfe's creative experience is best described by Wolfe himself in *The Story of a Novel.* In Paris in the summer of 1930 he felt the "naked homelessness" that great cities always caused him, and in sheer effort to break the spell of time and distance that separated him from home, Wolfe's creative process began. Recalled by the image of some "familiar, common thing" in the past, "the million forms and substances" of Wolfe's life in America swarmed in "blazing pageantry" across his mind, issuing even from the "furthest adyt of his childhood before conscious memory had begun," yet transformed with the new wonder of discovery; and confronted by these blazing forms, Wolfe set himself the task of bringing them to life in a "final coherent union." In *The Story of a Novel* Wolfe explicitly names the "door" of his search as the door to creative power.

This process is dramatized in *Look Homeward, Angel.* Again the images of dark and light suggest *lostness in time* and *being found.* Along with his sense of time as a fading light, Eugene finds within himself a living pattern of certain experiences originally separate in time but fused by imagination beyond the dis-

tinctions of the time-space world, the "many" become "one."
". . . These images that burnt in him existed without beginning
or ending, without the essential structure of time." They have a
"white living brightness" compared with "the ghostliness of all
things else." It is among these living images that Ben, although
dead, takes his place, no longer a ghost, but bright and alive.
"And through the Square, unwoven from lost time, the fierce
bright horde of Ben spun in and out its deathless loom." A horde
of Eugenes, too, "which were not ghosts," troop past. "And
now the Square was thronging with their lost bright shapes, and
all the minutes of lost time collected and stood still."

Eugene has not only recovered Ben but found himself. The
symbols of "ghost" and "angel" suggest, respectively, a spirit lost
in death and a spirit secure in eternal life. In *Lycidas* the Angel
is asked to look nearer home and to have pity on the drifting
corpse of Lycidas. By analogy Ben's role in *Look Homeward,
Angel* would seem to be the angel's, while Eugene is Lycidas; but
throughout the novel Ben is also a ghost in that, like every person, he cannot be known even to his brother. In the last chapter he
is restored to a "life" that he did not have while alive; he is no
longer a ghost because no longer a stranger. At the same time he
is also an angel in the sense that he can now direct Eugene "home."
"*You* are your world," says Ben to Eugene, directing him to the
bright world of fused experience. Ben is not explicitly named
"angel," but the identification is further implied by the stone
angels' coming to life when Ben returns. In their marble deadness,
the angels in the shop stand for Gant's frustration as an artist.
But with Ben's return the angels come alive and with them
Eugene's creative power. The title, therefore, is appropriately
addressed to Eugene as well as Ben.

In "God's Lonely Man" Wolfe again describes his creative
process as breaking through the dark isolation of time to unite
the creator with a bright permanence. But even in his creativeness the lonely man is still lonely. In *Look Homeward, Angel*
Eugene has only exchanged one kind of loneliness for another:
the inescapable, involuntary loneliness of all humanity for the
voluntary loneliness of the creator. In *Of Time and the River* the

"spell of time," although it has recaptured the images of life in
America, becomes an "evil dream." Remembered human relationships are not an adequate substitute for actual human relationships. Time immutable, as well as past time, denies Eugene
and later George the complete and significant relationships they
are seeking. The people they want to know, like the books they
want to read and the women they want to love, are all too many
and the time too short.

Wolfe's solution of this problem is necessarily symbolical;
unable to know the plurality of experience, Eugene and George
must choose the representative singular, the symbol. This solution is implied by the subtitle of *Look Homeward, Angel*: *A Story
of the Buried Life.* The "buried life" of Matthew Arnold's poem
is the essential self wherein all men are one, brothers not strangers,
a self which is realized in moments of love which, in turn, make
man articulate and give his life direction. Again, as in the pre-
existence-and-return myth, there are the familiar opposites of the
many and the one, isolation and unity, false self and true self,
weakness and power. The ending of *Look Homeward, Angel*
stresses the articulateness and the direction rather than the unity
and the love, although the latter are implicit in the final interview with Ben. In *Of Time and the River* Eugene clearly recognizes, with pleasure, that the commonality of man's experience
resists the sorcery of time and space. Especially during those days
in Tours when the bright images of America rush back into his
consciousness, Eugene feels the similarity of all human experience everywhere and the consequent abridgement of the time and
space that separate him from home. Many a scene in the little
French towns seems to Eugene "intolerably near and familiar
. . . and something that he had always known." As he rediscovers
"the buried life, the fundamental structure of the great family of
earth to which all men belong," he is filled "with quiet certitude
and joy."

It is this archetypal quality that George feels deeply in the
experiences of the little unknown men in *You Can't Go Home
Again.* The face of his neighbor across the street, "immutable,
calm, impassive, . . . became for him the symbol of a kind of

permanence in the rush and sweep of chaos in the city. . . . That man's face became for him the face of Darkness and of Time. It never spoke, and yet it had a voice — a voice that seemed to have the whole earth in it." The man's face is a symbol of permanence in flux, but still dark in its suggestion of the pain and struggle that must precede a final peace. In the last two novels the frantic race with time gradually subsides as George realizes that to know a part of the earth well and to understand the life of that part is to know the whole earth. Through a sympathetic identification George, in *The Web and the Rock*, has come to love "life" and his "fellow men" and to feel at one with "the family of the earth."

The permanent and qualitative, therefore, may be found in the temporary and quantitative, for transient multiplicity reflects timeless uniformity. The repetition of the archetype through numberless forms is a cyclical concept of time inherent in the pre-existence-and-return myth and in the metaphor of the buried life. With the cycle of time Wolfe frequently unites the earth symbol, which usually suggests permanence. Earth's cycle of growth preserves for Eugene something of past time, for after Ben's death Eugene knows that Ben will "come again . . . in flower and leaf. . . ." Growth as the solution to the time problem is further suggested by the "self" to which Ben directs Eugene's search, a self of accumulated experience which has not simply been but which is always becoming. Eugene's and George's delight in train rides and Wolfe's frequent image of the train rushing through the night in time with time imply even in the earlier novels that synchronism was the magic needed to break the spell of time. It is to this conception of permanence in change — of growth with time and the repetition of eternal forms through growth — that Wolfe turns for his final solution of the problem of the individual and society in relation to time.

Like the other novels *You Can't Go Home Again* ends with a kind of soliloquy, but compared with the endings of the other novels, George's closing letter to Foxhall Edwards is a straightforward piece of exposition with less than usual of narrative, scene, image, or symbol. But the symbols of time still appear.

The river has its beneficent aspects; time as "Flow" has become definitely good. The earlier George, like Eugene, had tried to fix time or turn it back: to keep the past, to hoard up all experience within himself, to halt time until all space was his. Now George knows that "the essence of faith is the knowledge that all flows and that everything must change." Such immutability as man may attain is in growth.

This is the point at which, George discovers, he and Fox must part. Fox is Ecclesiastes. He believes that mankind is condemned to irremediable evils. But George believes that "man's life can be, and will be better" if "Men-Alive," although only the creatures of Now and not forever, take up the battle of truth against "fear, hatred, slavery, cruelty, poverty, and need. . . ." George finds his own life a symbol of the growth that synchronizes man with the river of time, giving him the stability of time. Fox is "the rock of life"; George is "the web." Fox is "Time's granite"; George is "Time's plant." Fox is "mankind"; George is "Man-Alive." George is not denying Fox's kind of stability, but he is claiming validity for his own kind. "You and the Preacher may be right for all eternity, but we Men-Alive, dear Fox, are right for now."

Wolfe never abandons the river symbol — in fact, it occurs in the closing sentence of *You Can't Go Home Again* and on the last page of Wolfe's last and uncompleted novel, *The Hills Beyond* — but the circular rather than the linear concept of time gains in emphasis. Like Fox, George reflects some of the wisdom of Ecclesiastes: ". . . Unto the place from whence the rivers come, thither they return again." In his letter to Fox, George's life has become a "circle," which George feels he has now rounded out. His "whole experience" has swung round, "as though through a predestined orbit. . . ." As the earth, the symbol of permanence, manifests its life in the cycle of growth, so has George made his life a symbol of permanence. He had to work himself out of the "giant web" of the past, but with the "plant" of this recollective-ness finally "unearthed," the "circle" of George's life has finally "come full swing. . . ." This comparison of his cycle of creative-ness with the earth's cycle of creation suggests the organic vitality of his accomplishment — "complete and whole, compacted of the very earth that had produced it, and of which it was itself the last and living part" — and the resulting sense of integration with the earth.

The ultimate resolution is not, however, in George's creativeness as a novelist. The themes of fraternity and movement with time are combined to resolve the problem of society. Like the individual, society must grow with time. To realize the brotherhood of man society must let its old forms die and create new ones. His visit to Hitler's Germany has shown George that the disease of Nazism is a virulent form of the disease that has struck America. America is lost, and only through growth may she find herself. ". . . The enemy is single selfishness and compulsive greed," and only through a change in the structure of society may the enemy be defeated.

I think that the life which we have fashioned in America . . . was self-destructive in its nature, and must be destroyed. I think these forms are dying and must die, just as I know that America and the people in it are deathless, undiscovered, and immortal, and must live.

The brotherhood of man, like the life-principle in nature, reveals its vitality in a succession of ever-changing forms.

Whether this pattern of man in relation to time is always adequately dramatized in character and action is, of course, an important question but one outside the scope of this article. The purpose here has been simply to analyze the time problem and to define the unity suggested by Wolfe's metaphors of time.

The unity of each novel, and of the four novels as one, is clarified by the opposition of the linear and the cyclical concepts of time. These two metaphors parallel each other throughout the four novels, the first representing the problem and the second its solution. The linear concept (that what passes is gone forever) is dominant in *Look Homeward, Angel*, *Of Time and the River*, and *The Web and the Rock*. In *Look Homeward, Angel*, however, it is combined with the pre-existence myth; pre-existence in bright, permanent unity and descent to a dark, transitory isolation. The return to brightness, permanence, and unity, which historically is implied in the pre-existence myth, is suggested only at the end of *Look Homeward, Angel* by Ben's return in "flower and leaf" and more definitely by Eugene's creative memory and, through it, his integration with the past. Likewise, in *Of Time and the River* and *The Web and the Rock*, the river symbol is opposed by the recurrent representations of the buried life, although, despite the ending of *The Web and the Rock*, the emphasis in both novels is on flux, and the dark images of transience and isolation are dominant. Finally, in *You Can't Go Home Again*, the cyclical concept solves the problem of both the individual and society in relation to time. To suggest the apparent evanescence and disunity of man's life, the images of darkness persist, but the now-beneficent river, the fecund earth, and the cycle of growth emphasize man's permanence and men's organic unity.

Wolfe's preoccupation with time is expounded here not by the critic but by the scholar. By the presentation of numerous quoted passages from Wolfe's four major novels, the scholar concludes that the books "echo the voice of time." Throughout the essay, Wolfe's treatment of the time element is contrasted and compared with that of Marcel Proust, whose concern with time is one of the most celebrated in contemporary literature. Margaret Church, of the English staff of Duke University, among other articles has written "Thomas Mann: Time" in the Spring 1950 "Johns Hopkins Review."

DARK TIME

by

Margaret Church

And time still passing . . . passing like a leaf . . . time passing, fading like a flower . . . time passing like a river flowing . . . time passing . . . and remembered suddenly, like the forgotten hoof and wheel. . . . — *The Hills Beyond*, p. 348.

In two passages of his recent book on *Thomas Wolfe* (1947), Herbert J. Muller has briefly, but incisively, dealt with the time concepts of Wolfe and Proust. He points out that while both writers depended upon sensory impressions to recall the past, Wolfe lacked the keen subjective analysis of Proust and stayed closer to the actual experience that produced his memories. Wolfe's interest was in fixity and change as they are in real life, while Proust "aspired to the realm of Essence or Being, where change is mere appearance" (p. 75). It is important, I believe, that these distinctions be made, for Wolfe, unlike Proust, was no

From *PMLA*, September 1949. By permission of the author.

philosopher and would without question have been confused by an array of Bergsonian metaphysics. While outwardly the time concepts of Wolfe and of Proust seem somewhat alike, a closer examination reveals that these concepts are in many respects different. But no distinctions were made, for instance, by Mary M. Colum in her article on "Literature of Today and Tomorrow" (*Scribner's*, Dec. 1936, p. 102), which stated that Wolfe's work might well be described as "Remembrance of Things Past" — that "like Proust he tells us of his struggles with Time elements." And Joseph Warren Beach, in *American Fiction 1920–1940* (1941), while acknowledging that Wolfe could not have accepted fully the implications of Proust's theories, found that Wolfe and Proust had had a common psychological experience. "It is found in the recall by means of present sensations or impressions of closely similar impressions received in extreme youth" (p. 192).

I intend, therefore, in this article to present a discussion of time concepts in Thomas Wolfe's work, to deduce if possible their exact quality, and to show how they differed from the Proust-Bergson concepts but at the same time had many points in common with them. For purposes of convenience and clarity I present Wolfe's time concepts in a much more orderly fashion than that in which they occur in his works. It should not be inferred from this essay, therefore, that Wolfe consciously worked out a philosophy of time which he then expounded in his novels. His references to time are haphazard and often mere clichés which he uses again and again because of his partially subconscious obsession with the time idea.

"The Story of a Novel" (*Sat. Rev. of Lit.*, Dec. 21, 1935) is Wolfe's manifesto of his literary creed and his tale of his experiences with writing. In it he mentions the quality of his memory which like Proust's could "bring back the odors, sounds, colors, shapes, and feel of things with concrete vividness." For instance, as he would be sitting in the Avenue de l'Opera and watching the people move past, suddenly he would remember the railing at Atlantic City. "I could see it instantly just the way it was, the heavy iron pipe; its raw, galvanized look; the way the joints were fitted together." The exact dimensions, an entire scene, would thus return through a certain street, the sound of a train whistle, the sight of muddy banks or a particular bridge. And so, Wolfe continues, he wished to find words for this experience with memory, to write words so vividly that the past would be re-animated for the reader. But these assertions contain nothing of Proust's metaphysical theories that the past exists; they simply state that Wolfe vividly recalled the past.

In a later passage Wolfe says that in the embryonic form of his book there would be a section entitled "Where Now?" in which he would record all the lost moments of the past, "the flicks and darts and haunting lights that flash across the mind of man." These flashes of the memory would concern more than man's immediate past, for they would go back into "the farthest adyt of his childhood before conscious memory had begun." Often, Wolfe continues, these flashes seem of no consequence, but they live with us longer than apparently more important events. This kind of memory brings unity to life and human experience. These flicks and darts of the past are like Proust's glimpses into lost eras; in fact they are caused by the same kind of sense impression which caused Proust's. It is difficult to point out any great difference here between Proust and Wolfe, for although Wolfe had no abstract concept of Bergsonian metaphysics, he actually put into practice much the same system of recall that Proust used. The difference is that Wolfe did not write pages explaining his metaphysical solutions of the time question; he applied them. For as J. P. Bishop notes (*Kenyon Review*, Winter 1939, p. 8), "He could . . . displace the present so completely by the past that its sights and sounds all but destroyed surrounding circumstances. He then lost the sense of time." For an example Bishop cites the scene on the terrace in Paris where Eugene recalls about all America, his early life, his parents. In him all experience existed.

In "The Story of a Novel" Wolfe goes on to explain his experience with *Of Time and the River*, where he found time elements baffling. There were three elements: present time; past time, which showed people "as acting and as being acted upon by all the accumulated impact of man's experience"; and time immutable, "the time of rivers, mountains, oceans, and the earth; a kind of eternal and unchanging universe of time against which would be projected the transience of man's life, the bitter briefness of his day." Thus simply he explains his time concepts. His definition of a past where everything experienced up to the present influences man explains his interest in memory and the recall of certain scenes. For, as he wrote the novel, the two and a half years it actually took extended into centuries. Experience built upon experience as black and bottomless as the ocean depths "which no ordinary scale of hours would ever measure."

Look Homeward, Angel contains several passages worth noting in a discussion of time. Early in the book Wolfe mentions a theme which is to stand behind the entire tetralogy. His urge to return to the past through actual experience with it, not through second-hand information, is closely connected with his acute realization of the past which exists in each one of us and which needs only night or nakedness to reveal it. Each of us, he cries, is the sum of many things we have not known or counted. Look behind the screen of the present, return to the darkness of the womb, to night, "and you shall see begin in Crete four thousand years ago the love that ended yesterday in Texas." At first glance one recognizes Bergson in this passage, but it is Bergson modified by Wolfe's earthiness. Wolfe's emphasis is on the individual as a result of the generations that preceded and framed him. He says that if you could really examine your love affair ended yesterday in Texas, you could see elements it had in common with one begun in Crete four thousand years ago by a remote ancestor. Bergson, on the other hand, would have said these two love affairs exist simultaneously; Texas and ancient Crete exist simultaneously; all matter has a fourth dimension which is its existence. These are statements quite different from Wolfe's simple assertion that one's hereditary past helps to make the present.

Further on in *Look Homeward, Angel* (p. 192) Eugene reflects on the vision of a passing scene while riding on a train, the train that for Wolfe from boyhood denoted freedom from mountain fastness, the train where alone he felt the security that fixity never gave to him, yet whose whistle sounding in the reaches of the night filled him with longing and terror. "And it was this that awed him — the weird combination of fixity and change." As he passed a town, a slattern standing in a doorway, both seemed suspended or frozen in time. For within him these images were fixed, motionless "without the essential structure of time. Fixed in no-time, the slattern vanished, fixed, without a moment of transition." This passage is nearer Bergson than the preceding one, for here Wolfe states that an instant, captured, although vanished in space, remains in time or "no-time" which is something like Bergson's *durée*. The difference is that Wolfe fixes his moment through the mind, the individual's consciousness, while Bergson says it is the nature of matter itself to have these properties of fixity and change. All matter exists simultaneously, but it is we who make it appear to change. At certain times it is possible, according to Bergson, to achieve a consciousness of his *durée*, at a moment like that of Proust's when the hero tasted the madeleine. But Wolfe's moment with the slattern and Proust's with the madeleine differ in that Wolfe simply makes the immediate past continually present in his mind while Proust makes two moments simultaneous in the sense of *experiencing* both at once. The incident in Proust leads further to long subjective analyses of the experience of which Wolfe was entirely incapable. With no intention of subtlety Wolfe was merely restating that the "mind is its own place" and yet the captured instant of Wolfe is fixed in "no-time."

Thomas Wolfe's two scenes in the square of Altamont, where time is suspended, can serve to continue the comparison of Wolfean and Bergsonian time techniques. In the first one, Gant standing on his porch looking over the square suddenly feels as if all action were arrested. Fagg Sluder, a policeman, the firemen, a farmer, Yancey stop simultaneously their activities. The fountain, which plays in the center of the square, is suspended. And Gant feels as if he were looking at a photograph of himself taken years earlier and as if he alone were moving toward death in this world of shadows of reality.

In contrast to this scene there is the one at the end of *Look Homeward, Angel* when Eugene meets the ghost of Ben in the square. In this scene (p. 623) "the fountain pulsed with a steady breezeless jet." Here time is in a way the duration of Bergson, for (to use Zeno's arrow) there is change of position but there is no arrow. In the square this night "all the minutes of lost time collected and stood still," lost shapes, lost events, lost meetings; all the life of the square existed simultaneously during these moments with Ben. But in the scene where time is suspended for Gant the present is merely arrested momentarily so that it seems like the past to the observer of the scene. Wolfe differs from Bergson and Proust in that they would have said Gant lived in the present and past at once; he did not *seem* to experience them simultaneously. To Proust the past was never like a photograph, for he could smell it, taste it, even see it in four dimensions.

But the description of Eugene's meeting with Ben seems the purest Bergsonian philosophy in this book. Eugene sees fabulous cities, Thebes, the temples of Daulian and Phocian lands. He sees all the life and death of all time. Nevertheless, once again it must be noted that Eugene is here the observer, not the taster of madeleine and lime juice. Furthermore, Proust never returned to Phocis or Daulis, but merely to points of his own personal past. Wolfe's scene is fantasy based on a conception of the simultaneous occurrence of events in a ghostly land. But has not eternity always been timeless? And Ben was in the land of the dead to which he transported Eugene until the cock crew and the stone angels in Gant's shop became frozen once more and Ben faded away.

In *Of Time and the River* Wolfe presents more fully than in his first book his concepts of time. It is, as the title indicates, a kind of time-epic. Wolfe's main preoccupation with time concerns, of course, its fleetingness, its grandeur, its pathos — "the immense and murmurous" sound of time which rises over great railroad sheds or over huge cities (p. 136). But he was sometimes concerned with the nature of time and its properties. Passages which inquire into its nature are more frequent in this second novel than in the others. At the opening of the book Wolfe thinks, for instance, of the relative qualities of space and time on his trip between Asheville and New York. The distance, he says, is more than seven hundred miles. "But so relative are the qualities of space and time, . . . that in the brief passage of this journey one may live a life."

Again in the train the present fades and, as he fingers the watch which Ben had given him, the image of Ben appears and the scene changes to his twelfth birthday when he had received the watch from his brother. He wonders what time is. The watch is to keep time with. "What is this dream of time, this strange and bitter miracle of living?" This scene with the watch (p. 52) is reminiscent of Proust. Here the watch instead of the madeleine recalls the past into the present and fuses them into one timeless instant. And once again on the train present and past time fuse when he thinks of his life with his father. Suddenly the thousand images of his father become as "one terrific image." But in contrast to the preceding scene with the watch, there is no key, no magic word with which to unlock the past. Only in his memory does time become a unit, not in his experience as with the watch.

But it must not be forgotten that Eugene Gant and, consequently, Wolfe were persistently searching for a key which would admit them into the past. Through the memories and tales of his mother Eugene comes closer to the actual past than he is able to come by other means. When he meets Bascom Pentland in Boston he thinks that his uncle will reanimate for him all the scenes and faces of old about which he wanted to know. But Bascom could not do this; he had somehow lost the key and was unable to give Eugene a feeling of the reality of his past life. This intense desire on Wolfe's part to reanimate things lost and dead is probably closely connected with his search for a father or an antecedent. And it is ironical that it is his mother who most nearly fulfills his desire with her stories of the Pentland tribe. Yet recall that his seekings into past time almost exclusively concern men, Ben, his father, the Joyner brothers, "The Four Lost Men," Garfield, Arthur, Harrison, Hayes. "Who had heard the casual and familiar tones of Chester Arthur?" he asks in *From Death to Morning* (p. 121). This familiar and exact quality of the living was what

Wolfe sought to capture in much the same way that Proust desired to, but Proust succeeded better, for Wolfe never ceased to feel that the past was irrevocably lost. Change was but appearance to Proust, while to Wolfe it was a bitter fact of existence, separating him from all life.

Loneliness was another condition which often made Eugene see time in unusual perspective. At Harvard and later in Tours there were times when he would spend days or weeks by himself without seeing a face he knew. These days were like dreams and during them weeks seemed like a single day, and then he would awake and find time once more in normal perspective.

His childhood recurred frequently during these years: "A voice half-heard, a word far-spoken, a leaf, a light that came and passed and came again. But always when that lost world would come back, it came at once, like a sword thrust through the entrails, in all its panoply of past time, living, whole, and magic as it had always been." This description of the return of the past (p. 200) reminds one of Proust's description of recalling bygone days. In fact, it becomes increasingly clear as we further examine *Of Time and the River* that Wolfe had heard of and probably read Proust. And although Wolfe did not grasp Proust's full meanings or aspire to the "realm of Essence," he tried to incorporate into this book some of the aspects of time that he understood in Proust.

That he had become curious about the whole matter of time and of its nature is apparent in the excerpt from his notebook which he included near the end of the novel. He believes that his query about the nature of time has been finally answered after a visit to the American Library in Paris where he reads the *Americana* and William James. Here he discovers, however, the theory of relativity: "the time-units of both time and space are neither points nor moments, but moments in the history of a point." The significance of the title of the book becomes clearer if we examine this statement (pp. 670–671) in the light of certain passages. He speaks, for instance (p. 510), of "the moving tide of time as it flows down the river." Again and again the river and time are connected, especially in the scenes in which he travels up the Hudson to meet Joel. Time, for Wolfe, is an unchangeable, unalterable thing, like a river, but paradoxically it always changes. Bergson's *durée* would represent the river of Wolfe. Its change or flow would be Bergson's space. Because we are in the river and not on the bank, we cannot see the true nature of time.

Now in the passage quoted above on the theory of relativity, "moments in the history of a point" would apply to either time or the river. Time-units and the waters of the river are only the superficial make-up of a larger reality. Bergson and other theorists on relativity put the emphasis on the larger unit while the rest of us swimming or sinking in the river and time worry about the waves and income taxes. Wolfe at least implies then that his book is to deal with time in both its aspects, fixity and change. The fixity of change constantly impresses Eugene, the stillness of the macrocosm and the disturbing fluctuation of the microcosm. Life, he says (p. 245), is "like a river, and as fixed, unutterable in unceasing movement and in changeless change as the great river is, and time itself." The earth, sweeping past a train on which he rides, has this same quality of "unchanging changefulness," but time is "as fixed and everlasting as eternity." And for Abe's mother seven thousand years, "yesterday, tomorrow, and forever [are but] a moment at the heart of love and memory" (p. 492).

In Book VII, "Kronos and Rhea: The Dream of Time," Wolfe invokes the past by means of music as Swann does in Proust. "Play us a tune on an unbroken spinet" is Wolfe's thematic sentence (p. 853). And through this tune of the spinet he recalls Athens as it actually was, people in the Middle Ages, their casual words, the trains in Baltimore in 1853. The difference between Wolfe and Proust here is that Wolfe wishes to reproduce all time, for a recurrent dream while he is in France would take Eugene back to the days of Homer, while Proust was interested only in his own segment of it.

Finally, as the sexton rings the church bell in Dijon, sounds of another bell come to Eugene. He is once more ringing the college bell "and now the memory of that old bell, with all its host of long-forgotten things, swarmed back with living and intolerable pungency." This (p. 896) seems like an illustration of

Proust's assertion that the past is hidden in some material object. The difference is that Proust would say the college bell was still there, that he had unconsciously been carrying its sound with him, for time only served to obscure the true perspective in which things stand, while Wolfe meant that one bell reminded him of another, although his actual experience may not have been unlike Proust's.

For as he watches the scene in Dijon the lonely sounds of his native Catawba awaken in him, and there in the square in the French village he sees the square of his own town, Altamont, hears his father slam their iron gate, feels "the magic of full June," smells turnip greens, and hears the slamming of screen doors. The life of twenty years past is thus recalled to him, but it is *recalled* and not *recaptured*. Wolfe understood at least the outward aspect of Proust, but he either did not understand or was not interested in his metaphysics. Never does Wolfe make an attempt to explain at length a metaphysics of time as Proust does. He is content with its mystery, "the mystery of strange, million-visaged time that haunts us with the briefness of our days" (p. 899).

In *The Web and the Rock* and *You Can't Go Home Again* Wolfe treats the subject of time much less fully than in his second novel. Nevertheless several passages in *The Web and the Rock*, which are worth mentioning here, repeat or further develop Wolfe's thoughts on time. Aunt Maw is, of course, substituted for Eliza, and it is through her that George hears "lost voices in the mountains long ago" (p. 8). But George laments Aunt Maw's callousness, for he says she cannot know "the eternity of living in a moment" (p. 24) or the swift flash of change. The old problems of fixity and change and the desire to recall lost voices continue to haunt Wolfe. For Aunt Maw's words bring to George the voices of his Joyner ancestors, the smell of pine blaze, but somehow, like Uncle Bascom's words, they fail actually to recreate the past.

During his trip to Richmond to see the football game Monk takes part in events that happened during the Civil War. He hears Grant and his soldiers fighting their way into Richmond; he knows that Lee is digging in at Petersburg, that Lincoln is waiting to hear the news, that Jubal Early "was swinging in his saddle at the suburbs of Washington" (p. 153). But Monk and his friends did more than just imagine these events, for "they felt, they knew, they had their living hands and hearts upon the living presence of these things" (p. 183). Thus Richmond reanimates for Wolfe a past era; he sees no ghostly procession of historical events but rather the living images of them. Like the memories of his childhood, these memories become "living, whole, and magic." But in Wolfe no matter how live memories become they are still memories and images, not actual events. The difference between Proust and Wolfe is, however, often very slight, for the question of exactly how complete is Wolfe's recovery of the past is unanswerable in many cases.

Wolfe recognized the immobility of time, its immeasurableness, its relativity. For he describes an estuary of the sea as "motionless as time"; the fight between Firpo and Dempsey lasts a three minutes which seem like hours; men measure immeasurable time by arbitrary symbols, they even measure the timeless sea; and "every man on earth held in the little tenement of his flesh and spirit the whole ocean of human life and time" (p. 262). Then suddenly a sound, an odor, a city square will bring to him the "streets of noon some dozen years ago" (p. 276), the shuffle of leather on the pavements, the shouts of children, the smell of turnip greens, the slamming of screen doors. And constantly he cries out that he may find the lost eras of time, knowing his wish impossible of accomplishment, for man is but "that little, glittering candle-end of dateless time who tries to give a purpose to eternity" (p. 299).

Even Esther fits into his schemes for recovering the past, for in his manhood it is Esther, and not Eliza or Aunt Maw, who regales him with tales of bygone days. It is Esther who gives him "a blazing vision of lost time," Esther who makes "ghosts of forgotten hours" move about her (p. 367). As she talks, all life awakens for Monk, all the lost and secret recesses of the past are opened, and she brings her living warmth and presentness to reanimate lost faces, her father's world of the theater, her first party. "She was like time," Monk says, for she could give the feeling of distance and memory to events that had occurred only an hour before. But sometimes during her descriptions of her childhood days he would think that there was no way actually to bring back even a few seconds of her lost eras. Always he is haunted by past moments, by a devouring curiosity which makes him go to any lengths to secure a peep hole through which he can view bygone days. For the time of each man is different; there is the time of great bells in a tower, the time of a tiny wrist watch, the time of each human being. And the "dark rich river [is] full of strange time, dark time, strange tragic time" (p. 427).

That spring in New York with Esther and the new novel he is writing, he feels that both mistress and novel make "the past as real as the present." He is living "the events of twenty years ago with as much intensity and as great a sense of actuality as if they had just occurred" (p. 541). There is no *now* and no *then*, for George feels unity with the larger purposes of time and destiny. And as he looks at the green tree which stands outside his window, he feels as if it had the magic qualities which had unlocked the past. Like the madeleine for Proust, the green tree is the key which admits Wolfe into lost days. Wolfe comes very close to Proust here, for in this passage change is mere appearance to Wolfe; and the green tree, like the madeleine, unlocks memories which the author is to record in a book. But still this process of recall is not the central theme of Wolfe's tetralogy, though an important coulisse of the central theme, his past. For Wolfe never tires of repeating that each man has his own time, that there is the time of clocks, of mountains, of rivers, of individual man, for time has ten thousand faces and yet is a fable, a mystery.

In the last section of *The Web and the Rock* the hero flees to Paris. I say *hero* here purposely, for by the end of Wolfe's third book one knows that Eugene and George have become Eugene-George. For example, in Paris George feels "that he has been here before," and he immerses himself in the "fixed and living eternity of the earth" (p. 631). Eugene-George came to stand, I believe, in

Wolfe's mind as a symbol, the kind of symbol that Thomas Mann's Joseph was. Mann uses Joseph as a figure who represents many, who is not sure even of his own identity, and Wolfe eventually sees his hero as the summation of all young men's experience and especially of the experience of the creative artist of the 1920's. For the episode in the French town of *Of Time and the River* is repeated in *The Web and the Rock*. Instead of the bell, here the laughter of a woman recalls to him a scene from his childhood in Old Catawba, the sound of a distant train, the sleeping streets, and the start of a motor. Furthermore, Proust's main character was never named, and like Joseph was the timeless hero of timeless tales. For mortal time is clock time, George knows, as he lies in a German hospital and listens to a clock strike "with a solemn and final sweetness" (p. 674).

From *You Can't Go Home Again* it is necessary to mention here only one incident, a scene from the party at the Jacks'. The description of the arrival of the guests reminds one of Proust's description of the party at the Guermantes, while George, like Proust's hero, stands broodingly in the background observing and commenting. And as George looks at a portrait of Mrs. Jack as a young girl, the mystery of time passes over him. It seems to him that 1901, when the portrait was painted, was centuries ago. "Yes, he had lived and died through so many births and deaths . . . that . . . the sense of time had been wiped out" (p. 48). Those years had become a "timeless dream." For had they not been Thracian captives together? Had she not launched the ship? And had she not (p. 253) "come to charm remission from the lord of Macedon"? And now she had stepped out of these former selves and stood before him. The portrait here is the means of momentarily freeing George from the present. He travels far, into the days of Thrace and Macedon, and all time is for him vivid and immediate. Esther represents here the eternal beautiful woman, and George is the symbol of her everlasting admirer.

Thus the four novels of Wolfe's tetralogy echo the voice of time. Like the great railroad sheds, they harbor its sound. For Wolfe was secure only when he was in motion and never so sure of himself as when he was on a moving train. His books came from the huge railroad stations of his mind where "the voice of time remained aloof and imperturbed, a drowsy and eternal murmur," and where the train whistle "evoked for him a million images: old songs, old faces and forgotten memories." Involved with Proustian metaphysics Wolfe was not, but as the taster of life and time his experience was much the same as Proust's. And for both of them the sudden and vivid resurrection of the lost moment, through a present sensory impression, was the central time-experience: "time passing . . . and remembered suddenly, like the forgotten hoof and wheel."

In spite of the fact that Proustian analogies have received con-
siderable attention from commentators, Wolfe's avowed admis-
sion to the influence of Joyce was the most significant admission
he made. More than a mere comparison of the two novelists,
this essay has a discussion of Wolfe's "motifs" and of the trans-
formation in the last two major novels. Nathan Rothman,
teacher of English in the Richmond Hill High School in New
York City, is completing a book on Joyce's influence in American
writing, of which this is a chapter.

THOMAS WOLFE AND JAMES JOYCE:
A STUDY IN LITERARY INFLUENCE

by

Nathan L. Rothman

If Stephen Dedalus were eight inches taller, and if he shouted
his pride and his hungers instead of letting them gnaw at him
under his Spartan cloak, he would be twin to Eugene Gant, who
is Thomas Wolfe as surely as Dedalus is Joyce. The differences
are less significant than the likeness; they rise out of the differences in the two writers, physical, hereditary, and environmental:
Joyce, the proud, bitter, introvert, disciplined Irishman, and
Wolfe, the lusty, free-spirited, uncontrolled man of vigorous
Carolina and Pennsylvania stock. Yet at the roots of their minds
they are the same. Inside the large, turbulent frame of Eugene
Gant there is the secret, scathing spirit of Stephen.

Disillusion had come so often that it had awakened in him a strain of
bitter suspicion, an occasional mockery, virulent, coarse, cruel, and

From *A Southern Vanguard*, edited by Allen Tate, copyright 1947 by Prentice-
Hall, Inc. By permission of the author and publisher.

subtle, which was all the more scalding because of his own pain. Un-
knowingly, he had begun to build up in himself a vast mythology for
which he cared all the more deeply because he realized its untruth.
Brokenly, obscurely, he was beginning to feel that it was not truth that
men must live for — the creative men — but for falsehood. At times
his devouring, unsated brain seemed to be beyond his governance: it
was a frightful bird whose beak was in his heart, whose talons tore un-
ceasingly at his bowels. And this unsleeping demon wheeled, plunged,
revolved about an object, returning suddenly, after it had flown away,
with victorious malice, leaving stripped, mean, and common all that
he had clothed with wonder.

Is this not Stephen? It is a description of Eugene Gant, in Wolfe's
first novel, *Look Homeward, Angel.* The suspicion, the subtle
mockery, the secret mythology, the unsated brain, the stripping
of joy and wonder — this is a strange transplanting of that bitter
Lokian spirit in the body of one who might well have glowed
with the whole, majestic soul of Jove. From the first that kinship
was recognized; Wolfe served a glad apprenticeship. Most
marked of the books upon his desk was a copy of *Ulysses,* and
we find the following in one of the diary entries of young Eugene:

I was born in 1900 — I am now 24 years old. During that period I
think the best writing in English had been done by James Joyce in
Ulysses. . . .

Later, in a little book he wrote about the creative process that
went into the making of his first two novels, he said,

Like every young man, I was strongly under the influence of writers
I admired. One of the chief writers at that time was Mr. James Joyce
with his book *Ulysses.* The book that I was writing was much influenced, I believe, by his own book, and yet the powerful energy and
fire of my own youth played over and, I think, possessed it all.

His books, of course, make all such explicit citation of influence
unnecessary; I have quoted them to indicate not the influence
but Wolfe's conscious recognition of it, his conscious embracing
of the greatest literary influence of his time, for as long as he
needed it. I think the latter part of his statement just above is
quite true and worth noting at every step of his work. The fire
of his own youth — and I will say of his own genius — possessed

his work throughout. He was never swallowed up by Joyce. He was too conscious of his own strength, of the materials that sprang from his, not Joyce's, life, of the American voice that flowed through him, the inheritor of Whitman as well as of Joyce. Wolfe used all of Joyce that he could, and some elements of Joyce's that no one else had attempted or perhaps understood; yet Wolfe remained always free of purely derivative writing, always indigenous, personal, creative.

The appearance of that first novel in 1929 was a remarkable phenomenon, to be compared, I think, with the appearance in 1855 of *Leaves of Grass*. (I shall have something to say later of Wolfe and Whitman.) It should be remembered that Wolfe's work is not to be regarded as a piecemeal product, as a series of separate and successive volumes, like other men's. That is the way his books were published, of course, but that is not the way they were conceived. It is well known by now that Wolfe planned, from the very beginning, a gigantic autobiographic work of at least six volumes, of which the titles and approximate time-periods had already been chosen. In the writing he regarded them as a unit. He never planned one book, with a start, plot-curve, finish, but he wrote out of his experiences and passions large blocks of prose that were sustained upon a tireless, ecstatic level of inspiration, thousands of words, hundreds of pages, many of them among the best in our literature, torn out of a feverish creative consciousness. The duty of shaping devolved upon his publishers and editors, in whom Wolfe was very fortunate throughout. *Look Homeward, Angel* was not only the first of his novels to be published, but also in many ways the most unified, the most solidly shaped. For both of these reasons, and because it was the first revelation of a great talent, it is still regarded by most readers as their favorite among Wolfe's books. It came to them as no ordinary first novel, neither tentative nor unformed. It appeared to spring fully grown from the mind of a conscious artist. It was as rich, fine, sure, as though he had written it after a long apprenticeship. Dos Passos and Faulkner had to push forward, to their best work, through a period of uncertainty and in some ways downright incompetence; Wolfe began his novels at the peak of power and never left it. The effort cost him a great deal, as we know. He had to do it that way; he was wholly possessed by that literary conscience which flays the pupils as it did their master, Joyce.

The themes of Joyce are everywhere in Wolfe, from *Look Homeward, Angel* straight through. Viewing Wolfe's books as one body of work, one odyssey of Eugene Gant, we will do well to trace the themes through the volumes wherever they lead. We note the smaller indications first, the Ulyssean signatures such as Wolfe's phrase about Oliver Gant's "hot lion-breath of desire," recalling Joyce's phrase, "lion reek of all male brutes." There are many of the Joycean inversions, such as this: "Twittered with young bird-laughter, on bank and saddle sprawled, all of the Bard's personae," or this very familiar image which seems to come directly out of the consciousness of Leopold Bloom: "Smiling with imperturbable tenderness Mrs. Selborne thrust out her heavy legs slowly to swell with warm ripe smack his gift of flowered green-silk garters." And how startling and stirring it is to come once more upon "Brightness falls from the air," which we remember in both *A Portrait of the Artist as a Young Man* and *Ulysses*, or upon such a fragment of Dedalus-like musing as this:

King Solomon's mines. She. Proserpine. Ali Baba. Orpheus and Eurydice. Naked come I from my mother's womb. Naked shall I return. Let the mothering womb of earth engulf me. Naked, a valiant wisp of man, in vast brown limbs engulfed.

More significant are the larger forms and ideas of Joyce, all here and some of them reappearing for the first time. The stream of consciousness appears throughout in many guises. Its simplest form is most derivative, the associative stream darting from object to object, idea to idea. The best illustration of this comes early in *Look Homeward, Angel,* as we follow the thoughts of Oliver Gant, Eugene's father, returning home. He has just been told of the death of an old acquaintance:

In the prime of life, thought Gant. Myself like that some day. No, for others. Mother almost eighty-six. Eats like a horse, Augusta wrote.

Must send her twenty dollars. Now in the cold clay, frozen. Keep till Spring. Rain, rot, ruin. Who got the job? Brock or Saul Gudge. Bread out of my mouth. Do me to death — the stranger —

This will do very well to represent the many such passages devoted to Oliver Gant. Two observations need to be made about them. First, these Bloom-ish musings give but one small and far from inclusive aspect of Oliver Gant, an aspect querulous and fearful. Gant, of course, was as unlike Bloom as could be, a lusty, storming animal of a man. Whereas Joyce's Bloom is wholly contained in the conscious stream, for a whole view of Oliver Gant we must turn to other minds than his own, chiefly to that of his son Eugene. It is when Eugene is thinking and speaking of him that the wind of Oliver Gant's wild spirit really blows. For old Gant the stream of consciousness is an inadequate device, serving at best to add a little weight to the other side, give him some of the weakness of mortality. This leads us to reiterate what Wolfe has already said of himself. He employed the devices of Joyce, but it is plain that his own fire possessed everything he wrote. No device could contain the characters of Oliver or Eugene or Eliza or Ben Gant; their real and passionate life resides in and springs from the passionate life in Wolfe.

This is clear again as we observe another use of Joyce's stream, this time of the long, trance-like, contemplative brooding of Marion Bloom. Now it becomes a vehicle for the mind of Eliza Gant, Eugene's mother. She, like Oliver, is realized more fully in the narrative and dialogue of the books, but there is one large section of writing in which Wolfe has given her the center of the stage and let her speak, or think, unhindered. It is called *The Web of Earth* and is part of the volume of shorter pieces, *From Death to Morning.* I imagine it was originally a portion of the manuscript of *Look Homeward, Angel.* Eliza is presumed to be speaking to Eugene, but he is all but silent throughout and her memories and nervous energies impel her restlessly forward and along every tangent that appears, in a tremendous monologue. It is more successful than the Oliver Gant stream because it has more in it of the thinker's essential vigor and mental tone and accent. It is really Eliza Gant, thinking of her past and her people

and of remembered beauties. She is starting to tell Eugene of a
strange portent that came to her once out of the spirit world; she
dramatizes, interrupts herself, interrogates and answers:

> . . . In the year the locusts came, something that happened in the
> year the locusts came, two voices that I heard there in that year. . . .
> Child! Child! It seems so long ago since the year the locusts came, and
> all of the trees were eaten bare: so much has happened and it seems
> so long ago. . . .
> "What say?" I said.
> Says, "Two. . . Two," says, "Twenty . . . Twenty."
> "Hah? What say?"
> "Two . . . Two," the first voice said; and "Twenty . . . Twenty,"
> said the other.

It is more than eighty pages later that she comes back to the
opening phrase:

> That was the year the locusts came: it seems so long ago since the
> year that the locusts came, and all the earth was eaten bare, it seems
> so long ago. But no (I thought) the thing kept puzzlin' me, you know
> — it can't be that, there hasn't been time enough for that, it was only
> the year before in January — Lord! Lord! I often think of all that I've
> been through, and wonder that I'm here to tell it. I reckon for a fact
> I had the power of Nature in me; why! no more trouble than the earth
> takes bearing corn, all of the children, the eight who lived, and all the
> others that you never heard about — all the children and less married
> life than any woman that I knew — and oh! to think of it, to think that
> he should say the things he did — cursin' and tauntin' me and runnin'
> wild with other women, when he had done it all, and like a devil when
> he saw what he had done. Lord! Lord! he was a strange man, a wild
> and savage man; . . . Oh! the good, the bad times, all of the happiness
> and bitter weepin', and there is something now that can't be said. . . .

She relapses now into a peace and tenderness born of all memory:

> Lord, boy! What's that I hear now on the harbor? Hah? What say?
> A ship! — Now it will soon be April, and I must be going home again:
> out in my garden where I work, the early flowers and blossoms will be
> comin' out, the peach trees and the cherry trees, and the dogwood and
> the laurel and the lilacs. I have an apple tree and it is full of all the
> birds there are in June: the flower-tree you planted as a child is bloom-
> ing by the window where you planted it. (My dear child, eat good
> food and watch and guard your health: it worries me to think of you

alone with strangers.) The hills are beautiful and soon it will be spring
once more. (It worries me to think of you like this, alone and far away:
child, child, come home again!)

> O listen! . . .
> Hah? What is it? . . .
> Hah? What say? . . .
> (Lord God! A race of wanderers!)
> Child, child! . . . what is it?
>   *Ships again!*

In mood and extension this whole passage, ninety-two pages in
length, stems from Marion Bloom's closing solo; this, too, closes
a book. Yet the special rhythms and intonations of Eliza Gant are
the characteristics that give the passage flow and flavor. (To see
how marvellously faithful this is to the actual quality of Eliza's
[Mrs. Wolfe's] speech, compare it with a recording made by Mr.
John Terry of some of Mrs. Wolfe's spoken reminiscences.) Her
tenderness and strength, and the American anecdotage that fills
the pages I have not quoted, are the original materials of Wolfe.
He needed to borrow nothing but a form, and that only so that he
might press his own pattern upon it.

Ulysses is a history given to us largely through two minds,
those of Stephen and Bloom; Wolfe's novels are centered upon
one, that of Eugene Gant. There is nothing of Bloom in him, as
there is in so many of the derivative studies you will find in modern American writing, in Conrad Aiken, Melvin P. Levy, Nathan
Asch, others. And even the Stephen in him is tempered by the
exuberant physical vitality that is foreign to Stephen Dedalus.
Stephen's physical lassitude, almost enervation, quite shadows
the fire of his mind. Gant has a huge virility that lifts the
Stephen-mind within him into the sun. This is the contradiction
that makes Eugene Gant an even more unpredictable character
than Dedalus, less disciplined, reaching higher flights of ecstasy
and deeper despairs, more violent of speech, and steadily, as he
matures through the books, more assertive of life, more yea-saying
as Whitman said yea, and with Whitman's great sea-flow of
poetry. But first we search out the essential Stephen.

Early in *Ulysses* Stephen thinks, as he bandies words with

Buck Mulligan, ever in defense of his pride, his secrecy, his cunning:

Parried again. He fears the lancet of my art as I fear that of his. The cold steelpen.

Stephen wages against the philistine world the war of the picador against the bull: light, agile, provocative, inserting the little darts and getting away before the beast knows it is hurt, drawing blood by adroit gestures, sly insertions of the blade, no battle but secret victories. In literary expression this is the attack of irony, satire, and, when skillfully done, the burlesque. Spoken, it is the killing word, the feared lancet. In thought the attack broadens and calls up secretly the heavy bludgeon of burlesque. Stephen wages his war on both fronts. In those early sections of *Ulysses* his tormentors have reason to fear his wit; and his thoughts as they are revealed to us flay with steady acid the society that holds him prisoner. Eugene wages the same war largely upon its silent, secret front. He is not the cold disciplined jesuit that Stephen is by training; he cannot hurl the calculated dart at the precise instant of its greatest effectiveness; he is too emotional, clogged with feeling. Yet inside him the image of Stephen dwells, and along the channels of his thought we come upon the irony, the satire, the destructive burlesque, used as Joyce used them. We will remember, for example, how Joyce used a faithful rendering of the prose of the sentimental two-penny fiction, scarcely heightened since it provides its own burlesque, to give us the color of Gerty MacDowell's mind, in the Nausikaa episode. And through the mind of the youth Eugene Gant there runs a corresponding stream of images created out of cheap American fiction. In his case he is all too aware of their character; it is not his mind we are beholding mirrored in the stream of this sweet, sloshy fiction, but rather his judgment upon the reading and thinking of his overbearing contemporaries. Like Stephen, he is taking his own silent revenge upon them, as he concocts this orgy of sentimental posturing in the exact verbiage of the dime novel:

"I am going," he said presently.
"Going?" she whispered. "Where?"

The organ music deepened.

"Out there," he gestured briefly to the West. "Out there — among His people."

"Going?" She could not conceal the tremor of her voice. "Going? Alone?"

He smiled sadly. The sun had set. The gathering darkness hid the suspicious moisture in his gray eyes. . . .

Eugene turned his wet eyes to the light that streamed through the library windows, winked rapidly, gulped, and blew his nose heavily. Ah, yes! Ah, yes!

And so forth. There are dozens of such images scattered through *Look Homeward, Angel*, and in one furious mental outburst toward the end, the images fuse into one huge extravaganza.

Me! Me! Bruce-Eugene, the Scourge of the Greasers, and the greatest fullback Yale ever had! Marshal Gant, the saviour of his country! Ace Gant, the hawk of the sky, the man who brought Richthofen down! Senator Gant, Governor Gant, President Gant, the restorer and uniter of a broken nation, retiring quietly to private life in spite of the weeping protest of one hundred million people, until, like Arthur or Barbarossa, he shall hear again the drums of need and peril.

This brings us to another aspect of Joyce's burlesque, and we recall his trick of inflation, one word setting off an uncontrollable and mounting series of images that are swollen with detail and finally leave the original concept far behind. The above quotation reminds us of that moment in the Nighttown episode when Bloom's mind, at some provocation, releases a series of fancies in which he is successively Major Bloom, General Bloom, King, Bishop, Pope. It is in the business accompanying the dialogue of this incident that Joyce achieves the effect of incredible nightmare sanity by multiplying his absurd data in business-like fashion:

(Bloom holds up his right hand on which sparkles the Koh-i-noor diamond. His palfrey neighs. Immediate silence. Wireless intercontinental and interplanetary transmitters are set for reception of message. — Thirty-two workmen wearing rosettes, from all the counties of Ireland, under the guidance of Derwan the builder, construct the new Bloomusalem. It is a colossal edifice, with crystal roof, built in the shape of a huge pork kidney, containing forty thousand rooms —)

Less violent and thorough-going, but in the same mood of satirical inflation is Eugene's inner vision of a singer's closing note —

Jay's golden voice neared its triumph, breaking with delicate restraint on the last note, into a high sweet falsetto which he maintained for more than twenty seconds. All of the butchers stopped working, several of them, big strong men with grown-up families, dashed a tear out of their eyes. — Somewhere in the crowd a woman sobbed and collapsed in a faint. She was immediately carried out by two Boy Scouts who happened to be present and who administered first aid to her in the rest-room, one of them hastily kindling a crackling fire of pine boughs by striking two flints together, while the other made a tourniquet, and tied several knots in his handkerchief. Then pandemonium broke loose. Women tore the jewels from their fingers, ropes of pearls from their necks, chrysanthemums, hyacinths, tulips and daisies —

There are others of these passages of inflated burlesque, depending for their effectiveness, here as in Joyce, upon their straight-faced presentation of every-day data impossibly massed. And always there are the little spurts of bitter commentary, couched often in satirical phrases, bitterly mouthed:

Eugene thought of the beautiful institution of human slavery, which his slaveless maternal ancestry had fought so valiantly to preserve. Bress de lawd, Marse! Ole Mose doan' wan' to be free niggah. How he goan' lib widout marse? He doan' wan' stahve wid free niggahs. Har, har, har! Philanthropy. Pure philanthropy. He brushed a tear from his een.

This is inwit's agenbite, American style.

Closer to the actual tone of Stephen's thinking is another of Eugene's secret mental devices. We will recall Edmund Wilson's apt description of Stephen's mind as a "weaving of bright poetic images and fragmentary abstractions, of things remembered from books —." It is thus that Stephen wields in silence his cold steel-pen; particularly in his discourse with Mr. Deasy, with Mulligan and Haines, with the scholars in the library scene, he hurls at them his unspoken fragments of phrase and literary line. There is a large section of *Look Homeward, Angel*, particularly the twenty-fourth chapter, in which Eugene does exactly that, in Stephen's vein. Again we must note that he is younger than

Stephen and less intellectual; his poetic images are more apt to be
remembered from books than to be the abstractions of Stephen's
Aristotelian logic-chopping. But the mood, the method, are the
same. All through the chapter there is this counterpoint of
mundane dialogue and unuttered poetic commentary:

"Well, if it ain't ole Handsome," said Julius Arthur. He grinned
squintily, revealing a mouthful of stained teeth screwed in a wire
clamp. His face was covered with small yellow pustulate sores. How
begot, how nourished? . . .
Julius took the twist, wiped off his mouth with a loose male grin,
and crammed a large quid into his cheek.
He brought me roots of relish sweet.
"Want one, Highpockets?" he asked Eugene, grinning.
I hate him that would upon the rack of this tough world stretch me
out longer.
"Hell," said Ralph Rolls. "Handsome would curl up and die if he ever
took a chew."
In spring like torpid snakes my enemies awaken.

They are his enemies who would stretch him indeed upon the
rack, the crowd against the artist maverick. They do not fear the
lancet of his art — it is not yet sharp enough. He must bear their
raillery and answer meekly in their own tongue, inutile upon his
lips. But within he draws upon his army of friends, Shakespeare,
Drummond, Pope, Wordsworth, Milton, Herrick, the German
poets, and flings his barbs silently. It is a remarkable and revela-
tory chapter, and the most Joycean.

The satire and the burlesque and the barb are Wolfe, yet they
are not the Wolfe we think of, remembering what we have read.
Wolfe was a poet. The man and his spirit are most alive for us in
all the varied display of lyric power his books afford, stemming
alike from Joyce, from Whitman, from his own inspiration. Even
the psychological technique of the conscious stream is permeated
with the diction, accents, inversions of poetry. Whereas the
thoughts of Oliver Gant refer us directly to Bloom's mental
rhythm, this short passage dipped from Eliza's conscious stream
brings to us again the rich poetic texture of Stephen's mind —

Roofing the deep tides, swinging in their embrace, rocked Eliza's life Sargassic, as when, at morning, a breath of kitchen air squirmed through her guarded crack of door and fanned the pendant clusters of old string in floating rhythm. She rubbed the sleep gently from her small weak eyes, smiling dimly as she thought, unawakened, of ancient losses. Her worn fingers still groped softly in the bed beside her, and when she found it vacant she awoke. Remembered. My youngest, my oldest, final bitter fruit, O dark of soul, O far and lonely, where? Remembered O his face! Death-son, partner of my peril, last coinage of my flesh, who warmed my flanks and nestled to my back. Gone? Cut off from me? When? Where?

This is quite transcendent expression; it is not the conscious Eliza who speaks; we have discovered the pattern of her mind in *The Web of Earth*. This is not her own diction or rhythm, but those of her son, Eugene, who speaks for her: Wolfe. We are only discovering again that the stream of consciousness offers him at best a limited and strangled expression. It is when we turn from the stream to his fresh use of Joyce's poetic diction, the word as theme, the free poetic passage (swelling, in Wolfe, to great paeans; Joyce's muse is always cool and disciplined), the thematic idea, that we hear the full accents of his voice.

We will recall that Joyce used the word or phrase as motif, in the musical, repetitive sense, generally within a passage to unify it and give it a desired emotional tone. Outside this restricted area, his employment of the word-motif is rare; the "agenbite of inwit" comes now to mind as perhaps the sole repeated theme. Wolfe has gone greatly beyond Joyce in this. No writer has worked so powerfully with the evocative echoes and re-echoes of a sounded theme. I want to quote here the passage he set down by itself upon the fly-leaf opposite the opening page of *Look Homeward, Angel*. Its significance cannot be overestimated. It contains the words and themes that are to reappear again and again throughout the books of Wolfe.

. . . a stone, a leaf, an unfound door; of a stone, a leaf, a door. And of all the forgotten faces.

Naked and alone we came into exile. In her dark womb we did not know our mother's face; from the prison of her flesh have we come into the unspeakable and incommunicable prison of this earth.

Which of us has known his brother? Which of us has looked into his father's heart? Which of us has not remained forever prison-pent? Which of us is not forever a stranger and alone?

O waste of loss, in the hot mazes, lost, among the bright stars on this most weary unbright cinder, lost! Remembering speechlessly we seek the great forgotten language, the lost lane-end into heaven, a stone, a leaf, an unfound door. Where? When?

O lost, and by the wind grieved, ghost, come back again.

I will not enlarge here upon the sensory beauties of this prose. This is what we mean when we speak of Wolfe's Biblical eloquence, the organ-tone which is not incomparable with the organ-tone of the Elizabethan poet he loved most. What holds us now in the passage is its freight of themes, like seeds that are to sprout through the thousands of pages to come. They are blended here into one emotional chant of spiritual grief and wanting; when we search out its components we discover, first, that searing grief for a dead brother, a remembered hero (which runs also through Faulkner's work, a similar constant vein). "Which of us has known his brother?" The portrait of Eugene's brother, Ben, is to my mind the most poignant element in Wolfe's writing. Alive he is seen as already gone. Dead, he is forever alive in Eugene's mind, the remembered gestures, words, ways. He, most of all, is the cherished image. It is of him that Wolfe cries out always, "O lost, and by the wind grieved, ghost, come back again!" The words "O lost," detached, carrying the grief for Ben and for all else that is gone and mourned, appear again many times; I cannot catalog them all. "Return! O lost, and by the wind grieved . . ." Eugene cries again upon Page 456, "O lost, O far and lonely, where?" upon 522, and on 583, "And Ben will come again, he will not die again, in flower and leaf, in wind and music far, he will come back again. O lost, and by the wind grieved. . . ." These are only three. The words sing again wherever the emotion is once more evoked.

Ben himself is a theme to bind the books together. At a gesture or a sound the whole body of the narrative must pause while the vision of Ben rises to haunt us, as, in *Of Time and the River*: "Bitter and beautiful, scorn no more. Ben stands there in the window. . . ." The month of October, the date of his birth and death, never fails to evoke the memory:

> For now October has come back again, the strange and lonely month comes back again, and you will not return.
> Up on the mountain, down in the valley, deep, deep, in the hill, Ben — cold, cold, cold.

These last words are inscribed upon the fly-leaf of *From Death to Morning*, and the opening phrase, "For now October has come back again," is the theme of one of Wolfe's most profound and sonorous poetic passages, with its blending of October, Ben, all remembered, all lost. I must not carry this further, except to speak of the fortieth chapter of *Look Homeward, Angel*, in which Eugene, walking in the cemetery and filled with his emotions, holds ghostly converse with Ben. We have heard the dead speak in Joyce's Nighttown episode, in James T. Farrell's history of the O'Neills, in Conrad Aiken's *Coming Forth of Osiris Jones*. It is one of the marks of Joycean influence. Here again the meeting of life and death produces its terrific apocalyptic climax; mortal emotions and immortal vision flood the pages and bring the book to its ecstatic close.

So also might we trace that other pregnant phrase, "a stone, a leaf, a door," through the books. It appears everywhere (see, for example, the opening story in *From Death to Morning* called "No Door"; or the second page of "Gulliver" in the same volume; or page 604 in *Of Time and the River*), an echoing motif of search and desperation, carrying now the burden of old Oliver's groping, now the passionate thrust of Eugene, and always with added weight as the echoes and overtones are multiplied and blended with more and more of the thematic material that Wolfe steadily introduces. It is only such poetic weaving of themes that can produce, finally, the richness and incomparable impact of this brief climatic passage, near the very end of *Of Time and the River*. Eugene's mind is at this moment a cavern ringing with remembered words and voices:

> . . . Garfield, Arthur, Harrison, and Hayes . . . time of my father's time, life of his life. "Ah, Lord," he said, "I knew them all — and all of them are gone. I'm the only one that's left. By God, I'm getting old."

. . . In the year that the locusts came, something that happened in the year the locusts came, two voices that I heard there in that year. . . . Child! Child! It seems so long ago since the year the locusts came, and all of the trees were eaten bare: so much has happened and it seems so long ago. . . .
"To keep time with!" — To Eugene Gant, Presented to Him on the Occasion of His Twelfth Birthday, by His Brother, B. H. Gant, Oct. 3, 1912. . . . "To keep time with!" . . . Up on the mountain, down in the valley, deep, deep, deep in the hill, Ben, cold, cold, cold.

Three themes are joined here in grief and memory, the father, the mother, the brother lost. I have already shown the latter two in earlier uses. The words "Garfield, Arthur, Harrison, and Hayes" are the central theme of a story called "The Four Lost Men," in *From Death to Morning,* a story devoted to the remembered voice of Oliver Gant exactly as "The Web of Earth" is to that of Eliza. As these words reappear now at the head of this quoted passage in *Of Time and the River,* they carry with them the whole aura of emotional content of that story; and just so "the year of the locusts" and "deep in the hill, Ben — " set up in us the accumulated emotion of all the other times we have read them.

All of this is a great, loose application, sprawling across three books, of the tight musical technique of Joyce's Sirens episode in *Ulysses.* That opening passage in *Look Homeward, Angel* is Wolfe's statement of his main themes, later to be developed individually and together in various forms, exactly as the fifty-eight fragmentary lines which Joyce places at the head of his Sirens episode are later deliberately expanded, like theme-fragments first heard in an overture and heard again in the music's full development. Wolfe continues to introduce other themes as he goes along, playing backward and forward upon them and bringing many of them together at last, as above, with magnificently enlarged harmonies — an effect Joyce did not employ. It is a demanding technique; it demands that we attend as we do to music, hearing all at once, past and present, and making our syntheses every step of the way. Beyond doubt it is a successful technique, and especially because it does not seem a technique at all but a natural way of expression: poetic, musical, the only possible vehicle for these great mortal emotions.

We return again to the opening inscription: "Which of us has looked into his father's heart?" This is Wolfe's early statement of a Joycean motif that has gone untouched from *Ulysses* to *Look Homeward, Angel.* The theme of paternity is one of the most significant in *Ulysses*, stemming in its turn from the search of Telemachus for his father, in Homer's *Odyssey.* (Book Three of *Of Time and the River* is named "Telemachus.") That search, in *Ulysses*, is not the search for a physical father, but for a spiritual, culminating in the meeting of Stephen and Bloom at the end of their day. The whole problem of spiritual paternity here is subtle and engrossing; for the best discussion of it I refer the reader to the little chapter in Stuart Gilbert's book. It is one of the great themes in *Ulysses* — indeed the one that serves most to hold the narrative together and give it direction. The part it plays in Wolfe's work is less definitive; there were many reasons why Eugene Gant found more of satisfaction, more of spiritual root, in his physical father than Stephen Dedalus did in his. Yet there was the same essential hunger, for a more perfect *omphalos* of the mind, that drove both in identical search. Reading this in Wolfe's *The Story of a Novel*, it may well seem to us Stephen who speaks:

From the beginning — and this was one fact that in all my time of hopelessness returned to fortify my faith in my conviction — the idea, the central legend that I wished my book to express had not changed. And this central idea was this: the deepest search in life, it seemed to me, the thing that in one way or another was central to all living was man's search to find a father, not merely the father of his flesh, not merely the lost father of his youth, but the image of a strength and wisdom external to his need and superior to his hunger, to which the belief and power of his own life could be united.

I do not feel that this was, as Wolfe expressed it, the central legend of his work, but it was one of the strong currents in it. Like those word-themes we have been tracing, this spiritual motif inherited in its exact meaning from Joyce appears again and again in varied forms — in the actual dominant theme of the physical father (Oliver Gant himself cries out, "Here, Father! Here!" at the moment of his death) as well as in the symbolic use of the father image to designate the unknown, the desired, the cherished haven. Wolfe uses it so in his evocative sketch, "The Men of Old Catawba":

> The earth is a woman, but Old Catawba is a man. The earth is our mother and our nurse, and we can know her, but Old Catawba is our father, and although we know that he is there, we shall never find him. He is there in the wilderness, and his brows are bowed with granite: he sees our lives and deaths and his stern compassion broods above us. Women love him, but only men can know him: only men who have cried out in their agony and their loneliness to their father, only men who have sought throughout the world to find him, can know Catawba: but this includes all the men who have ever lived.

This is Wolfe's brooding and impersonal image of the Telemachan search. More direct, more impassioned comes the personal cry, in *Of Time and the River*:

> Shall your voice unlock the gates of my brain? Shall I know you, though I have never seen your face? Will you know me, and will you call me "son"? Father, I know that you live, though I have never found you.

This is one of the great tensions, in the entire history of Eugene Gant, that remains ever poised in mid-air, pent and crackling. I think it may be said that the whole unbearable effect, which some critics have found in Wolfe's work, of endless acceleration, of curves never descending, is due to this characteristic unreleased tension, of which the unsatisfied father-theme is one looming instance. Whether or not this search must be, in reality, doomed to remain fruitless, Joyce knew that it had to find its ripening in art. At that fatal moment in *Ulysses*, when Stephen and Bloom stand face to face an understanding, unuttered then or after, flashes between them, the tension of the whole book is released in a crash of illumination, expressed most temperately by the accompanying crash of masonry. The book leaps into integration. Wolfe failed in this, to create for Eugene Gant what Thomas Wolfe had not known. The great Telemachan theme rises in his books, endlessly, and never finds its resolution.

There are others of Joyce's methods still to be found in Wolfe. You will remember, for example, the nameless, garrulous Citizen,

Joyce's man of the street, main spokesman in the twelfth episode of *Ulysses*. This episode has been called the Cyclops, with reference to the Homeric parallel, and with good reason, for see how the Cyclops story is suggested at once:

I was just passing the time of day with old Troy of the D. M. P. at the corner of Arbour hill there and be damned but a bloody sweep came along and he near drove his gear into my eye. I turned around to let him have the weight of my tongue when who should I see dodging along Stony Batter only Joe Hynes.
— Lo, Joe, says I. How are you blowing? Did you see that bloody chimneysweep near shove my eye out with his brush?

This lively Dublin Citizen serves to provide one more angle, in vigorous vernacular, from which may be viewed the history of Leopold Bloom; and it is fascinating to observe how often he reappears in the work of Joyce's major pupils. I cannot resist citing, for example, this paragraph from Aiken's *Great Circle*:

And who should be standing at the bar, eating little-neck clams as usual, but Jitter Peabody, that ruined scion of a noble race, half-shot too as always, leaning with supercilious languor against the bar, his long horseface flushed with gin, his drooping mustache dripping clam-juice on to his weak chin.
— Hello, One-Eye!

That salutation rivets the analogy home with finality; it is Aiken's signed tribute to *Ulysses*, although, indeed, Joyce's signature is written on every page of the book. And what of Wolfe? Aiken has decked out Joyce's Citizen in all-too-nice a phraseology, but Wolfe returns him to his original status, in the story, "Only the Dead Know Brooklyn."

"So like I say, I'm waitin' for my train t' come when I sees dis big guy standin' deh — dis is duh foist I eveh see of him. Well, he's lookin' wild, y'know, an' I can see dat he's had plenty, but still he's holdin' it; he talks good and is walkin' straight enough. So den, dis big guy steps up to a little guy dats standin' deh. . . ."

The same thing is carried out at length in still another story, "Gulliver," in which a whole chorus of these earthy Citizens are called upon to stare, exclaim, jeer, conjecture, upon this outcast from the common mold. The legend of Gulliver is substituted for that of Polyphemus, but the method and intent are the same: an oblique view of Gant, such as Joyce gives in the Citizen's view of Bloom. (Upon page 71 of *Look Homeward, Angel* there is an early touching upon the Gulliver theme, referring this time to Oliver Gant.)

Wolfe makes use also of the familiar time-scheme of Joyce's Wandering Rocks episode in *Ulysses*. It is the tenth episode, and named, once more, after a parallel episode in Homer. In twentieth-century Dublin the rocks are people, crossing and recrossing one another's paths within the space of one hour. We observe one character for a few moments, rapidly shifting then to another, then to another, all the while catching oblique glimpses of some of those we have already seen, in the instant of saying the words or making the gesture that identified them at first. The characters are placed successively at the center and the outer fringe of attention, they change places, they are spatially dispersed, they are most often unaware of one another, their thoughts and movements seem a succession of free and disconnected tangents. But there at the core is the centrifugal force that holds them together. They are parts of a picture that is shot with one instantaneous flash of the lens. The whole point of this tenth episode is that all spaces and lives are relative parts of one Time history. Time is everywhere at once, and if we could be everywhere with it, as are God and the writer, as this episode permits us to be, we could see this history at a glance.

The entire fourteenth chapter which opens Part Two of *Look Homeward, Angel* is devoted to this same technique of telescoped Time, and the latter half of the twenty-fourth chapter. Both instances are dedicated to exactly the same purpose served by Joyce's episode, to give an instantaneous, panoramic view of the life of the town — in this case Wolfe's Altamont. We are everywhere at once, all paths cross, all voices speak; these are the most objective sections in Wolfe's work, always remembering that even these are written by Eugene. Their indebtedness is plain in the way they are arranged, that same sequence of smaller items introducing the different characters at a fixed point in time, and is

perhaps underscored by a passage such as this, which has proven
to be a kind of Joycean talisman:

At this moment, having given to misery all he had (a tear), the very
Reverend Father James O'Haley, S. J., among the faithless faithful he,
unshaken, unseduced, unterrified, emerged plumply from his chapel —

From Joyce (Father Conmee) to Farrell (Father Gilhooley) to
Wolfe (Father O'Haley) we have watched the successive appearances of the Reverend Father.

It cannot be doubted that Wolfe gave a great deal of thought
to that problem of Time which Joyce approached in so many
ways. The Wandering Rocks technique was one answer, but it
answered only the demands of actual present time. Wolfe saw
that there were two other Times to be considered, and wrote of
them in that same remarkable little essay, *The Story of a Novel*:

The second time element was of past time, one which represented
these same characters as acting and as being acted upon by all the
accumulated impact of man's experience so that each moment of their
lives was conditioned not only by what they experienced in that
moment, but by all that they had experienced up to that moment. In
addition to these two time elements, there was a third which I conceived as being time immutable, the time of rivers, mountains, oceans,
and the earth; a kind of eternal and unchanging universe of time. . . .

It was from a basic texture of these two Times that Joyce evolved
his *Work in Progress (Finnegans Wake)*. Out of this concept of
Time came the title of Wolfe's second novel, *Of Time and the
River*, and to it are devoted many passages in which Wolfe
escapes from the immediate impact of the present and ranges
backward into a past both personal and racial, striving always to
encompass them simultaneously as though they were indeed one
immutable and unchanging universe. Joyce found this unity by
receding to the dream world of H. C. Earwicker, but Wolfe
sought it in the waking world, in such conscious drawings-
together of all memories as the passage quoted above (page 276)
and in the actual permanent stuff of the physical world, in the
mountains and rivers themselves, repositories of memory, in the
body of America. And it was in this second way that he found the

solution closest to his wants, turned at last from the methods of
Joyce to that other source of which he is inheritor: Whitman.

When we discussed Wolfe's failure to bring his Telemachan
theme to any climax, we were noting a symptom of the one great
gap in Wolfe's art that even Joyce could not teach him to bridge.
Wolfe was conscious always of huge insatiable hungers — physical, mental, spiritual — and scarcely knew how to lay upon them
the discipline of his mind, and scarcely desired to. In his reading,
observing, writing, he yearned gigantically to swallow up all
life, all books, all experience, and to disgorge it all, in entirety.

He read insanely, by the hundreds, the thousands, the ten thousands,
yet he had no desire to be bookish; no one could describe this mad
assault upon print as scholarly: a ravening appetite in him demanded
that he read everything that had ever been written about human experience. He read no more from pleasure — the thought that other
books were waiting for him tore at his heart forever. He pictured himself as tearing the entrails from a book as from a fowl. . . .
And he would rush out in the streets to find it, be hurled through
the tunnel into Boston and then spend hours in driving himself savagely
through a hundred streets, looking into the face of a million people,
trying to get an instant and conclusive picture of all they did and said
and were, of all their million destinies, and of the great city and the
everlasting earth, and the immense and lonely skies that bent above
them. . . .

The words were wrung out of him in a kind of bloody sweat, they
poured out of his finger tips, spat out of his snarling throat like writhing
snakes; he wrote them with his heart, his brain, his sweat, his guts;
he wrote them with his blood, his spirit; they were wrenched out
of the secret source and substance of his life. . . . flung down upon
paper like figures blasted by the spirit's lightning stroke, and in them
was the huge chronicle of the billion forms, the million names, the
huge, single, and incomparable substance of America.

Such were the gargantuan ambitions of Wolfe. They would have
wrecked the work of any other man, less fit to house them; I
think they wrecked his body at last. They were not Wolfe's
ambitions solely. You will find them stated by James T. Farrell in
his introduction to the Lonigan trilogy in terms more temperate
and controlled, and I feel that John Dos Passos, ever since *Forty-*

Second Parallel, has been working to set down in a variety of forms the "incomparable substance of America." That Wolfe had more genius than either of them, that his headlong, blasted, writhing flood of words is greater upon every page than their superior discipline, seems incontrovertible to me. Yet he might have wrought greater than he did, if he had only learned to shape his passions to his purposes, not by cramping them but by building forms large enough to conserve and direct his energies. He himself came to see something of this, as when he wrote,

I actually felt that I had a great river thrusting for release inside of me and that I had to find a channel into which its flood-like power could pour.

This was written after *Of Time and the River* was published, yet there are indications in that book of the beginnings of the channeling, passages and pages wherein the flood-like power begins to converge and flow in one direction. These are the long passages that have seemed so clearly to be infused with the moods and rhythms of Walt Whitman. Let us note here that this is the great distinction which sets the first two novels apart. There are power and beauty and poetry in both, but in *Look Homeward, Angel* it is the poetry of Joyce; I do not find any Whitman in it. Now in *Of Time and the River,* as Wolfe sets about, still unsuccessfully, to curb the torrent, he begins to block out pages of his manuscript and devote them to pure poetic chant — no longer the blind rushing narrative, but now the marginal commentary of, shall we say, the impersonal, racial voice, the all-embracing, the disembodied, the timeless. This is the voice he invokes now to speak for him, and when it speaks we are hearing, for the first time in Wolfe, the accents of Whitman: the great catalogs of times and years and places, names, occupations, men and women, sounds and smells, words and gestures of America.

It may be a directly addressed poem to all of these, five incomparable pages — or it may begin with that familiar lament, "October has come again —" (a time which to him was always inexpressibly dear and painful) and blend then into a panorama of America everywhere as October passes over it — or he may be sitting in a train, hurtling through the darkness (an experience he celebrates many times in the book) and hears the voices of his forbears speaking out of the ground:

Who sows the barren earth, their voices cried. We sowed the wilderness with blood and sperm. Three hundred of your blood and bone are recompacted with the native earth: we gave a tongue to solitude, a pulse to the desert, the barren earth received us and gave back our agony: we made the earth cry out. One lies in Oregon, and one, by a broken wheel and horse's skull, still grips a gunstock on the Western trail. Another one has helped to make Virginia richer. One died at Chancellorsville in Union blue, and one at Shiloh walled with Yankee dead. Another. . . .

You can hear and feel the pulse of marching iambics, the free line and Biblical sonority. If this is not as plain an echoing of Whitman as can be desired, let us turn to those two ringing pages of names and places at the end:

For something under our feet, and around us and over us; something that is in us and part of us, and proceeds from us, that beats in all the pulses of our blood.

Brother, for what?

First for the thunder of imperial names, the names of men and battles, the names of places and great rivers, the mighty names of the States. The name of the Wilderness; and the names of Antietam, Chancellorsville, Shiloh, Bull Run. . . .

Then, for the continental thunder of the States: the names of Montana, Texas, Arizona, Colorado, Michigan, Maryland, Virginia, and the two Dakotas; the names of Oregon and Indiana, of Kansas and the rich Ohio; the powerful name of Pennsylvania, and the name of Old Kentucky; the undulance of Alabama; the names of Florida and North Carolina.

Read that whole passage, and hear again, unmistakable, the old Americano himself — "I will make a song for these States." In the very process of writing *Of Time and the River* Wolfe was finding new ground to stand upon, and a fresher vigor was coursing through him. Stephen was dropping from him, a pale, bitter cast of secret thought, and he was joining hands now with the robust, bearded lover. He was looking about with lover's eyes upon the great varied continent of America, looking with affection even into the teeming city and using Walt's own word — "Million-footed Manhattan." He was going into the streets, among taxis, down into the subway, and looking with tenderness and brother-hood upon the little man, obscure in life, dignified in death, and writing then one of his best stories, "Death the Proud Brother." And even in the midst of an interpolated section of diary which owes its form to Stephen's diary at the close of the *Portrait* (there is an entry covering two pages, made of broken musical themes, never developed, like those that usher in Joyce's Sirens episode), there are signs here and there that he is coming into the clear —

I am getting a new sense of control — millions of books don't annoy me so much. . . .

Instead of whining, that we have no traditions, or that we must learn by keeping constantly in touch with European models, or by keeping away from them, we should get busy telling some of the stories about America that have never been told. . . .

Never has the many-ness and the much-ness of things caused me such trouble as in the past six months. But never have I had so firm a conviction that our lives can live upon only a few things, that we must find them, and begin to build our fences.

All creation is the building of a fence.

But deeper study always, sharper senses, profounder living; *never* an end to curiosity.

The fruit of all this comes later. I must think. I must mix it all with myself and with America. I have caught much of it on paper. But infinitely the greater part is in the wash of my brain and blood.

The intimation of these reflections is borne out by the strong, calm, certainty of the Whitman-like passages, and the broadening note of sympathy and comradeship which appears in many of the tales in *From Death to Morning* and has its final expression in the closing Credo of his last novel, *You Can't Go Home Again,* to which I shall return. Wolfe seemed about to find the balance he sought. He was building his fence. His electric tension was re-solving. The problem of Time was finding its answer too, Time was history, was America past and present, all the men and blood and tradition that had seeped into the soil and lived there yet. All of these problems that had tortured Wolfe were being drawn together now; he seemed to be shedding his subjective preoccu-

pations, his frustrate hungers for the unobtainable, his desperate
sense of isolation. He was finding his way to an integration from
which would have proceeded work beyond our conjecture.

This work did not come to us in *The Web and the Rock*, or in
You Can't Go Home Again; we shall never see it. *The Web and
the Rock* is a good novel for anyone else to have written; for
Wolfe it was a deviation. He wrote it to prove to certain critics
that he could do the things they said he couldn't. In the chorus of
praise that came to him from the day *Look Homeward, Angel* was
published, there were the dissenting voices that said he could
write only in one vein, only subjectively, autobiographically,
about Eugene Gant, that he could not invent, that he would soon
write himself out. And of all the critics he read, it was these to
whom he reacted most. He was sensitive beyond measure to their
cavilling. He smarted, and swore he would disprove everything
they said. One of his friends has written of this:

The suggestions by some of the reviewers that in *Look Homeward,
Angel*, so patently autobiographical, he had possibly written himself
out, maddened him with a determination to prove to others the faith
he had in himself that as long as he might live he could never write
himself out. He would "show them too that he could compress, maybe
like Dostoevski," that he could write short stories to conform to "any
damned acceptable pattern they wanted." He said he would write a
Gargantuan fable for them, without a recognizable person in it, with
New York as setting, portraying the struggle of an artist against the
attempts of literary people to cheapen and kill him —

They had goaded him into writing for "them," when he should
have continued along the path he was finding for himself. The
books he finally wrote for them only prove how wrong they were.
The Web and the Rock and *You Can't Go Home Again* are by no
means weak books, but they are built upon concessions to his
critics, and they are deflected from the course Wolfe's work was
taking at the end of *Of Time and the River*. He dropped, for example, the character of Eugene Gant, and created a new one
called George Webber — a shorter man less symmetrically made,
with the nickname "Monk" for his stooped shoulders. He endowed
Webber with a new history and background; this would show

them he could invent! But this was simply not the kind of invention with which Wolfe could function. He started with Monk Webber, but by the time *The Web and the Rock* is half written, by the time Webber is in New York carrying on his battle against the "literary people," all pretense at invention is gone and Eugene is alive again, chafing inside the innocuous disguise. By far the finest thing in the book is the long history of the relations between Webber and Esther Jack; but then Esther is the woman whom Eugene Gant glimpsed for the first time aboard ship, at the rhapsodic close of *Of Time and the River*. The junction is complete here, and that part of *The Web and the Rock* belongs to the Gant history. For the rest, with its abortive attempt to create George Webber, its easy lampooning of literary critics and literary teas, little theater movements, brash publishers (Rawng and Wright), presumptuous intellectuals generally, it all adds up to work any talented young writer could turn out. Wolfe was working with his left hand. There are new characters, plenty of them, but nobody of memorable stature save Esther Jack, who belongs to the history of Eugene Gant, and Foxhall Edwards, who came later into the life of Gant and Wolfe. "They" had done this for him, impelled the creator of Ben Gant, of Helen and Luke, of Oliver and Eliza, of Horse Hines, Doctor McGuire, Bascom Pentland, Francis Starwick, to waste two novels to show them he could create characters.

Had Wolfe lived it would not have proved a costly deflection, but costly it was because at thirty-eight Wolfe was dead, with his work not done. We feel he knew what that work was to be. It was to Foxhall Edwards that he addressed his long and significant Credo at the close of *You Can't Go Home Again*. In it he reviewed the development of his thinking from the days of early awareness at college to the growing sense of social consciousness that was coming upon him even as he was finishing the pages of this novel.

There came to me a vision of man's inhumanity to man, and as time went on it began to blot out the more personal and self-centered vision of the world which a young man always has. Then it was, I think, that I began to learn humility. My intense and passionate concern for the interests and designs of my own little life were coming to seem petty, trifling, and unworthy, and I was coming more and more to feel an intense and passionate concern for the interests and designs of my fellow men and of all humanity.

This is a weather change in the Eugene Gant we have known in the first two novels. No longer the Byron, the Stephen Dedalus, the wandering Telemachus. His eye now is outside himself, upon men, his brothers. He is seeking for an answer to *their* needs now, not his any longer. He thinks he has it:

And the essence of all faith, it seems to me, for such a man as I, the essence of religion for people of my belief, is that man's life can be, and will be, better; that man's great enemies, in the forms in which they now exist — the forms we see on every hand of fear, hatred, slavery, cruelty, poverty, and need — can be conquered and destroyed. But to conquer and destroy them will mean nothing less than the complete revision of the structure of society as we know it. They cannot be conquered by the sorrowful acquiescence of resigned fatality. They cannot be destroyed by the philosophy of acceptance. . . .

And he closes with the magnificent paean on the last two pages, beginning, "I believe that we are lost here in America, but I believe we shall be found." Wolfe had something else to tell us now. He saw that in the wash of his blood and brain, but also in the wash of human experience about him, were all the meaning of America, Time, Art. He could dip endlessly into these, go on to work upon that huge project, the history of the Gants and Pentlands, go on to wring from this the elements of an American philosophy. His two great novels attest that no one since Whitman has been so well endowed to express it. There remain to us now only some brief sketches of a western journey he made, some posthumous fragments, and the melancholy reflection that seventy-five years intervened between *Leaves of Grass* and *Look Homeward, Angel.* We shall be hugely fortunate if seventy-five years more bring us another such man.

In addition to their publication in England, one or more of Wolfe's books have appeared in translation in Norway, Sweden, Denmark, Holland, Czechoslovakia, Russia, Switzerland, France, Italy, and Argentina. But his greatest acclaim abroad was in Germany following the publication in Berlin of "Schau heimwärts, Engel" in March 1933 but bearing a 1932 imprint. About that time, Franz Schoenberner, editor of the anti-Nazi magazine "Simplicissimus," slipped away from Germany into France and finally came to America. The account of his stumbling upon Wolfe's novels is one of the most superb tributes ever paid the American writer.

MY DISCOVERY OF THOMAS WOLFE

by

Franz Schoenberner

It is a strange thing that I should discover Thomas Wolfe only seventeen years after his glorious debut in the literary world and seven years after his untimely death. I could hardly have missed him for so long, had he occupied the predominant place in modern letters which, I think, is rightly his.

More than twenty years ago, while I was still living in Germany, I became interested in American literature, and until 1933, when I left Germany, I often used to write or talk on the radio about the latest translations of new books by Upton Sinclair and Sinclair Lewis, by Sherwood Anderson and Theodore Dreiser, by Thornton Wilder, Ernest Hemingway, Dos Passos, and other important

First appearance as "Wolfe's Genius Seen Afresh" in the *New York Times Book Review*, 4 August 1946. Revised selection from Franz Schoenberner's *The Inside Story of an Outsider*, copyright 1949 by Franz Schoenberner and used with the permission of The Macmillan Company, the publisher.

American writers. Thomas Wolfe, it is true, was translated into German only at a time when I had cut myself off entirely from the book-burning Third Reich and was living in France, where the interest in foreign literature was much less developed than in Germany. But it seems surprising to me that, arriving in the United States in the summer of 1941, I was not told immediately by everyone of my well-educated American friends: "First of all you must read Thomas Wolfe."

Perhaps I would have missed him all my life, had it not been for the coincidence that as editor of the OWI, looking through German-language broadcasts prepared by another section, I found among the badly mimeographed scripts on yellow paper a feature about Thomas Wolfe which quoted from his posthumous novel *You Can't Go Home Again* some phrases of the great farewell to Nazi Germany. It struck me like a flash of lightning and I knew at once: This is it, this is a great writer, a true genius, something entirely different from all I knew of American literature. Strangely enough, I could not find the title in the main catalogue of the Public Library, though, as it later turned out, a copy was available in the Circulation Department. But I soon discovered this novel and even his earlier ones in cheap reprint editions at the corner drugstore among dozens of outdated popular best sellers. Reading one of his books after another, I failed more and more to understand that the indubitable literary success of Thomas Wolfe had evidently hardly survived his death and that this timeless work had only had its short season of fashion, soon to be displaced by other literary fashions. Probably not one of his great books had ever reached the circulation of those pseudohistorical trash novels which, year after year, roll from the literary assembly line and sometimes sell more than a million copies.

But even among the most famous representatives of the more serious contemporary literature that I know, Thomas Wolfe, it seems to me, occupies a place all his own. Endowed with the prophetic ethos and poetic pathos of the true genius, he consciously transmutes his personal discovery of life and of the world into a message of religious intensity. He had consented to be "God's lonely man." He knew from the start that "genius can bring death"; he knew that "giants die early and things which are too great in nature for the measure of the world destroy themselves." There must have been in him from his early youth this feeling of being consecrated, fated and inevitable. Even beyond his own artistic testimony, it is the most poignant human experience to witness this pilgrim's progress from the exalted, rhapsodic lyricism, the youthful turmoil and ecstasy of his first book to the manly composure, the profound ethical awareness of his "Credo" in the last chapter of *You Can't Go Home Again*. This long letter of farewell to his old friend Fox was written in the foreboding of death. "Something has spoken in the night and told me, I shall die, I know not where." It was his last will and testament and he expected America to be his executor. It would be even more tragic than the cruel tragedy of his untimely death to see this last will unfulfilled. Today it seems more timely than ever to remember his great prophetic message:

I believe we are lost here in America, but I believe we shall be found. . . . I think the true discovery of America is before us. I think the true fulfillment of our spirit, of our people, of our mighty and immortal land is yet to come. I think the true discovery of our democracy is still before us. And I think that these things are as certain as the morning, as inevitable as noon.

But I could just as well quote thousands of other passages from his work, because it is one great confession of faith in life and in the holy spirit of truth.

It is for now and for us the living that we must speak and speak the truth, as much as we can see and know. With the courage of the truth within us, we shall meet the enemy as they come to us and they *shall* be ours. . . . In the continuance of that unceasing war is man's religion and his living faith.

Perhaps it was all for the good that my discovery of Thomas Wolfe started with his last book *You Can't Go Home Again*, which like *The Web and the Rock*, repeats on a new level of artistic achievement the life cycle of his first two books *Look Homeward, Angel* and *Of Time and the River*. The mental vision of the whole pattern of his life and work becomes clearer and clearer, for himself and for the reader, the higher he mounts toward the summit after having fought his way through the virgin forest and the wild jungles of his early youth. It is an unspeakable tragedy that his progress ended when he was on his way to even higher goals, when he had found himself and was prepared, in full possession of his artistic means, to give his all and his best "out of the last secret source and substance of his life." He was far from being exhausted by the superhuman, frantic effort of his early work when, at thirty-eight, he died.

He did not belong to those who pride themselves on, and secretly enjoy, the sheer power of their ecstatic feeling, a danger which even Walt Whitman did not escape. He was involved in a lifelong, deadly serious struggle to channel and to master the titanic forces of emotion which threatened to overwhelm him and to sweep him away into insanity. But he never was afraid to express himself with all the exuberance and eloquence which was so natural to him. He did not mind using what most Americans, with a sort of embarrassment, would call "big words." He was not hiding his feelings or even his immense erudition beneath a disguise of understatements or of craftily exploited naïveté in the manner of the "I-am-dumb school of Hemingway," to use an expression of his unforgettable Seamus Malone. He was not afraid of thinking and of ideas and not ashamed of his "A-1" in philosophy or of his "1" in logic. He was not content to be merely a reporter or a sort of press photographer, giving meaningless "slices of life." For him, fiction was "fact, arranged and charged with purpose." And this purpose became more and more clear when, turning from the self-centered introspection of youth to the deeper understanding of his surrounding world, he became aware of "man's inhumanity to man," of the "hollow pyramid of a false social structure," of the whole "world that Jack built," Jack the great banker and businessman.

But even his social criticism was not, as so often in modern literature, the criticism of a snob just clever enough to see how ridiculous and how wrong other snobs are, but who never would think of separating himself from this sham world. Thomas Wolfe never belonged to any circle or any clique, he always belonged entirely and exclusively to himself and to his artistic task; he always was trying to "achieve the highest life on earth, the life which can be won only by the bitter toil and knowledge and stern living — the life of an artist."

But spending his life "in solitude and wandering," he "always possessed the whole of life." He only had to look at people and it was as if he had known them forever. Caught in the X-rays of his inner vision, world and man became transparent. For the truly great artist, the god and creator of his own universe, "knoweth the heart," he is all-seeing and omniscient, full of superior justice and understanding.

His "powerful indignation at the cruelty and injustice in the life he knew," this "burning indignation which is one of the dynamic forces in the artist's life," could never induce him to paint oversimplified propaganda posters in black and white, like so many well meaning "social writers." He saw through the "glorious unreality" of the "river people" and the feverish world of speculation "honeycombed with privilege and dishonesty." But even the cruel lucidity of his hate was animated not only by passion but compassion, by deep human tolerance and understanding.

On the other hand, he was entirely free from the romantic escapism of so many disillusioned literary revolutionaries who, like Steinbeck and others, tend to believe that true life and true humanity can finally be found only among social outcasts and misfits, among irresponsible "children of nature" or among bums and drunkards and whores, the eternal objects of nostalgic bourgeois sentimentality. He knew the "trackless jungle of the city" not only from the secure vantage point of some esthetic sight-seeing car. He had lived for years in the slums of Brooklyn in a kind of self-imposed exile, as in earlier times prophets went into the desert, "driven by a resolution to seek out the most forlorn and isolated hiding spot that he could find." He knew the "desolate emptiness of city youth," the "murderous rages of drunken Irishmen on Saturdays," the whole "squalor and filth and misery and despair, the violence and cruelty and hate" of "suffering helots." He suffered with them, he understood them much better than they could ever understand themselves, but he did not insult them by melo-dramatizing them, by finding them interesting, picturesque, and touching or even kind of cute. Thomas Wolfe was never in danger of becoming a sort of specialist like so many talented writers who, throughout their lives, limit themselves more or less to one topic, to one type of human being and usually end up in repetitious monotony.

The "terrible Faustian fever of the tortured spirit," the insatiable urge "to read all the books, eat all the food, drink all the wine, see all the great pictures" had given him an almost universal treasure of experience. He had a larger frame of reference than most other modern writers I know. He knew not only the famous "hundred great books" of St. John's College but almost the whole world literature. He had accumulated within his vast mind the literary heritage of Western culture, from the great classics of antiquity to Joyce and Proust. He had not only traveled but actually lived in France and England, in Germany, Italy, and Switzerland. He learned to understand and partly even to speak French and Ger-man. And, wherever he was, he knew the world of the waiter and the doorman no less intimately than the world of the "idle rich," of the businessman, and the literary snob.

He was involved in the superhuman task of continuously trans-muting the reality of his life into the higher reality of art. With millions of words, he painted, panel by panel, the enormous panorama of his life as he lived it, always trying to jump over his own shadow and almost succeeding in catching up with himself. It is significant that he used to refer to the whole of his writing as "the book"; it was the book of his life, rounded out and com-pleted by his creative imagination. This apparently most sub-jective and autobiographic writer had such a power of intellectual and artistic objectification that, looking into the mirror, he could see his own image with the same superior detachment and know-ing justice as any other object of his world. Even in all the madness and fury and frenzy of the tormented agonies which he reflects, there is nothing morbid, nothing pathological, and cer-tainly nothing of the coquettish self-indulgence of narcissistic neurotics who eagerly convert their interesting complexes into a literary case history. Even his madness is nothing but an excess of health and vitality. His basic concept of the world and life is as simple and natural as that of a child and full of an almost cruel innocence and "nakedness of the spirit."

Out of his "torrential recollectiveness" and out of the vast sea of all the sensations and impressions of his "unnaturally absorptive senses," he distilled the "inner essence of truth," the central core of a reality so real that it became magical. He developed a sort of sixth sense, an unerring instinct for artistic or generally human values measured in terms of the highest ethical and esthetical standards. He could not be deceived by anything or by anybody that was not entirely genuine, authentic, and true. He could not even deceive himself. Perhaps he would have ended in blind despair, in nihilistic misanthropy, had it not been for the liberating power of his Gargantuan humor, exploding again and again in the irresistible wild laughter of a great satirist. But even his most grotesque satirical exaggeration remained true to life and convincing as a still more intensive view of reality. He knew that "satiric exaggeration belongs to the nature of life and particularly American life."

Perhaps Hatcher's class at Harvard, Miss Potter's art party, the American expatriates in Paris or the Rhodes scholars in Oxford, the lion hunters in New York, the portraits of Starwick or of Mr. Lloyd McHarg (alias Sinclair Lewis), the nocturnal Frenchman Alec or the countess and "La Marquise" at Orléans — all these innumerable scenes and figures are not grotesque distortions of truth, but have the savage, almost tragical comicality, the fierce and revealing authenticity of concentrated life. Perhaps I am not yet entirely qualified to judge the veracity of Thomas Wolfe's American scene. But I have lived long enough in Germany and in France to know with what an almost terrifying clairvoyance he was able to see and to reflect the very substance and essence of these countries: Munich and the Octoberfest, with all its exuberant animality; the universe of Paris; the dry and brittle atmosphere of a provincial town in France; and, finally in the closing part of his last book, Nazi Germany and Berlin during the Olympic Games of 1936 — the whole ominous picture of a great nation "infested with the contagion of an ever-present fear," with a "plague of the spirit — invisible but as unmistakable as death."

This last poignant farewell to Germany, which had been for him "a geography of heart's desire, an unfathomed domain of unknown inheritance," was written at a time when other foreigners returning from Berlin used to tell us German refugees in France that Nazi Germany was the greatest and happiest country on earth; that Hitler was a political genius, a benefactor of mankind; and that it was just silly for some poor emigrants to hurl themselves against the irresistible "wave of the future." In not quite one hundred pages of *You Can't Go Home Again*, he gave us a deeper insight into the much discussed "German problem" than all the endless cables and reports of all the legions of American correspondents combined, not even mentioning some German refugee writers doing their best to out-Vansittart Mr. Vansittart.

I wish I could have talked with him about Germany and about a thousand other things. It seems unbelievable to me that we never met during the twenties in Munich or the thirties in France; it may even be that, indeed, our paths did cross, perhaps in the Theresienstrasse near the Pension Burger or in the Café Neue Börse in Munich, perhaps in Nice in the café on the Avenue de la Victoire, while he was observing the two French monks carrying on their flirtation with two pretty street walkers. I remember so many scenes and so many places pictured in *Of Time and the River* or *The Web and the Rock*, but I cannot remember him. It evidently belongs to the ironical pattern of my life that I should have missed him, God knows how often, when we were so near each other in space and time. But what if I had met him in one of his black hours of despair, dead drunk or raving mad, unrecognizable even to himself? Perhaps it was meant to be that, so many years after his death, I should encounter only his immortal part, the great reflection of his genius left in his work.

If the essays in this collection are not already sufficiently indicative of the antithetical nature of Wolfe criticism, Miss Thompson's summary will at least be conclusive on that score. The round-up mentions not only many of the selections in this volume but numerous others. Also there is a comparison of the book-length studies of Wolfe by Herbert J. Muller and Pamela Hansford Johnson. Miss Thompson, presently a resident of New York City, spent two summers at the Kenyon School of English and was later director of publicity at Wesleyan College and Emory University in Georgia.

THOMAS WOLFE: TWO DECADES OF CRITICISM

by

Betty Thompson

The tenth anniversary of the death of Thomas Wolfe on September 15, 1948, was unmarked by critical fanfare in erudite journals which observe historical events in connection with their favorites. The interest in the North Carolina writer, who was one of the most controversial literary figures of the thirties, was no less vigorous in the forties, but the pattern of the argument had not changed significantly. As early as 1929, when *Look Homeward, Angel* appeared, the outline for the long critical debate was apparent; after 1935, when Wolfe published *Of Time and the River*, a continuation of the story of the protagonist of the first novel, and *From Death to Morning*, a volume of short stories, both

From the *South Atlantic Quarterly*, July 1950, copyright by Duke University Press. By permission of author and publisher.

attack and defense were monotonously predictable. Bernard DeVoto, the most vociferous of the dissenters, published his "Genius Is Not Enough" article in 1936 as a belligerent review of Wolfe's *The Story of a Novel*, a slender volume concerning his methods of writing. At the time of Wolfe's death a decade ago in the Johns Hopkins Hospital in Baltimore, his implacable enemies had their manifesto, and his equally fanatic admirers had been told that he resembled everyone from Melville to Proust.

With every new account we read of the "depressingly familiar" legend of Thomas Wolfe. It is almost impossible for a biographer or critic to begin without reviewing it. Despite Wolfe's lack of attention from the "new critics" and space in their journals, two book-length critical estimates have been published. Herbert Muller, whose *Thomas Wolfe* surprisingly turned up in 1947 in a New Direction series featuring more esoteric and fashionable modern writers, plunged into the legend in the first paragraph to get rid of it. *Hungry Gulliver*, the "English critical appraisal" issued in 1948, is British novelist Pamela Hansford Johnson's summary of the myth in a two-word title and less than two-hundred pages of discussion. Even those most weary of the legend, Maxwell Geismar, who wrote the Introduction for the *Portable Wolfe*, and James K. Hutsell, who told the story of Thomas Wolfe and Asheville in the *Southern Packet* for April, 1948, had to repeat in order to refute.

According to Mr. Hutsell's version:

Here was a man too big for ordinary beds. Here was a man so outsize that, in an alien basement flat in the Assyrian quarter of South Brooklyn, he wrote standing up — with the top of a refrigerator for a desk — and literally tossed millions of words (pencil-scrawled on yellow paper) into a packingbox in the middle of the floor. Here was life's hungry man, insatiable in his hunger for food and drink and more insatiable still with a hunger to know all places, all hearts and all of fury and chaos.

All of these things about Thomas Wolfe are true. But they are a portion of the truth. . . . Gargantuan has become a favorite adjective for him in the dozens of Wolfe clubs that dot American campuses. It is almost time that somebody should object.

It is true that Wolfe by his own gusto, his own turmoil, his own undisciplined flow of words has been partially responsible for this twisted view of him. He was full of raptures and incontinences. His real weakness was not perhaps that he dramatized his life, but that Wolfe the writer dramatized it more than Wolfe the man.

After the Wolfe legend must come the comparison of Thomas Wolfe and his heroes, Eugene Gant and George Webber. Although Wolfe denied from the start that he was merely a diary keeper, in the preface to his first novel he said he had no answer for the charge that his book was autobiographical, as were all works of fiction. He spoke of turning over half the people of a town to make a single figure in a novel. That he turned over considerably less than half became painfully obvious when the citizens of Asheville recognized not only Tom Wolfe and his family but themselves and each other. Their reactions have been described by Wolfe in *The Story of a Novel* and in the portions of *You Can't Go Home Again* (his fourth and last novel, published posthumously in 1940) that deal with the reception accorded by the people of "Libya Hill" to "George Webber's" book, *Home to Our Mountains*. It is now evident that Wolfe's incessant war against the term *autobiographical* was not merely resentment at the accusation that he wrote "unconsciously boring catalogues of details and meaningless autobiographical reminiscences." He was concerned over the outraged reaction of Asheville people against his work and over the pain his frank portraits caused his friends and family.

Eugene Gant was the son of a lusty, rhetorical stonecutter and a driving, acquisitive mother, who kept a boarding house, Dixieland. Like William Oliver Gant, W. O. Wolfe, Tom's father, was a monument shop proprietor, who was born in Pennsylvania and who liked to quote Shakespeare and Gray's *Elegy*. Julia Elizabeth Westall Wolfe is hardly distinguishable from Eliza Pentland Gant by those who know both or who have read either Hayden Norwood's conversational biography *The Marble Man's Wife* or *Thomas Wolfe's Letters to His Mother*, edited by his friend and biographer, John Skally Terry. Visitors to Asheville flock to the Old Kentucky Home, which Mrs. Wolfe kept as a boarding house until her death in 1945. This house at 48 Spruce Street has become a memorial to the writer according to the plans of the Thomas Wolfe Memorial Association headed by Don Shoemaker, editor of the Asheville *Citizen*. Little is heard these days from the individuals who thought that Wolfe should be tarred and feathered. Sight-seers are directed to places described in Wolfe's novels, and the outrage of twenty years ago is less important than the fame Wolfe has brought to North Carolina.

The Thomas Wolfe issue of the *Southern Packet* is demonstration enough that Thomas and Eugene were one. The excellent photographs of buildings and people described in *Look Homeward, Angel* are accompanied by fragments of descriptions from the novel as captions. His teachers at the North State Finishing School are without question the Leonards of the novel; letters from Wolfe to his teacher and friend, Mrs. J. M. Roberts, which were published three years ago in the *Atlantic Monthly*, increase the certainty. The reminiscences of his friends mention persons and events we have read about in the chapters of his first two novels that deal with Eugene at "Pulpit Hill" and Harvard.

Eugene Gant and Thomas Wolfe were born on October 3, 1900. Their parents have been described; Eugene's hill-rimmed city was Altamont, Tom's Asheville. Eugene had twin brothers named Benjamin Harrison and Grover Cleveland. So did Tom. Their brothers and sisters correspond in personalities and ages. Youth in Asheville and Altamont was lost and lonely. The years at the state university were anguished but successful. As a bridge between these biographical facts and the treatment of Wolfe by the critics, it is convenient to use one of the many anecdotes.

In 1916 a gangling, overgrown boy not quite sixteen years old left his Asheville home to go to the University of North Carolina at Chapel Hill. The boy was filled with the wild, furious energy of genius and a lust for knowledge and experience which by its intensity set him apart from his fellow-students as decisively as his wild looks and excessive tallness separated him from them physically. He felt that he was different, and that feeling made him lonely and unhappy. He felt that his difference was due to his superiority, and he exulted in his variation. By his own admission, he performed brilliantly in those things which touched his interest and dully, or not well at all, in those subjects which did not.

Being a genius, he knew before Mr. DeVoto told him, was not enough. He longed to be accepted by the smooth, confident fraternity men whom he envied. By spring of his junior year, this story goes, one of the most exclusive fraternities had been forced by urgent financial difficulties into admitting boys who were not hereditary Greek-letter material. One day a brother brought in a possible pledge who was a trifle too unkempt, the gangling youth from Asheville. Just as he was about to be blackballed it was reported that a visiting celebrity had commented that the strange youth was "probably genius." The chance was worth taking, the brethren decided, and Thomas Wolfe was elected to membership.

The story, like most of the Wolfe legend, is a mixture of fact and fiction, drawn from what he has written and what others have related about him. It could as easily be false as true, but the significant thing is that the attitude of the critics was much like that of the typical or mythical fraternity brothers. At the time of the publication of *Look Homeward, Angel*, there was much about his prodigious volume they did not like. Few, however, could deny his genius, so he was elected to the ranks of "great American novelists." The vote lacked unanimity, for there were those who distinguished betwen a genius's novel and a novel of genius.

The appearance of *Look Homeward, Angel* has been called the nearest thing to a literary thunderbolt in the twentieth century. Leo Gurko makes this exaggerated claim in the *Angry Decade*, his social and literary interpretation of the ten-year period 1929–1939. Since the selected reading list printed with this book includes such "criticism" as that of J. Donald Adams, Bernard DeVoto, and Granville Hicks, it is not hard to decide whether the social or the literary determines Gurko's judgment. His extravagant statement looks silly in the light of such real literary "thunderbolts" as James Joyce's *Ulysses* or T. S. Eliot's *The Waste Land*. Wolfe's millions of lyrical, undisciplined words, his power to create great living characters, and his vivid exploration of middle-class American life caused him to be labeled original. His talent was marvelous, but he was not a creator of new forms or new modes of expression. In fact, *Look Homeward, Angel* was less startling to the general public than *A Farewell to Arms* and *All Quiet on the Western Front*, both published in 1929. William Faulkner's *The Sound and the Fury* was also first issued that year, and critics who have long since washed their hands of the mighty Wolfe are still pondering the mysteries of his fellow Southerner. Alfred Kazin in *On Native Grounds* considers Faulkner and Wolfe together as exponents of "the rhetoric and the agony." If we are to trust the editor of the Penguin book edition of Wolfe's stories, Faulkner himself is a great admirer of Wolfe.

The first chapter of the Gant saga did receive appreciative reviews: John Chamberlain in the *Bookman*, Basil Davenport in the *Saturday Review of Literature*, and Geoffrey Hellman in the *New Republic*. In his speech of acceptance for the Nobel Prize in 1930, Sinclair Lewis cited Wolfe as one of the most promising of the younger writers and said that his novel was worthy of comparison with the best literature America had produced. But his defects did not go unnoticed. From the first there were critics for whom Wolfe was chaotic, exhausting, overemotional, and revolting.

None of Wolfe's books was ever praised more exorbitantly or criticized more unmercifully than *Of Time and the River*, which was published six years after his first. Mr. Muller in his balanced (too balanced for some who feel that he builds up Wolfe's defense only to tear it down himself) study finds the second novel something more than another slice of the life of Tom and Eugene. The difference, this diligent and thoughtful student of Wolfe thinks, is intellectual and moral rather than technical, because Eugene gets away from the unity given his first book as a description of the process of growing up and gets out into the world beyond his own state. *Of Time and the River* lacks plot but has greater depth and variety. The framework is still that of Wolfe's life; graduate study at Harvard, life in New York as a university instructor, travel in Europe. To Muller it is more than tales of wandering and Faustian hunger. He documents his claims for greater maturity by explaining the transition from the personal legend to the

American legend through Wolfe's realization of community in loneliness.

In the midst of the critical storm, Wolfe was compared to Whitman, Dostoevski, Dickens, the Bible, De Quincey, Homer, and Jack London! Robert Penn Warren reminded the melancholy Tar Heel that Shakespeare "merely wrote *Hamlet*, he was *not* Hamlet." DeVoto, obsessed by the psychological jargon of the period, found in Wolfe examples of manic-depression, infantile regression, and compulsion neurosis. The problem which Wolfe had to solve before most serious critics would put any final evaluation upon his work was stated by John Donald Wade in an essay entitled "Prodigal" and published in the July, 1935, issue of the *Southern Review*:

> So far his work has been the record of his passage through the world. Whether he can transfer his peculiar virtues to books in which he is not himself the protagonist, is something that the performance only can indicate.

The critical obituaries which appeared in 1938 judged Wolfe on the strength and weakness of his first two novels and the book of short stories published during his lifetime. The general conclusion was that Wolfe suffered from some very American complaints. He was endowed with a profusion of remarkable talents and extraordinary vitality, but he was, for all his energy and genius, a classic American failure. Waste and immaturity, indigenous faults, cancel out the virtues in the final equation. Many reviews of Muller's appraisal called Wolfe's reputation declining. Actually, critical opinion of Wolfe has not changed very much in the decade since his death. Not enough, Muller believes, since the books about George Webber, *The Web and the Rock*, 1939, and *You Can't Go Home Again*, 1940, attained the greater objectivity Wolfe had promised in *The Story of a Novel*. The unfinished historical novel, *The Hills Beyond*, differed in style and was chronologically impossible of autobiography. The performance, it must be admitted, did not demonstrate the transfer of the "peculiar virtues."

If critics have failed to take into account the change in Wolfe's attitude toward society and himself as set forth in the posthumous novels, the judgments of his work generally have been more temperate, if somewhat arrogantly regretful of his shortcomings. There have always been, and there will continue to be naïve, hysterical idolators proclaiming his tremendous powers at one end of the pole, while niggardly, unsympathetic critics expose his excesses at the other. Hamilton Basso, once among Wolfe's staunchest defenders, expressed in a *New Yorker* review of the *Portable Wolfe* his reluctance to enter the controversy, as though it were something of recent origin, and referred to Wolfe as the darling of one cult and the villain of another.

Both Mr. Muller and Mrs. Johnson believe that Wolfe's writing made for hyperbolic criticism. Says Muller:

His elemental powers are remarkable but they are also obvious; so are his elementary faults. He offers critics plenty of opportunity to exercise their eloquence in celebrating his powers, or their wits in ridiculing his faults; he offers little opportunity for acute analysis, subtle appreciation, or the knowing kind of criticism that distinguishes this age. Nor is the reader's judgment of his work likely to be affected much by criticism. Whether one is most impressed by his splendid gifts or by his shocking sins as an artist is chiefly a matter of temperament. One may have to learn to like caviar; one does not cultivate a taste for roast beef.

Of Wolfe's works generally, Mrs. Johnson says:

It is difficult to write with moderation, for the grandiose epithets persistently reiterated — "huge," "vast," "enormous," "fine," "rare" — tend to transfer themselves to relevant criticism. They are his words, expressive of his own height, his own thought, his own conception of America.

"Rooted in Adolescence" is Caroline Gordon's title for her review of these two books, which compares them only indirectly. Writing in the *New York Times Book Review*, Miss Gordon discounts Wolfe's myth-making powers as expounded by Mr. Muller in his "interesting" and "uncritical" study. As for Mrs. Johnson, she remarks that "Wolfe's characters seem to be accepted as typically American by those persons whose history and affections are not deeply rooted in America."

Miss Gordon's comments on Wolfe himself are of more interest, since she and her friends are among the chief practitioners of that "acute analysis, subtle appreciation, or the knowing kind of criticism."

Wolfe's intention was praiseworthy, but there was a lack of artistic intelligence. Webber's repudiation of Foxhall Edwards seems not so much a denial of the friend and father as a repudiation of the man's vision of life and art. The "testament" concludes with the words: "The wind is rising and the rivers flow," but the wind, one fears, is only the rustle of rhetoric, and a critic contemplating Wolfe's controlling image in *Of Time and the River* is reminded of Henry James's figure of the artist who, cultivating his instinct rather than his awareness, sits finally in a stale and shrinking puddle.

A critic contemplating Miss Gordon's remark is reminded that this knowing criticism can rarely get through even such a short article as that just quoted without reference to Henry James. It is by the standards of James that Wolfe is such a monstrous artistic failure. Certainly, his "point of view" fails to interest students of the Jamesian method. A further revealing insight is offered when Miss Gordon suggests that John Peale Bishop's article in the first issue of the *Kenyon Review* in 1939 probably remains the best thing written about his work. That article, "The Sorrows of Thomas Wolfe," is indeed a lucid and fascinating piece of criticism, comparing Wolfe and Hart Crane. Bishop, according to Miss Gordon, paid Wolfe the compliment his admirers rarely do, of measuring his intention against his execution. The Bishop article is mentioned by Muller as one of the critical obituaries unable to take into account the unpublished novels. Miss Gordon's belief that Wolfe's later work made no difference is reflected both in her choice of Bishop's interpretation and her comments on Wolfe's credo.

In an attempt to be objective Mr. Muller fills his book with references to critics almost wholly unsympathetic to Wolfe. To prove that Wolfe was more than a regionalist and nothing of the provincial, he chooses Allen Tate's distinction between regionalism and provincialism. Mr. Tate has said in the classroom and perhaps in print that Thomas Wolfe not only did harm to the art of the novel, but moral damage to his readers. Wolfe, for Mr.

Muller, becomes a myth-maker through Mark Schorer's definition of myth as a "large controlling image . . . which gives philosophical meaning to the facts of ordinary life, that is to say, which has organizing value for experience." Mr. Schorer in his recent article on "Technique as Discovery" gives a detailed demolition of Wolfe as artist:

The books of Thomas Wolfe were, of course, journals, and the primary role of his publisher in transforming these journals into the semblance of novels is notorious. For the crucial act of the artist, the unique act which is composition, a sympathetic blue pencil and scissors were substituted. The result has excited many people, especially the young, and the ostensibly critical have observed the prodigal talent with a wish that it might have been controlled . . . for until the talent is controlled, the material organized, the contest achieved, there is simply the man and his life.

The title of Wolfe's second book is for Schorer simply a euphemism for *Of Man and His Ego.* Had Wolfe had adequate respect for and been able to pursue technique, he continues, he might have been able to write a great novel on his true subject, the dilemma of romantic genius. "Like Emily Brontë, Wolfe needed a point of view beyond his own which would separate his material and its effect." Rather than as a great myth-maker, Wolfe appears to Schorer as a subjectivist, whose record of the bewilderment of the age is no more valuable to us than our own diaries and letters.

The sympathetic editor whose blue pencil and scissors are notorious was the late Maxwell Perkins of Scribner's, to whom Wolfe dedicated *Of Time and the River* and to whom many other writers, including Miss Gordon, have dedicated their books in appreciation for his services as editor and friend. Undeniably, Perkins, who is the Foxhall Edwards of the last Webber novel, helped Wolfe tremendously in preparing his manuscripts for publication, but the part of the Wolfe legend which deals with his methods of creation is the most enormously magnified of all. Edward Aswell, the editor who worked with Wolfe after he transferred to Harper's, refers to the belief "that when Tom was in the throes of composition all he had to do was to open the sluice

gates and the words tumbled forth in an irresistible torrent like
the surge of pent-up waters suddenly released." The popular
conception of Wolfe's methods of writing was described by Wolfe
in an amusing and touching letter to F. Scott Fitzgerald. Schorer
is not alone in believing Wolfe to be a cut-and-paste artist who
took his fictional diaries to Mr. Perkins to be made with infinite
patience into publishable books. When this "collaboration" was
discovered, Wolfe sought to disguise his methods by changing
his hero's name to Webber and taking packing cases filled with
thousands of sheets of paper over to Harper's where a new tailor
would attempt similar miracles.

In an article on which he was working at the time of his death,
which was published in the *Harvard Library Bulletin,* Autumn,
1947, as an introduction to the Thomas Wolfe Collection of
William B. Wisdom, Perkins explained his literary relationship to
Wolfe. The editor expressed his conviction that Wolfe made a
horrible mistake in changing his hero from Gant to the presumably
objective Webber. Perkins says that when he first read Wolfe's
manuscript he felt that it was autobiographical in the sense in
which *David Copperfield* or *War and Peace* is, but that he realized
as he worked with Wolfe that it was often almost literally autobiographical. The amount of cutting was far less than has been
supposed. The work was really a matter of reorganization. But
neither Wolfe's denials nor those of his editors have been able
to destroy the notions some critics have concerning his total dependence on his editors. John Terry found it necessary to state
again in a recent article that Perkins never rewrote a single word
of Wolfe's and that most of the cutting was done by the author
himself on the editor's advice.

Perkins in his exposition of their co-operative working methods
tells of an instance in which Wolfe ignored his advice and
turned out to be right. Working on the principle that Wolfe's
unity and form in *Of Time and the River* came through the senses
of Eugene, Perkins tried to persuade Wolfe that the episode of his
father's death was outside the perception and knowledge of the
general character, who was at Harvard at the time. Wolfe agreed
but wrote on as he planned, creating the magnificent death of

stoneman Gant. Perkins realized that it was he who was wrong, even if right in theory: "What he was doing was too good to let any rule of form impede him."

The schism between George Webber and Foxhall Edwards had, in addition to the philosophical undertones revealed by Webber, a very practical reason. He wanted to prove to his detractors and perhaps to himself that he could write an objective book without the aid of his friend. His editors have written truthfully of his constant rewriting, of the many versions before he was satisfied that a single episode was ready for print. Maxwell Geismar submits as proof that Wolfe was not purely a quantitative writer the three years he spent in writing his first novel, the complete abandonment of his next book, *K-19*, a novel about a train and its passengers, and the years of work on *Of Time and the River*. That he learned at least enough discipline to have plays he wrote as a result of three years of drama study under Professor George Pierce Baker of Harvard considered for Broadway production is for Muller an indication that he was capable of restraint. However, *Mannerhouse*, the recently published (1948) Wolfe play, contains most of his excesses of romantic feeling and rhetoric.

Regardless of what misconceptions they might hold concerning his methods of writing, the critics primarily interested in standards measured Wolfe by their criteria and found him a megalomaniac without form or real style. The strength of the opposition of the best critics is shown in the parenthetical remarks of their historian and critic, Stanley Edgar Hyman, in the *Armed Vision*. The critic of critics says of Van Wyck Brooks, "He is probably the most repetitious writer since Thomas Wolfe died." Of R. P. Blackmur's concept of the fallacy of expressive form he says that it has been employed consistently "to demolish writers like Thomas Wolfe and Carl Sandburg, as well as bigger game." He criticizes Harry Slochower by stating that "windy bores like Wolfe are treated as comparable to Kafka and Rilke." In the reviews found in most of the better quarterlies Thomas Wolfe is equated with artless raving.

Critical detestation of Wolfe was not limited to the aesthetic group. The other principal school of the thirties, the social critics who judged all literature by Marxist standards, found Wolfe equally abhorrent for different reasons. Edwin Berry Burgum called *Of Time and the River* an example of the third and worst of his categories of bourgeois novels. The rise of fascism was reflected in this type, which presented a distortion of contemporary society through the optimism of an idealistic or Nietzschean interpretation. It is interesting to contrast this utterance with Burgum's "Thomas Wolfe Discovers America" in the *Virginia Quarterly Review*, Summer, 1946. Rather than a sinister precursor of fascism, Wolfe is the voice of average American youth of the postwar period, "better than Hemingway (who represented the minority of the sophisticated), better than Dos Passos (who only described the appearance of things)." This reversal is perhaps less a sign that criticism takes a more tolerant view of Wolfe than a symptom of the widespread modifications and retractions of the social critics in the forties.

With accuracy Gurko has remarked that the width of Wolfe's scope and the abundance of his energy make him fuel for almost any thesis. Bella Kussey, writing in the *Sewanee Review* in 1942, found in Wolfe a sensual primitivism, a kinship with Whitman, Nietzsche, and the Nazis. Franz Schoenberner's article "Wolfe's Genius Seen Afresh" * appearing on the front page of the *New York Times Book Review*, August 4, 1946, was a German intellectual's affirmation of the belief that Wolfe alone among the most famous of contemporary writers was endowed "with the prophetic Ethos and the poetic Pathos of the true genius." The article praised Wolfe for discerning the terror of Nazism before it was fashionable to do so and for giving in the comparatively brief account of George Webber's visit to Germany a better insight into the problems of those days than the combined cables and reports of the correspondents there.

This eloquent defense by the editor of *Simplicissimus* and the author of *Confessions of a European Intellectual* was countered by the late Russell Maloney, who described himself as "Spokesman for a small number of cads who believe that Thomas Wolfe was only a part-time genius." His letter attacked Wolfe, whose

* Printed above under the title "My Discovery of Thomas Wolfe."

place among Germans as the American Homer was traced to anti-Semitism and other provincial prejudices. "Our theory is that he did not like the Third Reich only because he didn't properly understand it."

More than intellectual and temperamental differences in the readers cause Wolfe to appear a spiritual Nazi to one and a vigorous anti-Fascist to another. The explanation lies in the opposing emotions and thoughts which co-exist in Wolfe and his heroes. Diverse students of Wolfe realize these incongruities as a major key to his writing and to his unique personality. Gurko calls the constant alternation "the immutable counterpoint" and "this tormented interplay of opposites." As a sociologist, he is interested in the anti-Semitism, which is balanced by Gant's affection for his Jewish student, Abe Jones, in *Of Time and the River* and his anguished love for his Jewish mistress, Esther Jack, of the Webber novels, whom he both adores and despises for her Hebraic richness. Wolfe's slighting references to Negroes are matched by his bitterness at the cruel stupidity of lynchers. Paranoia and naïve egocentricity have their counterparts in common sense and humility.

As literary critic, Mr. Muller finds in Wolfe's handling of typical incongruities abounding in his work something like "the melancholy, ironic detachment" of Joseph Conrad. To Mr. Muller the constant stress upon incongruity is the peculiar quality of Wolfe's fiction, and in the death of Ben Gant in *Look Homeward, Angel* he finds a scene unsurpassed in contemporary literature for resolution of complex disharmonies. In her analysis of Wolfe's style, Mrs. Johnson is also aware of the incongruities. When the two critics arrive at similar conclusions, however, it is seldom by the same methods. Mrs. Johnson's book may be regarded as the one some critics, displeased with the emphasis Muller placed on Wolfe's failings, would have had him write. The adverse criticism in Muller deals legitimately with Wolfe's artistic failures, while his praise is directed more to his intellectual and moral development. On the other hand, Mrs. Johnson finds Wolfe acceptable as an artist, while she deplores the philosophy and middle-class prejudices she feels his environment bred. His saving force, she believes, was his natural optimism and his belief in the grandeur of mankind. She finds the purest expression of his optimism in Eugene Gant; of his conflict, in George Webber.

Growth is for Muller the theme of all Wolfe's work, and he is convinced that it is the explicit theme of *You Can't Go Home Again.* In the conclusion to this book he discovers the culmination of organic growth in the faith Wolfe has in the promise of America and in the dignity of man, which was implicit in his earliest work. But while the English critic calls the ending "one of the most flawless conclusions to any novel in the English language," the American considers the whole farewell to Edwards a personal postscript of more interest to the biographer than the novel reader, not "an artistically logical or effective ending."

The constant references to the new critics in Muller's book are not merely to impress the reader with his superior knowledge of them. Simply because he is a contributor to their journals and an admirer of their excellent work, Muller is much concerned with their values. He mentions William Empson on Proust, Cleanth Brooks on metaphysical poetry, T. S. Eliot on tradition, Constance Ruorke on the American character. Although his discussions often seem farfetched, the superiority of his method over the rhapsodic approach of Mrs. Johnson stands out in their very different final chapters. "Wolfe and the Tradition," Muller's conclusion, is a brilliant survey of American literature, measuring Wolfe against Hawthorne, Melville, Whitman, Emerson, and James as well as the Agrarians, Dos Passos, Sinclair Lewis, and other contemporaries. Mrs. Johnson, in a much briefer and more limited survey, finds Wolfe's comparative importance unassessed. "Beside him Faulkner appears neurotic and obscure, Hemingway oversophisticated and Steinbeck, a novelist of power and solidity, to have a certain recessive quality." Her further comments on these writers reveal a lack of understanding of them; all of them, she says, might easily have been Europeans. She follows Kazin in his belief that Wolfe was a perpetual boy. Mrs. Johnson's style itself is overblown, given to such extravagances as:

The words strike response from the heart as the sun strikes arrows of bronze from the shield. In their clangour, their grasping weight of effort, they force the imagination to the realization of Wolfe's whole being and desire, as narrowly, as nearly, as the battering ram breaches the walls which will not yield.

William B. Wisdom, whose vision and industry kept together the practically complete assembly of Wolfe's letters, manuscripts, publications, library, and other possessions of interest to the scholar, has donated his remarkable collection to the Harvard College Library. It is said to constitute a concentration of research material unsurpassed for a major literary figure. Here all the sub-literary questions on this intensely personal author can eventually be solved. Mr. Muller observes that personal taste and fashion, not eternal principles of prose, dictate verdicts.

Here in contemporary America is our first and last concern; for the immediate world is the only world we have. And here is the final significance of Wolfe for contemporaries; he made himself at home in this world.

Whether Wolfe's faults are the flaws of greatness or of a magnitude to preclude greatness is a decision the individual reader along with the conscious literary critic must make. He is out of the literary fashion; he fails by the standards of some of the finest critics of the age. But his significance for his contemporaries is that he did create with marvelous words and powerful emotions a world in which they also could be at home. And we can wonder how declining the Wolfe reputation is when David McDowell's sympathetic review of French translations appears among a group of articles devoted to the celebration of new critic John Crowe Ransom's birthday and when the income from the sale of his books is three times what is was in 1938.

83.
85
89